MEDITERRANEAN COOKING

MEDITERRANEAN COOKING

LYNNE GIGLIOTTI

Photographs by Ben Fink

THE CULINARY INSTITUTE OF AMERICA®

Houghton Mifflin Harcourt
Boston • New York • 2013

Photography copyright © 2013 by Ben Fink

The Culinary Institute of America

President	Dr. Tim Ryan '77, CMC, AAC
Provost	Mark Erickson '77, CMC
Senior Director Educational Enterprises	Susan Cussen
Director of Publishing	Nathalie Fischer
Editorial Project Manager	Margaret Wheeler '00
Editorial Assistant	Shelly Malgee '08

www.hmhbooks.com

Cover and interior design by Vertigo Design NYC

Library of Congress Cataloging-in-Publication Data:

Gigliotti, Lynne.
  Mediterranean cooking at home with the Culinary Institute of America / Lynne Gigliotti ; photographs by Ben Fink.
     p. cm.
  Includes index.
  ISBN 978-0-470-42136-9 (cloth)
  1. Cooking, Mediterranean. 2. Cookbooks. I. Culinary Institute of America. II. Title.
  TX725.M35G54 2013
  641.59182'2--dc23
                        2011038025

C&C 10 9 8 7 6 5 4 3 2 1

Contents

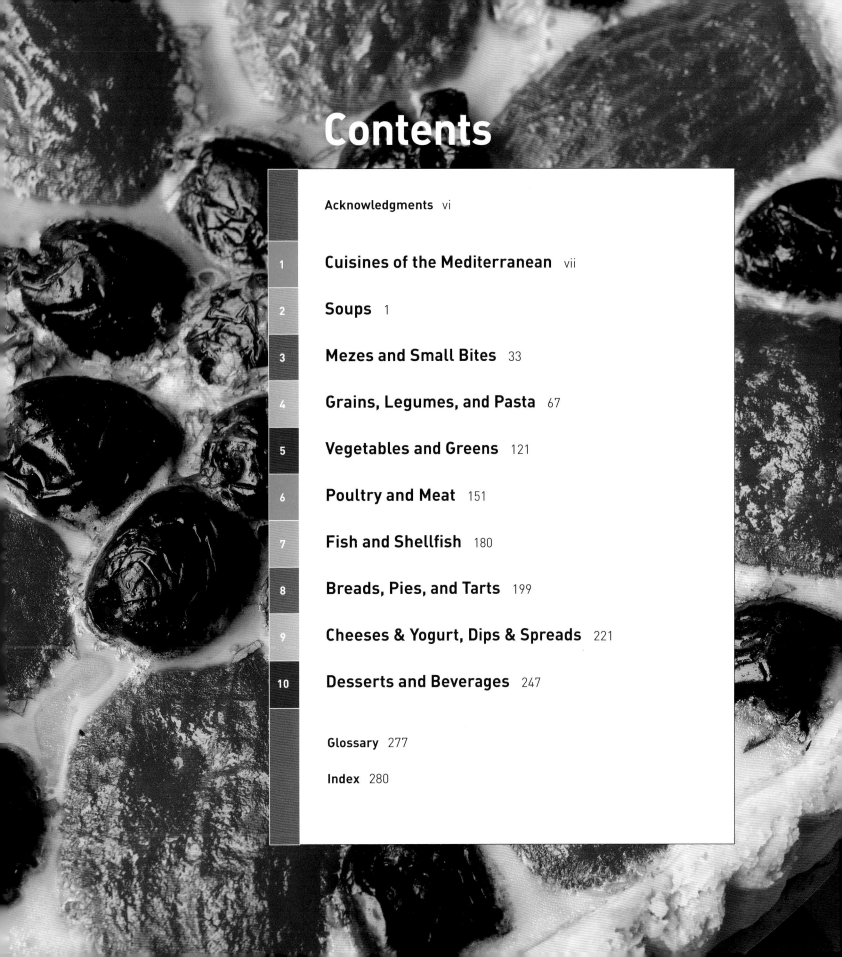

ACKNOWLEDGMENTS

For the past twenty years or so, my clients, colleagues, friends and family have been urging me to write a book. It's a large task to take on by oneself. Luckily for me The Culinary Institute of America had enough faith in me to offer me this project. For that I will be eternally grateful. And so I would like to thank Dr. Tim Ryan, our president and fearless leader, for giving me this opportunity.

Writing this book with the assistance of the publishing department at school has been a totally enjoyable endeavor. At the helm is Wiley Publishing and I would like to thank Pam Chirls, the editor at Wiley, for her expertise. The first person I spoke to about this project was Nathalie Fischer, director of our publishing department. Thank you, Nathalie, for your faith, humor, and camaraderie.

I would also like to thank Maggie Wheeler and Shelly Malgee for helping me along every step of the way. Shelly was at my house every Saturday for the photo shoots and she was a pleasure to hang out with, as well as an amazing source of moral support. Maggie gave me positive reinforcement when I was unsure and is a fantastic force in our publishing department.

Let me also thank our manager-in-training Rob Kristof for testing recipes, giving feedback and attending my 4:00 Coffee Club in whatever kitchen I happen to be found. In addition to Rob, we have had two externs tirelessly working on recipes throughout the process. Jamie Hall and Eleanor Martin would show up in my kitchen every day with four or five dishes to taste. They were always a pleasure to see and their recipe testing was quite a task—so I thank them. Jamie and Eleanor were also front and center at my house to assist with the photo shoots, which was a lot of fun.

The first few photo shoots were kind of brutal due to unforeseen circumstances, but thanks to Ben Fink—our photographer extraordinaire—for his patience, humor, and good spirit. I would also like to especially thank my neighbor Kerry Gordon, who, although only a high school student, came over, washed dishes, and basically threw herself into the whole process with amazing enthusiasm. She even took my dog, Lily, out for walks so that I could continue working.

Thank you to everyone in our editorial department for making this possible for me. You are a pleasure to work with and thank you is simply not enough.

On the home front, thank you to Noelle, my roommate, for putting up with the tornado that ripped through the house on a weekly basis. Thank you to my friend Steve Smith, who reached through 800 miles of phone line to give me a swift kick in the butt when I needed a push. Thank you to all of my family, extended family, and friends for letting me have enough space to work on this project. Most of all, I would like to thank my mom, Amelia, without whom I would not have been able to go to culinary school. For that I am eternally grateful. I would also like to thank Pesto and Taylor, the cats at my house, and my dog, Lily, for cleaning the corners of the kitchen after a day at the stove.

This book is for Keith, who showed me that dreams really do come true.

CUISINES OF THE
MEDITERRANEAN

The term "Mediterranean cuisine" might leave people living in one of the many countries that surround the Mediterranean Sea scratching their heads. This is because the region is so culturally and geographically diverse; twenty-one countries border the Mediterranean, among them France, Italy, Spain, Greece, Turkey, Syria, Algeria, and Egypt. What we consider Mediterranean cuisine is really a combination of the foods, cultures, and traditions from these different countries and regions. For the purposes of this book, we have embraced the ingredients, cooking methods, and flavor profiles of the various cultures in the Mediterranean basin, put them into a big pot, and stirred. Great culinary possibilities arise from combining the many spices, types of produce, and techniques from such a wide array of cooking traditions.

HISTORY

The Middle East

In ancient times, the area of the Middle East known as the Fertile Crescent played an important role in the development of Mediterranean cuisine. The Fertile Crescent ranges from modern-day Iraq to the Nile River Valley to the eastern Mediterranean coast (also known as the Levant). The area is semi-arid and was not conducive to agriculture. This changed with the development of irrigation systems by the ancient Egyptians. Suddenly land where nothing had previously grown became green and ripe with vegetation. Cultivated fruits and vegetables became an important part of people's diets. Subsequently, as time passed, more and more peoples settled in the Fertile Crescent and established cities. The great empires all had presences in the Fertile Crescent, among them the Mediterranean civilizations of the ancient Greeks and the Romans.

However, all good things must come to an end. By the fifth century A.D., the Greek and Roman empires had all but vanished. For the next three hundred years, the Mediterranean region, along with the rest of Europe, declined into what has become known as the Dark Ages. There was no longer a central unifying government and no common language. The Northern European Barbarians inherited the continent of Europe, where they established kingdoms and adopted Christianity as their religion. This was a volatile time for religion in the Mediterranean; Christianity was split between the Eastern Orthodox and Western Roman Catholic churches and the Jews were a leaderless and displaced people. In the Middle East, where the Byzantines—the last remnants of the Roman Empire and the neighboring peoples of Persia—controlled the area along the silk and spice trade routes connecting Asia to the Mediterranean, and a man named Muhammad began to call the people of the Arabian Peninsula to submit to Allah.

The Mediterranean region.

His message spread, moving among the many different races and creeds of the Middle East and converting them to one unified religion—Islam. As the Muslim population expanded and spread during the Islamic Golden Age, their culinary traditions had a great influence on Mediterranean food culture.

For more than seven hundred years the Islamic ruling dynasties dominated, influenced, and controlled most of the Mediterranean. During this time, the Muslim empire developed unique systems of trade that linked the countries of the Mediterranean basin with those of the Indian Ocean, introducing new products to the region. Due to its strategic position as the conduit between the Far East and the Middle East on the famous trade route known as the Silk Road, Persia (present-day Iran) became key in the development of Mediterranean cuisine. Persians created sophisticated methods of cooking that enhanced the textures, flavors, and colors of the bounty of ingredients available to them. In the eighth century A.D., Persia fell to the Bedouin Arabs, but the Arabs enthusiastically absorbed much of the Persian culture and culinary artistry. Indigenous food products, such as oranges, lemons, almonds, pistachios, lentils, grapes, eggplant, spinach, and rice, were all taken along in the Islamic expansionist trail.

In the Arab Levant, the direct descendants of Muhammad established their reign in Damascus, Syria, and Arabic cuisine began to develop. It combined the pastoral traditions and practices of the local agricultural population—the Bedouin tribes—with the more sophisticated culinary traditions of the elite class of the Byzantines and the newly annexed Persians. Olive oil was the supreme condiment, and dried beans and garden vegetables were held in the highest esteem. The hot, arid climate of the Levant inspired *mukhallalat,* or foods pickled with salt and vinegar, and grilled meats, like the log of spiced meat cooked on a rotating vertical rod known as shawarma. Today the Arab Levant is a melting pot of foods from many places throughout the Arab world and many traditional preparations that originated in the Levant are still widely available.

Africa

The western part of North Africa, which includes Morocco, the western Sahara, Algeria, Tunisia, Libya, and Mauritania, is sometimes referred to as the Maghreb. The Maghreb was transformed during the Islamic Golden Age (700 to 1200 A.D.), from an arid, nomadic grassland into a fertile, agricultural wonder. The Muslims introduced methods of irrigation that vastly increased the productivity of the land in the Maghreb, and subsequently had lasting influence on its delicately spiced cuisine. However, the Maghreb's agricultural progress was hindered over the next five hundred years by incursions from the Spanish, Italians, French, and English.

European exploration of the New World in the sixteenth century brought a tremendous bounty of new agricultural food products to North Africa. Foods such as potatoes, peppers, various bean cultivars, corn, chocolate, squash, and tomatoes were introduced to the Maghreb. These new trade products transformed not only the cuisine of the Maghreb itself, but also the existing cuisines from Portugal to Japan.

Turkey

In the fifteenth century A.D., the Ottoman Turks experienced substantial activity in agricultural trade and commerce. Foods that were indigenous to distant, remote areas of the world were now being cultivated in many parts of the Mediterranean, especially in the Ottoman domain. The Ottoman capital city of Istanbul was strategically located at the center of a network of trading routes, and as the urban center developed and expanded from the profits of trade, its population also soared. In this food culture, the sophisticated palace cuisine of the Ottomans filtered down to the common people in Istanbul, creating one of the first recognized and recorded restaurant cultures in the Mediterranean, as well as Europe.

Greece

No discussion of the history of Mediterranean cuisine is complete without mentioning Greece. Ancient Greek culture is still our classical model for government, philosophy, science, agriculture, religion, fine art, and the culinary arts. Archestratus, who was not a chef but a connoisseur, composed one of the first cookbooks around 330 B.C.; the work is in verse, and was probably intended to be read at a symposium—or at a party with copious amounts of wine. The commentary and recipes in his book indicates that while there was an advanced level of culinary sophistication enjoyed among the Greeks, the best way to appreciate truly good food is to respect the ingredients themselves and feature them in simple preparations that accentuate their quality. Historically, Greece was the Mediterranean's land link between Central Asia, the Middle East, and Europe. Greek food evolved over time, strongly influenced by the Persians, Ottomans, Byzantines, and Venetians. Classic flavors such as olives, olive oil, zucchini, lemon, dill, feta, oregano, and yogurt are utilized in other cuisines but their combination is a hallmark of Greek cooking.

Spain

The Iberian Peninsula, which is comprised of Spain and Portugal, has experienced many waves of invaders and settlers over the centuries. The first to arrive were the Iberians, a desert-dwelling tribal folk from North Africa who slowly settled in southern and central Spain in waves of migration, starting in the Bronze Age. By the twelfth century B.C.E., the Phoenicians were actively established in Spain. By the seventh century B.C.E., the Celts from northern Europe and the Greeks had arrived. A few centuries later, the Carthaginians began calling the country Ispania, which means "land of rabbits"—this may explain why rabbit stew is still one of the classic dishes of the Spanish countryside. When the Romans conquered the country in the third century B.C.E., they used the name Hispania, which has evolved into the modern España, or Spain, we know it in English. The Romans were great innovators and devised many agricultural advancements, which they brought with them to Spain.

After the fall of the Roman Empire in the fifth century A.D., the Northern Visigoths invaded the Iberian Peninsula and occupied it for the next two hundred years. The Visigoths did not contribute much to agriculture. The health as well as the culture of the Iberian Peninsula declined during the Goth period of occupation.

In the eighth century A.D., the Moors of North Africa invaded the Iberian Peninsula. (The term "Moors" is usually used as if the invaders were a single ethnicity, but they were in fact Arabs, Syrians, Egyptians, and North Africans unified by the Arab language and the Muslim religion.) The Moors defeated the Visigoths and ushered in what is known as the Golden Age of Islam, a time of great culinary advancement in Spain. The rest of Europe at the time was still involved in a system of feudal agriculture, and hence there was little innovation in food production. The Moors, on the other hand, were so agriculturally advanced that Spain started to experience what is called the Medieval Green Revolution. Due to their agricultural advancements as well as advancements in medicine, pharmacology, and botany, the health of the population greatly increased. The Muslim diet was rich and diverse, in direct contrast to that of the rest of Europe, where the diet was heavier in meat and wheat. The Moorish occupation also made Spanish cuisine distinctive from the cuisines of neighboring countries. They brought with them cinnamon, cloves, nutmeg, cumin, almonds, sugar, rhubarb, quinces, eggplant, spinach, artichokes, apples, quails, pomegranates, bitter oranges, lemons, figs, saffron, and rice, which were used in Spain centuries before they were available in other European countries.

By the eleventh century A.D., the Muslim Empire began to fall apart and split into smaller kingdoms. Because they were no longer unified, the Christians from the north of Spain systematically reconquered their southern lands. It took the Christians five hundred years to drive the Muslims out of Spain and by 1492 the last of them retreated from Grenada and never returned.

King Ferdinand of Aragon and Queen Isabella of Castile then joined forces to unify the people of Spain. During their reign, they charged Christopher Columbus with finding a more direct route to the Spice Islands in the East Indies.

Columbus set sail and found the Americas, specifically South America, the land of the Incan and Mayan empires. These civilizations introduced Columbus, and therefore Europe, to many new food products, including corn, tomatoes, chocolate, squash, potatoes, beans, and peppers.

Italy

Italy is a relatively new country. Until its unification in 1860 by Giuseppe Garibaldi, it was just a jumble of separate city-states, each controlled by an ever-changing roster of invaders. At any one time, the disparate regions were occupied by the Lombards, Saxons, Spanish, French, Arabs, and countless other groups who invaded, occupied for a time, and then disappeared.

The earliest settlers of the Tuscany region of Italy were the Etruscans, an advanced civilization that existed as early as 1000 B.C.E. They were sophisticated cooks, and frescoes inside Etruscan tombs illustrate pasta, cheese graters, pastry wheels, and colanders. Tuscany, the birthplace of the Renaissance, later had a profound influence on French cooking methods. In the sixteenth century A.D., Italian-born Catherine de Medici and her Florentine cooks laid the foundation for medieval French cooking, from which modern French cuisine later developed. Her cooks introduced crêpes, artichokes, frying, olive oil, béchamel, spinach, and the use of the fork to France. The Medicis also passed "sumptuary laws," which restricted the number of courses permitted to be served at banquets, where ostentatious displays with copious amounts of food were the norm. These changes eventually led to a cuisine that was balanced and simple, relying on the natural quality of ingredients.

France

The south of France borders Spain and has a stretch of coastline on the Mediterranean Sea. Thus, like the Iberian Peninsula, the region experienced waves of invaders and settlers, all of which had lasting influence on the culture and cuisine. The Greeks were the first to arrive, settling in the Mediterranean region of Provence. Eventually, the Romans conquered all of Gaul, as France was then known, and ruled it for nearly five centuries. After the fall of the Roman Empire, France devolved into a tangle of kingdoms until a monarchy was established in the tenth century A.D. During the late thirteenth century, the chef for King Charles V, Taillevent, wrote an extensive cookbook that codified both French and Italian dishes. In addition to the early cookbook, France pioneered many of the knives and cutlery that were adopted by Italy and countries in the New World. Eventually, French cuisine became widely synonymous with haute cuisine, although more rustic, peasant fare was prepared across the country as well.

THE ROLE OF REGIONAL CUISINES

France

The cuisine of a country varies by region as much as its landscape and its people; there is no simple definition of a national cuisine. The culinary traditions of most, if not all, countries can be broken into regional cuisines. This is especially true for the many regions of France, with its southern half having a strong Mediterranean influence.

Provence, located in southeastern France, borders the snowcapped Alps of Piedmont, Italy, to the east, the Rhône River to the west, and the Mediterranean coast to the south. The climate is subtropical with more hours of sunlight than any other region of France. Provençal cooking has a distinct style and flavor components. Garlic, tomatoes, olives, and olive oil are staples of the Provençal kitchen. Herbs grow abundantly and play a large role in seasoning foods. Sheep in this region are free to graze on rosemary, savory, lavender, thyme, and marjoram. This grazing is what gives the lamb of the region a distinct flavor that can't be found elsewhere. Due to the proximity of the Mediterranean Sea, there is also a rich assortment of fish. What these small fish lack in size they more than make up for in flavor. Anchovies, for instance, are the basis for tapenade—a purée that also includes olives, capers, and olive oil—and anchoïade—a dish of fish softened in olive oil with finely chopped garlic, sometimes served on grilled bread. Some common large fish include red mullet, sea bass, monkfish, and cod, which is often salted and used in dishes such as brandade.

The Vaucluse in the Rhône Valley of Provence is considered "the garden of France." Almost every variety of fruit and vegetable grows in the narrow fields between the dark cypress windbreaks. Apricots, cherries, plums, strawberries, figs, melons, and peaches are abundant due to the intense sunshine and the warm mistral winds that blow through the region. Much of the fruit is preserved in jams or as crystallized fruits. In the Vaucluse, the tomatoes, peppers, zucchini, and onions are not so much cooked as "melted" in olive oil, and the seasonings are as essential as the ingredients. The cheeses of this region are mostly small and, depending on the season, may be made with cow's, sheep's, or goat's milk. Some of the most popular cheeses are Picodon, Bossons macérés, Banon, which is wrapped in chestnut leaves, and fromage fort du Mont Ventoux, which is Banon mixed with wine, oil, and herbs.

Salade niçoise is a typical example of a Provençal dish that combines fresh produce and seafood, and is perfect on a hot summer day, served along with a chilled glass of rosé. Some other Provençal specialties include ratatouille and bouillabaisse.

Spain

Spain, unlike France, did not develop a cuisine of its own until the seventeenth century A.D. Up to that point, the foods eaten in Spain were the products of various other cuisines. Even today, a national cuisine is still very difficult to define. Spanish cuisine can be categorized into several different types of cooking, divided into six gastronomic zones.

The cuisine of the northern region of Galicia, Asturias, Cantabria, the Basque Country (Euskadi), and northern Navarre is built around fish and sauces. The great Cantabric region also shares similar gastronomic characteristics, particularly the emphasis on livestock from the vast green prairies and on fish from the Bay of Biscay and the Atlantic Ocean. Considered by some to be the best in Spain, the cuisine of the Basque Country is characterized by simple dishes of grilled fish and meat. A few regional dishes are *piperade* (pepper omelet), *toro* (seafood soup), *lotte à la basquaise* (monkfish prepared with peppers, onions, and tomatoes), and *jamón de Bayona* (the Basque region's cured ham).

The cuisine of Catalonia shares the same emphasis on fish as in Galicia, but the fish are from a different sea—the Mediterranean. Catalonia is also known for cazuelas, their regional casseroles.

The region along the south of Navarre, La Rioja, and Aragon is an area rich in pastureland and agriculture. The region's bounty of vegetables has given rise to a specialty known as chilindrones, a dish of sautéed peppers, tomatoes, and onions that is served alongside many other dishes.

The provinces of Castellón, Valencia, Alicante, and Murcia on Spain's eastern coast, along with the Balearic Islands, is a region known for the cultivation of rice and garden vegetables. This area is known for paella valenciana, the paella that most Americans recognize. However, every region in Spain has its own version of paella, not all of which contain seafood. Some versions of paella are strictly vegetarian, some feature rabbit, poultry, and other meats, but what they all have in common is Calasparra rice. Calasparra is short grain rice grown in Spain and is traditionally used in paella.

The cuisine of the central region of Spain, which includes Old Castile, New Castile, Madrid, and Extremadura included some major grazing lands. One area, known as the Dehesa, is the largest area for livestock production in Spain. This area is known for hogs, sheep, and cattle, as well as the production of cork, charcoal, and olives. This is the area famous for roasted meats. Roasted meats are simply prepared, roasted with olive oil, sometimes over olive branches, and often accompanied by bread and wine.

The Canary Islands and the province of Andalusia are both front and center to the Mediterranean Sea, and seafood is a big part of the cuisine. The food of this area is also heavy on fried foods because of the region's golden olive oil that is used to fry a vast array of items in the cuisine, even desserts.

COCIDO: SPAIN'S NATIONAL DISH

Although Spain displays extraordinary variation in its gastronomic regions, the six different cuisines within the country all share one unique dish called *cocido*. A cocido is a one-pot wonder whose ingredients may vary from region to region, with variations like *cocido madrileño,* from Madrid. The main ingredients are chickpeas, pork belly, beef shank, morcilla (blood sausage), chorizo, cabbage, carrots, turnips, and sometimes green beans or other vegetables. The final ingredient in a cocido is the bola, which is essentially a spiced meatball. Other fairly well known versions are *la pringá,* or Andalusian cocido, but the basic dish is a national tradition and varies greatly depending on which area of Spain you are in.

Italy

The first fully developed cuisine in Europe was that of ancient Rome, which, as the empire grew, acquired cooking techniques and ingredients from Greece and Asia Minor. It was, in fact, Italy that passed a love of good cooking and eating to France through the Medicis. The bible of the French kitchen, *Larousse Gastronomique,* goes so far as to make the concession that "Italian cooking can be considered, for all the countries of Latin Europe, a veritable mother cuisine."

Italy is a country of at least twenty diverse regions, each with its own distinctive dialect, culture, and cuisine. For example, Italy's southern regions and island regions share a common larder, yet each uses the ingredients in ways shaped by its climate, past occupiers, proximity to the sea or mountains, and other geographical factors.

Sicily, an island in the Mediterranean Sea that is very close to Africa, has a cuisine based on olive oil, the island's produce, and fish and shellfish. In the very early spring the island is abundant with lemons, oranges, almonds, tomatoes, and eggplant. Wine and sea salt are central products in Sicily and are renowned for their superb quality. For those on the Sicilian coast, the cuisine includes a variety of fish, such as sardines, anchovies, tuna, and swordfish. Influences remain from the 250-year Arab occupation of Sicily, such as marzipan, couscous, saffron, cinnamon, and the pairing of sweet and sour flavors. The Arabs also planted rice and brought better methods of irrigation. The art of ice cream– and sorbet-making was also learned from the Arabs, using ice from the slopes of Mount Etna.

Sardinia, an island off the coast of Sicily, has its own food customs and cuisine. Local specialties include *carta di musica* (a crisp, paper-thin bread) and fregola (a toasted form of couscous). Dried pasta is preferred to fresh, and, as in Sicily, olive oil is the primary cooking fat, although in recent years, more butter has been used. Lamb, pork, and goat are the principal meats, but quality beef and veal have become more available.

On the mainland of Italy, the region of Campania and its major city of Naples is home to an olive oil–based peasant cuisine. Fresh fish, the San Marzano tomato, and dried pasta are featured ingredients. Naples is the birthplace of pizza, made with fresh mozzarella di bufala and a crust blackened in a coal-burning or wood-fired oven. Sheep's, rather than cow's, milk cheeses are the norm in this area.

The favorite sheep cheese is pecorino, which is available in a number of ways, such as dry, soft, seasoned, or peppered.

In Italy, you will rarely see fish served in poorer inland regions; in Calabria, Puglia, Abruzzo, and Molise, the cuisine is based instead on lamb and pork. The mountainous terrain does not support the production of beef, so the region's cooking techniques adapted to suit their geography and local products. One dish found only in this region is *spaghetti alla chitarra*, spaghetti cut on a special piece of equipment called a chitarra, or "guitar," served with a lamb ragù and hot chili peppers in oil on the side. Other regional specialties include orecchiette ("little ears") pasta in Puglia and *scripelle* crêpes in Abruzzo, a product of the French occupation.

The discovery of the Americas also had a major influence on Italy. Florence has long been a major financial and cultural center in Italy, and was amongst the first cities in Europe to see the New World's tomatoes, beans, potatoes, corn, chocolate, and turkey. Some of the items brought from the Americas are now considered fundamental to Mediterranean cuisine—Italian or Spanish cuisine is hard to imagine without tomatoes!

Greece

The holy trinity of olive oil, grapes, and grains is omnipresent in the Greek diet, which can be broken down into three distinct styles: shepherd's cuisine, island cuisine, and Turkish-influenced cuisine. Shepherd's cuisine is from the interior mountains and was designed for the seminomadic lifestyle of a people moving continuously with the herds and the seasons. Food needed to travel well and be fairly simple in nature. Cheese, yogurt, grains, greens, cured meats, pickled vegetables, and savory pies met these needs. Due to the bountiful Mediterranean Sea surrounding the islands, seafood is a staple protein in island cuisine. The arid and rocky terrain on many of the islands also make sheep and goats a predominant farm animal. Vegetables in island cuisine are limited to what the dry terrain will grow. Turkish-influenced cuisine is common in eastern parts of the country, and includes tzatziki, stuffed vegetables, eggplant caviar, smoked fish, kebabs, and moussaka.

COOKING STYLES AND SPECIAL EQUIPMENT

There are a variety of specialized cooking styles and methods used in the various cuisines of the Mediterranean. In more arid areas, succulent vegetables and fruits are used to help keep people cool and hydrated. Though it may seem counterintuitive, the heat of spicy food can also help cool you down in a hot environment. Therefore, arid regions often serve more spicy dishes and spicy condiments, like zhug or harissa. In the warmer regions of the Mediterranean, sauces are usually not heavy; if they need to be thickened, nuts are often used, as with a muhamara. The intense heat also leads to more food being served at room temperature, for example, salade niçoise is a specialty in Provence.

Slow cooking is a method found in many Mediterranean cuisines. Tagines and stews need to be cooked very slowly in order to coax out the flavor and fully tenderize the tougher cuts of meat. Certain dishes are beautifully simple, while others are a bit more complex, but it is imperative in every recipe that you add each ingredient at the proper stage, so that the flavors layer upon each other in the best possible way. Other dishes have signature ingredients or certain cooking techniques that define the dish and without which the dish would not be the same. For example, when making paella (page 118) or chelow (page 72), it may seem strange, but it is absolutely essential, to get a crust to form on the bottom of the pan.

If you love kitchen gadgets or enjoy collecting pots and pans, you can add to your collection by purchasing some specialty items for the Mediterranean cook. But many people don't have a kitchen large enough to store all these extras or simply don't want to incur the expense. If that is the case with you, don't panic. Although certain dishes are traditionally made in special pieces of cooking equipment, there are plenty of inexpensive solutions that you probably already have in your kitchen.

A tagine is a cooking vessel with a heavy, flat bottom and a cone-shaped top traditionally made of glazed or painted clay. It is the perfect portable oven, which is why it is the cooking vessel of choice for Morocco's nomadic tribes. If you don't have a tagine, a Dutch oven with a tight-fitting lid will serve the same purpose.

A paiolo is an unlined copper pot specifically used to make polenta. It has slightly sloped sides like a jam pot and is often used on farms as an all-purpose tool, used for everything from making cheese to doing laundry. If you don't have a paiolo, you can make polenta in any sauce pot with a tight-fitting lid. Just remember that polenta is extremely sticky when it gets hot and can burn easily.

A cataplana is a hinged copper pot that is rounded on the bottom and top, making it look like a clamshell. It is traditionally used to cook shellfish in Spain, and it can be used on the stovetop or in the oven. If you don't have a cataplana, just use a sauce pot that is wider than it is high and has a lid.

A couscousière is a piece of special equipment used to steam couscous over a stew. The idea is that the steam from the stew cooks the couscous while flavoring it at the same time. You can achieve the same result by using a steamer basket lined with cheesecloth.

Paella pans are fairly common and not too hard to find in kitchen stores. They are flat and low, usually no more than 2 inches in height. The large surface area allows for lots of crispy rice and for the appropriate layering of the chicken, quail, and/or shellfish. If you are making a small paella, you can substitute a regular sauté pan on the stovetop, but if you are feeding a large crowd, I recommend purchasing a large paella pan and cooking the whole thing out in your backyard over an open flame.

In addition to being the name of a dish, a cocido is also the term used for the ceramic or clay pot in which the dish is cooked. Ceramic and clay allow for even cooking without any hot spots, but a heavy, cast-iron kettle will do the job just as well.

MEDITERRANEAN DINNER PARTIES AT HOME

When hosting a dinner party at home, a culinary theme can really pull your party together. The beauty of choosing a Mediterranean theme is that the possibilities it offers for entertaining are virtually endless. You have the choice of creatively combining the cuisines of different regions, staying strictly with traditional foods from one country, or simply focusing on a particular style of eating.

A Middle Eastern meze table will allow your guests to mingle over a large assortment of small items. A meze party will encourage conversation, and the fact that the table can be as small or vast as you wish will keep your guests coming back for more, further encouraging mingling.

If you have some help, you may want to try your hand at hosting a tapas party. Tapas are small bites usually eaten with an alcoholic beverage, like wine or beer. The thing to consider about tapas is that they require lots of small plates and little picks, forks, and spoons as well. If you don't mind the fuss, you can have a lot of fun with this kind of party. If you enjoy entertaining with tapas, it's smart to start purchasing small plates whenever you see them on sale—before too long you will have a sufficient assortment.

Should you decide to go with an Italian theme, be sure to choose plenty of antipasti, light pasta dishes, cheeses, and artisanal salumi. If you have a tight budget, you can create a beautiful assortment of pickled vegetables paired with some good-quality breads.

If you are in the mood for a French theme, choose some of the delicious and colorful foods of Provence. Decorate the dinner space in vivid, sunny colors, and don't forget a large bouquet of sunflowers. Keep things simple and serve large platters family style or buffet style. The summer temperatures and aridity of Provence often keep people confined to the shade during the day, enjoying cold or room-temperature dishes instead of hot foods. Bottles of French rosé on ice offer a cool complement the Provençal dishes.

A Greek islands party can provide you with the opportunity to serve simple seafood preparations. Fresh fish grilled with sea salt and lemon is a great summer dish. An assortment of dips and spreads alongside a simple Greek salad with some fresh pita bread make a beautiful and refreshing buffet spread. You can transport your guests to a beach in Corfu by serving some chilled ouzo and recreating a Greek-style taverna atmosphere on an outdoor patio.

Mix and match these cuisines or just stay with one region. There is so much to choose from that you will never be bored in the kitchen. You may have to go to some specialty shops or even procure ingredients online, but a Mediterranean theme is a sure winner. Your guests will be happy and at the end of the night, and so will you.

SOUPS

Every culture has its own soup, and since there are so many different countries in the Mediterranean basin, the flavors and possibilities for soup are endless. This chapter is just a sampling of some of those flavors. Soup is easy to make, freezes well in many cases, and, with the simple addition of some crusty bread and a salad, is a complete meal.

TYPES OF SOUP

A broth, made by simmering poultry, meat, fish, or vegetables in water, can be either a sustaining cup of soup on its own or the basis of countless other dishes. Broth-based soups include such classics as chicken noodle soup, onion soup, and bouillon. If your broth-based soup includes vegetables, grains, or pasta, add these ingredients in the sequence indicated in a recipe to ensure that everything finishes cooking at the same time. Finish a full-bodied broth with simple, carefully chosen garnishes: grilled or baked croutons, poached eggs, wontons or tortellini, a few sprigs of a fresh herb, or tender new peas.

Puréed soups and cream soups share several characteristics, although they also differ in a few essential ways. Puréed soups are made from dried legumes or starchy vegetables such as lentils, potatoes, pumpkins and other squashes, or carrots. Their hearty texture and substantial body come from these main ingredients. The base of a cream soup may be nothing more than a puréed soup, or it can be broth or milk thickened with flour in the form of a roux and simmered with the main ingredient, which might be chicken, broccoli, asparagus, or tomato, for instance. Both puréed soups and cream soups, whether or not they contain cream, are creamy when properly cooked. Cream soups can be strained for an elegant texture; puréed soups usually are not. Serve puréed soups with a plain garnish, like tiny croutons or a fine dice of ham. In a bisque, a type of cream soup, shells from shrimp, lobster, crab, or crayfish are cooked and puréed in the base. The base is then strained and finished with cream.

Hearty soups are sometimes classified as special regional soups and may combine the characteristics of more than one soup type. They usually feature an area's specialties, such as local seafood, or staples like cabbage, potatoes, or beans. Some are traditionally made to celebrate seasonal holidays. As these soups travel the globe, they are changed and adapted.

PREPARING AND SERVING SOUPS

Cook soups at a gentle simmer until they are flavorful and stir them as often as necessary to keep them from scorching. Pay special attention to soups made with beans or potatoes or those thickened with flour, as they scorch easily. If you are reheating a soup after storing it, be sure to bring it up to a vigorous simmer. Broth-based soups can be reheated over high heat, but puréed or cream soups should be placed over low heat until they soften, and then stirred frequently as they reheat. When making soup, sample it at every stage. To avoid "double dipping," ladle small amounts into a cup that you keep nearby along with a tasting spoon. When the soup is done, or after reheating, taste and adjust the seasoning one more time before ladling it into bowls and presenting it at the table. Kosher salt is used for all the recipes in this chapter and in the book unless otherwise specified. Table salt can be substituted if desired. Serve hot soups very hot in warmed bowls or cups. Serve cold soups very cold in chilled dishes.

MAKING A SPICE SACHET

These bundles of herbs and spices, also called sachets d'épices, are used to add flavor to a simmering broth, soup, or stew. A basic sachet that will flavor 2½ to 3 quarts of liquid contains 5 or 6 cracked peppercorns, 3 or 4 parsley stems, 1 sprig fresh thyme or ½ teaspoon dried thyme, and 1 bay leaf. Add or substitute other spices to complement the flavors in a specific dish. Place the herbs and spices on a square of cheesecloth large enough to contain them. Twist the corners of the cheesecloth together and tie securely with one end of a long piece of kitchen twine. When adding it to the pot, tie the other end of the twine to the pot handle for easy removal later. At the end of cooking, gently pull out the sachet, untie the twine from the pot handle, and discard the bundle. If you prefer, enclose the herbs and spices in a large tea ball, in place of the cheesecloth, and hook it to the side of the pot.

MAKING BROTH

A great soup starts with a good broth. Not everyone has the time to prepare homemade broth, so I have also included instructions for improving store-bought broth. This quick process will refresh the flavor and greatly improve the overall quality of any store-bought broth. But if you have freezer space and an available afternoon, it is preferable to make your broth from scratch. Make a large batch and freeze it so it is ready to use any time you want to make soup. When you are making a broth you will need a sachet (see page 3). Using a sachet will enable you to pull it out when the flavor of the broth is just right even if it has not finished cooking.

GENERAL TIPS ON MAKING AND STORING BROTH

The following tips can help to produce the most flavorful, nutritious broth. Don't be afraid to experiment with different ingredients in the broth to try a variety of flavor profiles that are suited to your taste.

- For good flavor and body, use meaty bones. Bones from younger animals contain a high percentage of cartilage and other connective tissues that break down into gelatin during simmering and give the stock body. Knuckle, back, and neck bones are good for broth as well.

- Cut bones into 3-in lengths for quicker and more thorough extraction of flavor, gelatin, and nutritive value.

- If the bones are frozen, thaw them before simmering for stock. Rinse all bones, fresh or frozen, thoroughly before putting them into the stockpot to remove blood and other impurities that can compromise the quality of the stock.

- Make sure to skim the broth to remove foam and other impurities.

- The flavor of the broth can be changed or deepened depending on the ingredients used. Many broths generally use basic vegetable combinations, but more ingredients can be added to produce the desired flavor. This is also true of the standard sachet d'épices, whose ingredients can be expanded to produce deeper and more varied flavors.

- Broth is an excellent way to infuse flavor into a dish without adding fat or excess calories. Use it to cook grains, vegetables, meats, sauces, or soups.

- Store broth in an airtight container for up to a week or in the freezer for up to 3 months.

VEGETABLE BROTH

A good vegetable broth is not hard to make. The key is slowly sweating the vegetables until their juices are released. Simmering, but not boiling, is also important to making a clear broth, be it vegetable or meat. Skimming is essential to remove impurities, so any foam that rises to the surface should be skimmed off and discarded. MAKES 2½ QUARTS

2 tbsp olive oil *or* unsalted butter

1 large yellow onion, thinly sliced

1 celery stalk, thinly sliced

1 leek, well washed and thinly sliced

1 carrot, thinly sliced

1 parsnip, thinly sliced

1 cup thinly sliced broccoli stems

1 cup trimmed and thinly sliced fennel bulb

3 qt water

1 spice sachet (see page 3)

Salt, to taste

1. Heat the oil or butter in a large soup pot over medium heat. Add all the vegetables and sauté until they start to release their juices, 10 to 12 minutes.

2. Add the sachet and water to the pot. Bring to a boil over medium heat, skimming any foam that rises to the surface. Once it is at a boil, reduce the heat and cook at a slow simmer. Cover partially and simmer for 1 hour, skimming the foam from the surface, as needed.

3. After 1 hour, taste the broth and season with salt, if needed. Strain the broth through a fine-mesh sieve and discard the vegetables. Cool down the broth as quickly as possible by putting the pot of strained broth into a sink full of ice water. Transfer to containers and store in the refrigerator for up to 5 days, or in the freezer for up to 3 months.

IMPROVED STORE-BOUGHT BROTH OR STOCK

If you just don't have the time to make broth from scratch, just take a little time to refresh the flavor of premade broth. It will perk up the flavor and make your soup taste that much better. MAKES 1 QUART

1 qt premade broth or stock

2 celery stalks, thinly sliced

2 carrots, thinly sliced

1 onion, thinly sliced

1 bay leaf

6 flat-leaf parsley sprigs

Combine all the ingredients in a large soup pot and bring to a boil. Skim off any foam that rises to the surface, then reduce the heat to establish a slow simmer. Simmer for 30 minutes and strain through a fine-mesh sieve and discard the solids.

CHICKEN BROTH

Some stores sell packages of chicken necks and backs that may be used to prepare broth. This broth may also be made with the carcasses of roasted birds. Save the carcasses from three birds after all the meat has been pulled or carved away. If you will not be making the broth within 2 days, freeze the carcasses or bones. MAKES 2½ QUARTS

---

4 lb stewing hen parts,
including backs and necks

3 qt water

1 large yellow onion, diced

1 celery stalk, diced

1 carrot, diced

1 spice sachet (page 3)

1½ tsp salt, or more to taste

1. Put the chicken and the water in a large pot. Add more water, if needed, to cover the chicken by at least 2 inches. Bring to a boil over medium heat, skimming any foam that rises to the surface. Once it is at a boil, adjust the heat to establish a slow simmer. Cover partially and simmer for 2 hours, skimming the foam from the surface, as needed.

2. Add the onion, celery, carrot, sachet, and 1½ teaspoons salt. Continue to simmer, skimming as necessary, until the broth is flavorful, about 1 hour more. Season with additional salt, if needed.

3. Remove the meaty parts and save for another use. Strain the broth through a fine-mesh sieve and discard the solids. Cool down the broth as quickly as possible by putting the pot of strained broth in a sink full of ice water. Skim the fat from the surface or chill the broth and lift away the hardened fat. Transfer the broth to containers and store in the refrigerator for up to 5 days, or in the freezer for up to 3 months.

Chef's Note *The onion, celery, and carrot used to make the broth are collectively known as* mirepoix.

ARTICHOKE AND LAVENDER SOUP

For me, this soup conjures up images of sunny days picking fresh lavender in Provence and misty nights spent looking out over the meadow with a chilled glass of rosé in hand. The combination of flavors may seem a bit unusual, but this unique soup is truly delicious whether served hot or chilled. MAKES 1½ QUARTS

SOUP

¼ cup olive oil

6 shallots, sliced

6 artichoke bottoms, cleaned, choke scooped out and discarded, stem peeled and thinly sliced

1 lavender sprig

3 cups Chicken Broth (page 6) or Vegetable Broth (page 4)

Finely grated zest and juice of 1 lemon

Salt, to taste

Freshly ground black pepper, to taste

2 tbsp lavender honey

GARNISH

Zest of 1 lemon

Heavy cream, whipped to soft peaks

Lavender honey, to taste

Lavender sprigs, to taste

1. To make the soup: In a small sauce pot, heat the olive oil over medium heat. Add the shallots and cook until soft and translucent, about 5 minutes. Add the sliced artichoke bottoms and lavender sprig, cover, and cook over medium heat until the artichokes are soft, about 20 minutes.

2. Add the broth, increase the heat, and bring to a boil. Skim off any foam that rises to the surface, then reduce the heat to establish a simmer. Simmer for 15 minutes, then remove from the heat. Add the lemon zest and juice and season with salt and pepper. Add the lavender honey.

3. Allow the soup to cool slightly, then process in a blender (not a food processor) until very smooth.

4. If serving the soup hot, first carefully fold the lemon zest into the whipped cream. Ladle the soup into warmed bowls and garnish with a large spoonful of lemon whipped cream, some drizzled honey, and a lavender sprig on top.

If serving the soup cold, fold the whipped cream into the chilled soup along with the lemon zest. Ladle the soup into chilled bowls and garnish with a drizzle of honey and a lavender sprig on top.

Chef's Note *True lavender honey is not infused. It has a sweet floral flavor because it is harvested from bees that extract the nectar from lavender blossoms. It can be found in natural and gourmet food shops and in many grocery stores. Plain honey can be substituted if you cannot find lavender honey.*

YELLOW TOMATO GAZPACHO

Swing by your local farmers' market to find heirloom varieties of yellow tomatoes in the fall. While you are there, pick up a few extra pounds to core and freeze whole so that you can make this soup throughout the winter. If you can't find yellow tomatoes, red beefsteak tomatoes will work just as well. MAKES 2 QUARTS

¼ cup olive oil

3 lb yellow tomatoes, cored

Salt, to taste

Freshly ground black pepper, to taste

1 hothouse cucumber, diced, seeds reserved

2 yellow bell peppers, seeded and diced, scraps reserved

4 celery stalks, peeled and diced, scraps reserved

1 yellow onion, diced, scraps reserved

4 plum tomatoes, peeled, seeded, and diced, scraps reserved

1 jalapeño pepper, seeded and diced

Rice wine vinegar, to taste

Juice of 2 limes

1 tbsp chopped cilantro

1. Preheat the oven to 350°F.

2. Lightly oil the yellow tomatoes. Place the tomatoes on a sheet pan and season with salt and black pepper. Roast the tomatoes in the oven until the skins pop open and the flesh is fairly tender. Allow to cool to room temperature.

3. Place the tomatoes, all the reserved vegetable scraps, and the jalapeño in a blender and purée. Press the purée through a fine-mesh sieve. Season with salt, black pepper, vinegar, and lime juice.

4. Combine all the diced vegetables. Stir the vegetables into the purée or reserve the vegetables and use them to garnish the soup. Refrigerate the soup overnight to allow the flavors to develop. Serve the soup chilled, garnished with the cilantro.

MINTED FAVA BEAN SOUP

This soup originally started as a first course, but it is also wonderful as a main course. On a warm spring day you may find favas at the market. Enjoy them while you can, because they won't be around for long. Although you can usually find them dried, fava beans are really at their best when fresh and in season. MAKES 1½ QUARTS

4 lb fresh fava beans

½ cup extra-virgin olive oil

12 shallots, thinly sliced

Zest and juice of 1 lemon

6 cups Vegetable Broth (page 4)

Salt, to taste

Freshly ground black pepper, to taste

2 tbsp shredded or chopped mint leaves

1. Prepare the fava beans according to the directions on page 35.

2. Heat the olive oil in a large soup pot over medium heat. Add the shallots and cook for 1 to 2 minutes until aromatic. Add the favas, lemon zest, and broth and bring to a boil. Skim the foam off the top and reduce the heat to establish a simmer. Simmer until the beans are tender, about 15 minutes. Add the lemon juice and season with salt and pepper.

3. Process half of the soup through a food mill, then return it to the soup in the pot.

4. Fold in the mint and refrigerate the soup for 1 hour to develop the mint flavor. Serve in chilled bowls with a nice bottle of Sancerre.

Chef's Note *If desired, garnish the soup with blanched fava beans and unsweetened whipped cream.*

KURDISH HOT AND SPICY LENTIL SOUP

This soup is delicious and comforting. If you want it to be a little more attractive, make it with red lentils. They will change the muddy brown color to a nice brick red, which is much more palatable. MAKES 2 QUARTS

2⅓ cups dried brown or red lentils

¾ cup fine-grain bulgur

⅔ cup long-grain white rice

3 qt Chicken Broth (page 6)

2 tbsp ground cumin

Salt, to taste

2 tbsp ground coriander

Pinch of cayenne

Freshly squeezed lemon juice, as needed

¼ cup extra-virgin olive oil

3 medium onions, thinly sliced

1. Rinse the lentils, bulgur, and rice.

2. In a soup pot, combine the lentils, bulgur, rice, broth, cumin, and salt. Bring to a boil over high heat. Reduce the heat to low, cover, and establish a low simmer. Cook until the lentils, bulgur, and rice are tender, about 20 minutes.

3. When the lentils, bulgur, and rice are tender, stir in the coriander, cayenne, and lemon juice. Taste the soup and adjust the seasoning, if necessary.

4. In a large sauté pan, heat the olive oil over medium heat. Add the onions and sauté until they turn a deep brown color, 25 to 30 minutes.

5. Serve the soup in heated bowls and top each with a generous helping of the caramelized onions.

TUNISIAN VEGETABLE BEAN SOUP

This Tunisian soup is really easy to make. It consists of dried beans cooked with vegetables and greens and flavored with some harissa paste. Toward the end of the cooking, you will add some broken pasta to the soup, which adds a different texture and flavor as well. This is a comforting and tasty soup, so go ahead and make a large batch and freeze some for a chilly day. Just be sure to save the addition of the pasta till the last minute whenever you thaw and reheat the soup.

MAKES 2½ QUARTS

SOUP

2 cups dried lima *or* butter beans

2 cups dried chickpeas

3 qt water

2 tbsp olive oil

1 onion, finely chopped

1 celery stalk, diced

3 garlic cloves, finely chopped

1½ cups Chicken Broth (page 6) *or* Vegetable Broth (page 4)

½ cup tomato paste

½ bunch Swiss chard, stems cut into 1-inch-long pieces and leaves roughly chopped

2 cups capellini or angel hair pasta, broken into bite-size pieces

1½ tbsp Harissa (page 14)

1 tbsp salt

¼ tsp freshly ground black pepper

GARNISH

¼ cup chopped flat-leaf parsley

1. Soak the beans and chickpeas separately overnight, each in 6 cups of water.

2. The following day, cook the soaked beans separately in two times their volume of water until they are tender, about 45 minutes. Drain the beans and reserve the cooking liquids.

3. Heat the olive oil in a large soup pot over medium heat. Add the onion, celery, and garlic and sauté until translucent, about 4 minutes. Add the broth, reserved bean cooking liquids, and the tomato paste. Stir until all the ingredients are well blended, then simmer for an additional 10 minutes. Add the cooked beans, Swiss chard, and pasta. Continue cooking until the Swiss chard stems and pasta are tender, about 10 minutes.

4. Add the harissa and stir until incorporated. Season the soup with the salt and pepper.

5. Serve the soup in heated bowls and garnish each bowl with the parsley.

HARISSA

Here in the United States, we have many condiments: ketchup, mayonnaise, Worcestershire sauce, and hot sauce. Harissa, however, is the primary condiment in the Maghreb. Harissa is a spicy pepper paste that adds depth to the flavor of your recipes in addition to spicy heat. MAKES ABOUT 3 CUPS

2½ lb fresh red chiles, preferably Fresnos

1 small red dried hot chile

2 oz sun-dried tomatoes

1 garlic clove, crushed to a paste with a pinch of salt (see Chef's Note, page 97)

½ tsp ground turmeric

¼ tsp ground coriander

¼ tsp ground cumin

¼ tsp ground caraway

1½ tsp freshly squeezed lemon juice

Extra-virgin olive oil, as needed

1. Seed and stem the fresh chiles. Toast the dried chile over low heat in a small saucepan until aromatic, about 1 minute.

2. In a small bowl, rehydrate the sun-dried tomatoes by covering them with hot water. Add the dried chile and steep for 15 minutes. Remove the chile from the water and remove the seeds and stem. Drain the sun-dried tomatoes and reserve the water.

3. Add the fresh chiles, dried chile, sun-dried tomatoes, garlic, turmeric, coriander, cumin, caraway, and lemon juice to a blender and blend until smooth, adding the tomato soaking water, as needed, to achieve a smooth consistency.

4. Adjust the seasoning with additional lemon juice and spices, if needed. Lastly add the olive oil and blend to achieve a pastelike consistency.

MOROCCAN PUMPKIN SOUP

Yes, you can use canned pumpkin and pumpkin seeds if you don't want to bother peeling the pumpkin, but the end result won't be quite as yummy—the fresh pumpkin gives this soup a deliciously deep flavor. It also has a touch of *ras el hanout,* the "king of spices." The unique flavor of this North African spice is hard to describe, but once you taste it, it is obvious why it is called "the king." MAKES 2 QUARTS

SOUP

2 tbsp olive oil

8 oz shallots, sliced (about 4)

1 lb pumpkin, peeled, seeded, and diced, seeds reserved

2 cups Chicken Broth (page 6), warmed

1½ tsp ras el hanout

Salt, to taste

Freshly ground black pepper, to taste

GARNISH

¼ cup pumpkin seeds

Salt, to taste

Ground cumin, to taste

½ cup plain Greek-style yogurt

2 tbsp pomegranate syrup

½ pomegranate, peeled and separated, seeds reserved

1. To make the soup: Heat the olive oil in a soup pot over medium heat. Add the shallots and pumpkin, cover, reduce the heat, and continue cooking until the pumpkin feels tender when poked with a fork.

2. When the pumpkin is tender, add the broth and ras el hanout. Bring the soup to a boil and skim off any foam that rises to the surface. Reduce the heat to establish a simmer and cook for approximately 30 minutes. Season with salt and pepper.

3. Allow the soup to cool for a few minutes, then process in a blender until smooth. Reserve until needed.

4. For the garnish, season the pumpkin seeds with salt and cumin. Toast the seeds in a 325°F oven until they smell toasted and begin to pop. Remove the seeds from the oven and allow them to cool to room temperature.

5. At serving time, reheat the soup, if necessary, and portion it into bowls. Spoon a dollop of yogurt into each bowl of soup and drizzle with some pomegranate syrup. Finish with a sprinkling of the pomegranate seeds and toasted pumpkin seeds.

CLASSIC MINESTRONE

Classic minestrone is one of the most refreshing soups you can make. The combination of fresh vegetables, beans, and pasta makes it light yet hearty. It is an Italian version of the French pistou. Be sure to finish each bowl of soup with a nice hearty spoonful of grated Parmesan cheese. MAKES 3 QUARTS

1½ cups dried chickpeas

2 tbsp unsalted butter

¼ cup olive oil

1 cup diced onion

1 cup diced carrot

1 cup diced celery

2 cups diced peeled potatoes

2 cups diced zucchini

1 cup green beans, cut into ¼-inch lengths

3 cups shredded savoy cabbage

2 qt Vegetable Broth (page 4) or Chicken Broth (page 6), warmed

One 3 by 3-inch piece Parmigiano-Reggiano rind, cleaned

1 cup canned plum tomatoes, seeded and diced, juice reserved

1 tsp salt

¼ tsp freshly ground black pepper

Grated Parmigiano-Reggiano, to taste

1. Put the chickpeas in a large bowl and add enough cold water to cover them by 2 inches. Immediately discard any chickpeas that float to the surface. Soak the chickpeas overnight.

2. The next day, drain the soaked chickpeas. In a medium pot, combine the water with the drained chickpeas and bring the liquid to a boil. Reduce the heat to establish a simmer and cover the pot. Cook the chickpeas until tender, 1 to 1½ hours. Drain the chickpeas and reserve.

3. In a soup pot, melt the butter and olive oil over low heat. Add the onions and cook until soft and translucent, about 4 minutes. Add the carrots and continue cooking for 3 minutes more. Add the celery, potatoes, zucchini, green beans, and cabbage. Stirring frequently, continue cooking until all the vegetables have softened but not browned, about 20 minutes.

4. Add the broth, cheese rind, and tomatoes and juice. Cover loosely with aluminum foil, reduce the heat to establish a low simmer, and cook for at least 3 hours, stirring occasionally. Add more broth, as necessary.

5. Add the chickpeas and season with the salt and pepper. Sprinkle with grated cheese before serving.

Chef's Note *If time is short, you can substitute canned chickpeas or other canned beans that have been rinsed and drained.*

ZUCCHINI AND POTATO MINESTRA WITH MUSHROOMS

My grandmother Helen was a really good cook. She was just a natural. One of the dishes that I most loved was her *minestra.* The following is a version of her recipe. It can be served as a side dish or as a first course. MAKES 1 QUART

½ cup olive oil

2 medium yellow onions, cut into medium dice

4 garlic cloves, pressed or sliced

2 cups sliced white mushrooms

2 russet potatoes, peeled, diced, and held in cold water to prevent oxidation

1 qt Chicken Broth (page 6)

2 thyme sprigs

Salt, to taste

Freshly ground black pepper, to taste

2 medium zucchini, cut into medium dice

1. In a soup pot, heat the olive oil over medium heat. Add the onions and garlic and sauté until aromatic, about 5 minutes. Add the mushrooms, increase the heat, and cook until the mushrooms release their liquid and dry out.

2. Add the potatoes, then immediately add the broth. Add the thyme and season with salt and pepper. Reduce the heat and allow the soup to simmer until the potatoes are half-cooked, about 10 minutes; the potatoes should be slightly softened but still firm when tested with a fork. Add the zucchini and continue to cook until the potatoes are tender enough to mash easily and the chicken broth has almost evaporated, about 10 minutes more. Serve the soup immediately in warmed bowls, if desired, but this soup tastes better if you make it a few hours before serving and allow the flavors time to mingle and intensify.

TUSCAN WHITE ONION SOUP

A version of this soup was a winter standard when I owned the restaurant Grappa in Atlanta. It pairs one of my favorite spices, cardamom, with white onions, crispy prosciutto, and shaved Parmigiano-Reggiano for a combination of sweet, salty, and buttery that will knock your socks off. MAKES 1½ QUARTS

SOUP

¼ cup olive oil *or* unsalted butter

2 lb sweet onions, sliced

2 shallots, sliced

2 garlic cloves, pressed or sliced

1 tbsp ground cardamom

2 cups Chicken Broth (page 6), warmed

Salt, to taste

Freshly ground black pepper, to taste

GARNISH (*OPTIONAL*)

1 cup heavy cream, lightly whipped

4 slices Italian or French bread, brushed with olive oil and toasted

6 slices prosciutto, thinly sliced and crisped in the oven (the same way you would cook bacon)

Parmigiano-Reggiano, shaved with a peeler, to taste

1 cup balsamic vinegar, reduced over high heat to ⅓ cup

2 tbsp chopped chives, or as needed

1. To make the soup: Heat the olive oil or butter in a soup pot over medium heat. Add the onions, shallots, garlic, and cardamom. Slowly cook until all the onions are soft and translucent with no color, about 5 minutes; be very careful not to brown the vegetables because this is a white soup.

2. Add the broth, increase the heat, and bring to a boil. Skim any foam that rises to the surface, reduce the heat, and allow the soup to simmer. Season with salt and pepper.

3. Allow the soup to cool slightly then process it in a blender until completely smooth. Strain the soup through a fine-mesh sieve. You may serve the soup alone at this point or add the garnish in step 4.

4. Ladle the hot soup into bowls and spoon a dollop of the whipped cream into each one; the whipped cream will spread out like a cappuccino's foam. Place a piece of crusty bread into each bowl to soak up the soup and crumble a crispy piece of prosciutto on top. Finish with some shaved Parmigiano-Reggiano, a drizzle of the sweet, reduced balsamic vinegar, and a sprinkling of chives.

LOBSTER BISQUE

You have enjoyed most of the lobster meat in the Lobster Ravioli on page 109 and now you have all of those shells. Don't throw them out! By using them for soup, you will end up with the most delicious lobster bisque and, since the main flavoring is in the shells, it did not even cost you that much. Make the bisque and freeze it if you are now on lobster overload—that is, if there is such a thing. MAKES 2 QUARTS

⅓ cup unsalted butter

⅔ cup all-purpose flour

¼ cup olive oil

4 small carrots, diced

1 cup diced celery

1 cup diced yellow onion

¾ cup chopped leeks

1 fennel bulb, trimmed and diced

5 garlic cloves, crushed

5 lb lobster shells, cut into 2-inch pieces

½ cup tomato paste

1 cup white wine

2 qt clam juice

¼ cup Italian rice

Salt, to taste

Cayenne, to taste

1 pt heavy cream, heated

Juice of 2 lemons, as needed

2 tbsp chopped tarragon

1. In a medium sauté pan, make a blond roux: Heat the butter over medium heat and then stir in the flour until the mixture is smooth and moist with a glossy sheen. Stir constantly to prevent scorching as you cook until it is a golden straw color and has a slightly nutty aroma. Reserve the roux.

2. In a large soup pot, heat the olive oil over medium-high heat. Reduce the heat to medium, add the carrots, celery, onion, leeks, fennel, and garlic, and sauté until tender, about 10 minutes.

3. Add the lobster shells and sauté for 10 minutes more. Add the tomato paste and stir to combine. Add the white wine and continue to cook over medium heat until the liquid has reduced by half.

4. Add the clam juice and bring to a boil over high heat. Add the rice and season with salt and cayenne. Cover and cook over medium-high heat for about 45 minutes, or until the flavors are fully combined.

5. Process the mixture in a blender until most of the shells and vegetables are broken up. Strain the mixture through a cheesecloth-lined sieve, return it to the soup pot, and bring it back to a boil over high heat. Whisk in the reserved roux until fully incorporated and cook 10 minutes more, whisking frequently. Reduce the heat, stir in the cream, and continue to cook until the soup has reduced to the desired consistency. If necessary, add the lemon juice to adjust the acidity and taste and adjust the seasoning. Pass the soup through a cheesecloth-lined sieve one more time.

6. Just before serving, stir in the tarragon. Serve the soup in warmed bowls.

PISTOU SOUP

This pistou soup is simply a French version of vegetable soup similar to Italian minestrone. Drop some *pistou,* or fresh "pesto," into the soup just before serving and enjoy the aroma of the fresh basil wafting out of your bowl. It will undoubtedly bring to mind the aroma of a new vegetable garden in early summer. MAKES 3 QUARTS

BEANS
1 cup dried cannellini beans

PISTOU
2½ oz basil leaves (about 4 cups, loosely packed)
3 garlic cloves
½ cup extra-virgin olive oil

SOUP
2 tbsp extra-virgin olive oil
2 cups diced yellow onion
2 qt water
1 tbsp salt
¼ tsp freshly ground black pepper
⅛ tsp cayenne
¾ cup medium-dice peeled yellow potato
½ cup tubetti pasta
4 oz haricots verts, cut into 1-inch pieces (about 1 cup)
1½ cups small-dice, seeded zucchini
1 cup small-dice plum tomato
½ cup grated aged goat cheese

1. To prepare the beans: Put the cannellini beans in a large bowl, cover with cold water by at least 2 inches, and soak overnight. The following day, drain and reserve the beans.

2. To make the pistou: Place the basil and garlic cloves in the bowl of a food processor fitted with the metal blade and process until the garlic is finely chopped. With the processor running slowly, drizzle in the olive oil and allow the mixture to combine until the basil can still be seen in small pieces; you do not want the mixture to be smooth and homogenous. Reserve until needed.

3. To make the soup: Place the olive oil in a soup pot over medium heat. Add the onions and sweat them, stirring occasionally, until translucent with no color, about 7 minutes.

4. Add the beans to the pot and cover with the water. Increase the heat to high and bring to a simmer. When at a simmer, reduce the heat to medium-low, cover, and cook until the beans are cooked halfway, about 25 minutes.

5. Add the salt, pepper, cayenne, and potatoes and cook, covered, until the potatoes are almost completely cooked, about 10 minutes.

6. Add the pasta and cook, covered, until almost al dente, about 7 minutes.

7. Add the haricots verts and zucchini and simmer, covered, about 3 minutes.

8. Turn off the heat, add ½ cup of the tomato and the cheese, and stir to combine.

9. When the cheese has completely melted into the broth, divide the soup evenly among eight soup bowls and garnish each with a tablespoon of the remaining tomato and 1 tablespoon of pistou.

CHILLED CUCUMBER SOUP WITH YOGURT AND LEMONGRASS

In hot Mediterranean climates, cucumbers are incorporated into many dishes because of their cooling properties and natural succulence. They are a great way to cool off in the summer and are a winning combination with lemongrass. You can also use lemon balm in place of the lemongrass. Lemon balm is difficult to find in food stores, though, so I grow it in my garden. The plant is a hardy perennial herb that can be found in most garden shops. MAKES 2 QUARTS

½ cup finely chopped lemongrass

1 cup warm water

1 hothouse cucumber, peeled and diced, but not seeded

2 shallots, finely chopped, lightly sautéed in olive oil and cooled

1 tbsp olive oil

Finely grated zest of 1 lemon

2 cups plain Greek-style yogurt

Salt, to taste

Freshly ground black pepper, to taste

1. Make an infusion by steeping the lemongrass in the water for 1 hour and then strain.

2. Place the lemongrass tea, cucumber, shallots, olive oil, lemon zest, yogurt, salt, and pepper in a blender and process to the desired texture, whether slightly chunky or smooth.

3. Refrigerate the soup for several hours or overnight. Taste and season with additional salt and pepper, if necessary. Serve in chilled cups or bowls.

Chef's Note *Raw shallots and onions can have a very strong sulfuric taste when processed in a blender or food processor, but cooking them first solves this problem.*

DUCK AND WHITE BEAN SOUP

We made a version of this soup when I worked at the restaurant La Terrasse in Philadelphia, and it has been one of my favorites ever since. Here, I have simplified the recipe for the home kitchen. The combination of white beans with duck is classic. Two of the standard ingredients for cassoulet are beans and duck, so it just makes sense. The original recipe had far too many steps for the home cook, but this version is just as good. MAKES 2 QUARTS

8 oz dried white beans

DUCK STOCK
One 2- to 3-pound duck
6 qt cold water
2 onions, cut into large dice
4 carrots, cut into large dice
4 celery stalks, cut into large dice
1 garlic clove, finely chopped
6 black peppercorns
1 bay leaf
4 parsley stems

SOUP
¼ cup reserved duck fat *or* olive oil
2 yellow onions, peeled and diced
4 garlic cloves, finely chopped
1 thyme sprig
4 rosemary sprigs
1 bay leaf
1 qt duck stock, or more as needed, warmed
Salt, to taste
Freshly ground black pepper, to taste
Reserved duck meat, diced

GARNISH
Extra-virgin olive oil, to taste

1. To prepare the beans: Put the beans in a large bowl, cover with cold water by at least 2 inches, and soak overnight.

2. To make the duck stock: Rinse the duck under cold running water and put it into a 2-gallon soup pot. Cover with the cold water and bring to a boil over high heat. Skim off any foam that rises to the surface, then reduce the heat to establish a simmer. Simmer, uncovered, for 1 hour, continuing to skim off any foam that rises to the surface. Add the onions, carrots, celery, garlic, peppercorns, bay leaf, and parsley stems and continue to simmer for 1 to 2 hours more.

3. Carefully lift the duck out of the pot and set it aside until it is cool enough to handle. Pick the meat off the bones and reserve.

4. Strain the stock through a fine-mesh sieve and cool down as soon as possible. Put the pot of strained stock into a sink full of ice water and stir until the stock cools down to 40°F.

5. After you cool the stock, carefully skim the fat from the surface and reserve it; the duck fat will really add to the flavor of the finished soup. Reserve 1 quart of the stock for the soup and freeze the rest for another use. Making the stock can be done up to three days in advance.

6. To make the soup: Drain and reserve the soaked beans. Heat the duck fat in a soup pot over medium heat. Add the onions and garlic and cook until soft and translucent, about 6 minutes. Add the beans, thyme, rosemary, and bay leaf. Cover with the duck stock and bring to a boil. Skim off any foam that rises to the surface and reduce the heat to establish a simmer. If necessary, add more duck stock as the soup simmers. Simmer until the beans are completely tender, about 40 minutes. Season with salt and pepper. Remove and discard the bay leaf.

7. Stir in the duck meat. Ladle the hot soup into warmed bowls and drizzle olive oil on top of each.

RED PEPPER SOUP WITH SUMAC

I love to eat this soup as a refreshing treat in the warm months of summer, but it is also delicious when served warm in the winter. Ground sumac is made from the dried berries of a plant that grows wild throughout the Mediterranean region. It is a beautiful deep red color and lends a tart, astringent flavor. Sumac can be found whole or ground. MAKES 1½ QUARTS

SOUP

2 tbsp olive oil

2 small yellow onions, sliced

4 red bell peppers, seeded and sliced

8 lemon verbena leaves

3 cups Vegetable Broth (page 4) *or* Chicken Broth (page 6)

1 tbsp ground sumac

Salt, to taste

Freshly ground black pepper, to taste

GARNISH

1 cup plain Greek-style yogurt

Thinly sliced lemon zest, to taste

2 tbsp chopped chives

6 small lemon verbena leaves

1 tsp ground sumac

1. To make the soup: Heat the olive oil in a soup pot over medium heat. Add the onions and sauté until translucent with no color, about 5 minutes. Add the bell peppers and lemon verbena leaves and continue to cook until both are somewhat soft.

2. Add the broth and increase the heat to bring it to a full boil. Skim off any foam that rises to the surface, then reduce the heat to establish a simmer. Add the sumac and continue to simmer for 30 minutes. Season the soup with salt and pepper and allow it to cool completely.

3. Remove the lemon verbena leaves and process the soup in a blender until smooth. Chill in the refrigerator overnight.

4. Serve the soup in chilled bowls. Garnish each bowl with a dollop of yogurt lemon zest, chives, and a lemon verbena leaf, and sprinkle lightly with the ground sumac.

Chef's Note *If you can't find lemon verbena leaves, you can substitute 1 stalk lemongrass cut into 2-inch sticks. It is best to crush the lemongrass sticks with a mallet and tie them into a bundle with kitchen twine so that it is easy to pull them out of the pot later.*

ROASTED GARLIC SOUP WITH ROSEMARY

The thought of eating garlic soup may sound strange, but when the garlic is roasted, it takes on a very sweet flavor, much like caramelized onions. This soup would be traditionally made in the French countryside. The beauty of this soup is its minimal ingredients, so it makes an easy midwinter meal. It is really comforting on a cold day and it is surprising how mild the garlic tastes. MAKES 1½ QUARTS

SOUP

8 whole heads garlic

¼ cup olive oil, plus more as needed

8 shallots, sliced

1 bay leaf

1 rosemary sprig

3 cups Chicken Broth (page 6), warmed

Salt, to taste

Freshly ground black pepper, to taste

1 cup heavy cream, warmed

GARNISH

1 garlic clove, finely chopped

2 tbsp olive oil

Six ½-inch-thick slices crusty French bread *or* **1 cup Rosemary Popcorn (page 27)**

1. Preheat the oven to 350°F.

2. To make the soup: Rub or brush the heads of garlic with 2 tablespoons of the olive oil and wrap in aluminum foil. Place the foil-wrapped garlic on a sheet pan and bake in the oven until the garlic is soft, 30 to 40 minutes.

3. Cut the top third off each head of garlic to expose the individual cloves. Allow the heads to cool enough to handle, then squeeze the pulp out of the papery skins.

4. In a soup pot, heat the remaining 2 tablespoons olive oil over medium heat. Add the shallots and cook, stirring slowly, until lightly browned and softened, about 10 minutes. Add the roasted garlic, bay leaf, rosemary, and broth. Bring the mixture to a boil, skim off any foam that rises to the surface, and reduce the heat to establish a simmer. Simmer for 30 minutes.

5. Remove and discard the rosemary and bay leaf and allow the soup to cool slightly. Process the soup base in a blender until smooth. Season with salt and pepper.

6. Reheat the soup base and stir in the heavy cream. Serve in warmed bowls.

7. To make the garnish: Whisk together the garlic and olive oil in a small bowl and brush the mixture evenly over the bread slices. Place the slices on a sheet pan and broil on both sides just until browned, about 2 minutes per side; watch carefully to prevent the garlic from burning.

8. Garnish each soup bowl with a crouton or a sprinkling of popcorn.

ROSEMARY POPCORN

Popcorn can be a wonderful soup garnish, and this easy variation is the perfect topping for Roasted Garlic Soup with Rosemary (page 26). The crunchy popcorn adds a surprising texture that can be a nice alternative to the usual crouton or cracker soup garnish. MAKES 1½ CUPS

¼ cup olive oil	2 rosemary sprigs, chopped
½ cup popcorn kernels	1 tsp salt

1. In a saucepan, heat the olive oil over medium-high heat. Add the popcorn kernels and cover the pan with a lid.

2. As the kernels begin to pop, shake the pan on the burner to keep them moving. While the kernels are still popping briskly, stir in the rosemary and replace the lid.

3. When the popping has slowed, remove the pan from the heat to keep the popcorn from burning. Sprinkle with the salt while still warm. The popcorn is now ready to be used as a soup garnish or eaten out of hand.

BOURRIDE

Bourride is a traditional fish soup served with aïoli, a garlic mayonnaise. The fish is cooked in a court bouillon, which is an acidulated liquid that has been infused with aromatics. Although it does have some fish bones in it, the court boullion will be lighter than a traditional fish stock. If you don't want to fuss with fish bones, you can substitute 2 cups of clam juice for 2 cups of the water. This soup is thickened with aïoli and additional egg yolks so it is important not to overheat it. But don't be intimidated by the egg yolks—this is easy to make and quite tasty. MAKES 2 QUARTS

COURT BOUILLON

2 lb fish bones

6 cups water

1 cup dry white wine

2 cups thinly sliced onions

2 leeks, white parts only, washed and thinly sliced

2 tbsp white wine vinegar

1 unpeeled lemon, preferably organic, thinly sliced

1 unpeeled orange, preferably organic, thinly sliced

2 bay leaves

1 fennel bulb, trimmed and thinly sliced

2 tsp salt

AÏOLI

1 tbsp dry bread crumbs

1 tbsp white wine vinegar

6 garlic cloves, finely chopped

½ tsp salt

Pinch of freshly ground white pepper

7 large egg yolks

1½ cups olive oil

1 tbsp freshly squeezed lemon juice

1. To make the court bouillon: Combine all the ingredients in in a 6-quart sauce pot. Bring the mixture to a boil, then immediately reduce the heat and establish a simmer. Skim off any foam that rises to the surface, then simmer for 30 minutes. Strain through a fine-mesh sieve and reserve.

2. To make the aïoli: Combine the bread crumbs, vinegar, garlic, salt, and pepper in the bowl of a food processor fitted with the metal blade and process to a fine paste.

3. Add 3 egg yolks and process until smooth. With the processor running, slowly drizzle in the olive oil and process until emulsified. Add the lemon juice and process to combine.

4. Reserve ⅔ cup of the aïoli in a small bowl and cover with plastic wrap. Place the remaining aïoli sauce in a 4-quart sauce pot.

5. To make the croutons: Preheat the oven to 325°F. Slice the baguette into twenty ¼-inch slices and toast lightly in the oven for 10 minutes. Reserve until needed.

6. To cook the fish: Bring the reserved court bouillon to a simmer and add the halibut first, followed by the cod and then the sole. Simmer, uncovered, for 5 minutes, or until the fish is just firm. (The fish are added in that specific order because of the cooking time of each individual fish.)

7. Transfer the pieces of fish to a warm serving platter and cover with plastic wrap.

8. Remove the court boullion from the heat and add the remaining 4 egg yolks to the aïoli in the 4-quart sauce pot.

9. Whisk the aïoli and the egg yolks together and then whisk in 1 cup of the court bouillon so that the egg yolk–aïoli mixture warms up slowly—this is referred to as tempering. Tempering the egg yolk–aïoli mixture brings it slowly up to the temperature of the court bouillon so that it does not curdle, or break.

CROUTONS

1 baguette

FISH

2 lb halibut fillets, cut into 2-inch pieces

2 lb cod fillets, cut into 2-inch pieces

2 lb sole fillets, cut into 2-inch pieces

10. Slowly whisk in the remaining broth until it is all incorporated. Whisk constantly over low heat until it thickens enough to coat the back of a wooden spoon. Do not stop whisking and keep the heat low.

11. Check the seasoning and add additional salt, pepper, and lemon juice, if necessary. Pour the soup into a warm tureen.

12. Uncover the fish and bring it to the table with the soup as well as the aïoli and croutons. Place two croutons in the bottom of each serving bowl and then a few pieces of fish on top of the croutons. Ladle the soup over the fish and croutons and finish with a spoonful of the remaining aïoli.

SAFFRON MUSSEL SOUP

The addition of saffron makes this soup a beautiful orange color. Add as much saffron as you like, but whatever you do, use real saffron threads. It makes a big difference, so steer clear of the powder, which may be a cheap imitation. You can also decide whether to leave the mussels whole or chop them up before putting them into the soup. I personally like to add some unsweetened whipped cream at the end to create a froth on top. MAKES 2 QUARTS

SOUP

½ cup olive oil

5 oz bacon, chopped

4 shallots, thinly sliced

2 celery stalks, thinly sliced

2 carrots, thinly sliced

½ cup all-purpose flour

4 lb mussels, cleaned and debearded

2½ cups white wine

2½ cups clam juice

2 cups Chicken Broth (page 6) or Vegetable Broth (page 4)

½ bunch thyme stems

2 bay leaves

2 tsp crushed black peppercorns

½ tsp crushed saffron threads

2 tsp salt

½ tsp freshly ground white pepper

1 cup heavy cream, whipped

½ cup finely chopped chives

1. To make the soup: Heat the olive oil in a 2-quart sauce pot over low heat. Add the bacon and render until it just starts to brown slightly, about 5 minutes. Add the shallots, celery, and carrots and sauté over low heat until very tender, about 15 minutes. Using a wooden spoon, stir in the flour and continue to cook for 5 minutes more, stirring constantly, to form a roux. Remove from the heat and reserve.

2. In a medium, tall-sided pan, combine the mussels, wine, clam juice, broth, thyme stems, bay leaves, and peppercorns, cover the pot, and bring the liquid to a simmer over medium heat. Cook until the shells open and the mussel meat inside is fully cooked, about 3 minutes. Strain through a fine-mesh sieve and decant the mussel broth to remove any sediment. Discard any unopened mussels. Remove the mussels from their shells and reserve in a small amount of the strained broth.

3. Whisk the strained mussel broth into the roux and bring to a simmer over medium heat. Simmer for 25 minutes, then add the saffron. Continue to simmer for 5 minutes more. Season the soup with salt and white pepper. Place the mixture in a blender and purée. Chill in the refrigerator.

4. Garnish the cold soup with the reserved mussels and a dollop of the whipped cream and chives.

SQUASH SOUP WITH ZUCCHINI BLOSSOMS

This soup just smacks of summer. When squash is growing, each one of them has a flower attached to it. The zucchini are fresh and just picked and the flowers are sweet and become super-crispy when fried. There are not a lot of ingredients in this soup, which makes it simple and it tastes just like zucchini. You can serve the fried blossoms on the side so that they don't get soggy. Let your guests add them. MAKES 1½ QUARTS

SOUP

3 tbsp unsalted butter

4 shallots, sliced

1 thyme sprig

4 small zucchini *or* yellow squash, diced or grated

3 cups Vegetable Broth (page 4) *or* Chicken Broth (page 6), warmed

Salt, to taste

Freshly ground black pepper, to taste

1 cup crème fraîche

GARNISH

2 cups olive oil *or* vegetable oil

3 tbsp cornstarch

8 zucchini blossoms

Sea salt or flavored finishing salt, to taste

1. To make the soup: Melt the butter in a soup pot over low heat. Increase the heat to medium, add the shallots and thyme, and cook until they are tender and aromatic, about 5 minutes. Add the zucchini and cook until tender and aromatic, about 5 minutes. Add the broth, increase the heat, and bring the mixture to a boil, skimming off any foam that rises to the surface. Lower the heat and simmer for 10 minutes. Season the soup with salt and pepper.

2. Purée the soup through a food mill or blender. Adjust the seasoning, if necessary.

3. To make the garnish: First line a plate with a layer of paper towels and set aside. In a large sauté pan or small frying pot, heat the oil to 350°F.

4. Place the cornstarch in a sealable plastic bag, add the zucchini blossoms, and shake the bag until all the blossoms are lightly dusted with cornstarch. If necessary, add more cornstarch to the bag.

5. Carefully place the blossoms into the hot oil and quickly fry them until they are crispy and not quite golden brown, about 2 minutes.

6. While the blossoms are frying, reheat the soup, if necessary, and whisk in the crème fraîche.

7. Remove the fried blossoms from the oil and transfer to the lined plate to drain. Season with a sprinkle of salt.

8. As soon as the blossoms are fried, portion the soup into bowls. Garnish each bowl with a fried blossom on top or serve them on the side.

Chef's Note *Fried zucchini blossoms should be served immediately—they can get soggy quickly.*

In the Middle East, you might hear small dishes referred to as *meze* and in Spain as *tapas*. Since different regions have slightly different definitions, the term *meze* is somewhat ambiguous. For example, in Persian, the word *maza* means "taste," but in Arabic it means "table." Likewise, a meze table may be the heart of a meal in Lebanon or Cyprus, while it is a number of small dishes served before the main meal in other parts of the Middle East. What you will find universally is an assortment of simple dishes including vegetables, cheeses, legume-based dishes, and seafood, but geographical location, culture, and seasonality will determine exactly what items you will find on a meze table.

In Spain, tapas originally consisted of simple slices of bread placed on top of a sherry glass as a sort of lid to keep flying critters out. Now it has evolved into a culture in and of itself. Stroll down the street at the end of any workday for a glass of wine at one of the many tapas bars in Spain and you will find a real communal event, as much about the social aspect as the food and wine. In France you may enjoy hors d'oeuvre in the afternoon before a later dinner, while in Italy you will find an antipasti table in most restaurants.

All the recipes in this chapter may be served as meze, tapas, hors d'oeuvre, or antipasti. Try the dishes on their own as small bites, or incorporate them with heartier items from other chapters for a true Mediterranean feast. If you are planning on serving a meze table or having a tapas party, the question is: How much should you make?

One thing you don't want to do is run out of food, so remember that all of these items are great as leftovers and can be enjoyed for several days after they are made. A meze table can really be the entire evening, so you need not follow with an entrée—think variety. A proper meze table should have at least ten items on it, and if you start with the standards—baba ghanoush, hummus, falafel, cucumber salad, fattoush, and fresh pita bread—you already have six items. It is easy to take it further to ten items; simply add zucchini patties, chorizo cigars, feta dip, and some spanakopita and you're there.

How do you decide what to put on the table? Think about contrasting flavors, colors, and textures and make sure you have a good variety. Creamy, crispy, rich, lean, sweet, sour, bright colors, neutral colors—these are all things to consider when designing a meze or tapas party. If you are considering tapas, consider all the little plates you are going to need, or consider having each of your guests bring an item along with their own small plates. How much to make? Well, think about how much you can eat over a certain period of time. If your event is to last a few hours, you might be able to eat about a pound of food, so if you are planning on six guests, try to think about making that much per guest plus a little extra so that you have leftovers. If each guest brings something, be sure to trade after the party and send everyone home with something that they did not make. That way they each get a different leftover. Regardless of what you do, the main thing to remember is to stay organized, think ahead, prep ahead, and have fun with it.

PREPARING FRESH FAVA BEANS

Fava beans are encased in a large, spongy, inedible pod and each bean inside also has an outer skin that needs to be removed prior to using the beans in a recipe. This additional step can be intimidating because of the extra work, but the flavor and texture makes it well worth the effort. When purchasing fava beans, look for pods that are not yellow or wrinkled; they can have some dark spots but the beans inside should be pale and plump.

To prepare the favas, shell the beans as you would peas in a pod. Prepare an ice bath. In a large pot, bring enough water to cover the shelled fava beans to a boil. Lower the favas into the water and quickly bring it back to a boil. Allow the favas to boil for about 1 minute, then drain the beans and immediately submerge them into the ice bath to stop the cooking process. Drain the favas and, using a paring knife, make a little cut along the side of each bean so that you can either peel it or squeeze the bean out.

MINTED FAVA BEANS

My friends Richard and Jen Gaskins have a wonderful farm in Connecticut. They grow just enough fresh favas to keep themselves happy. On one of my visits, I unknowingly picked half their crop to make dinner. I only found out after the meal that I had violated the "fava code," but as soon as they tasted this dish, they gave me full access to their crop. MAKES 5 SMALL-BITE SERVINGS

2 lb fresh fava beans

¼ cup extra-virgin olive oil

3 shallots, thinly sliced

Finely grated zest and juice of 1 lemon

Salt, to taste

Freshly ground black pepper, to taste

1 tbsp shredded or chopped mint leaves

1. Prepare the fava beans according to the directions on page 35.

2. In a medium sauté pan, heat the olive oil over medium heat. Add the shallots and cook until tender and aromatic, 1 to 2 minutes. Add the favas and lemon zest, remove the pan from the heat, add the lemon juice, and season with salt and pepper. Fold in the mint and let the mixture sit for a few minutes to allow the flavors to combine. Serve immediately or refrigerate until ready to serve.

Chef's Note *This dish pairs well with a bottle of Sancerre.*

ZUCCHINI FRITTERS

One of the keys to successful fritters is to squeeze the moisture out of the shredded zucchini so that the batter is not too loose. Another is not to crumble the feta too much because larger pieces will look better and add more flavor to the fritters. And be sure not to stack them when they come out of the pan, or they will become soggy. MAKES 8 SMALL-BITE SERVINGS

2 zucchini (about 1½ lb), coarsely grated

½ tsp salt

¾ cup crumbled feta

1 cup chopped flat-leaf parsley

½ cup chopped scallions

1½ tbsp chopped dill

1 large egg

1 large egg yolk

½ cup all-purpose flour

Pinch of freshly ground black pepper

1 cup extra-virgin olive oil

¾ cup plain Greek-style yogurt

1. Toss together the zucchini and the salt and let stand for 15 minutes. Place in a strainer or small colander and press out the excess moisture.

2. Combine the zucchini, feta, parsley, scallions, dill, egg, egg yolk, flour, and pepper and mix well, adding additional flour, if necessary, to achieve a batterlike consistency.

3. Heat the oil in a sauté pan to 350°F. Test the mixture by dropping a heaping tablespoon of the batter into the oil and frying it until golden brown. If the batter spreads a lot and will not hold its shape around the zucchini, adjust the consistency of the batter by adding more flour.

4. To fry, drop heaping tablespoons of batter into the hot oil and fry until golden brown on one side, 2 to 3 minutes. Turn the fritters over and fry until golden brown on the opposite side, 2 to 3 minutes.

5. Drain the fritters on paper towels and reserve in a warm oven until all the batches are fried.

6. Serve with the yogurt.

DATE AND ALMOND CAKE

Although this is not a baked cake per se, it is formed into a cakelike log. It is a great little snack out of hand, but it is also one of the tastiest accompaniments to cheese that I have ever had, so it makes a fantastic addition to almost any cheese tray. This "cake" gets better with age, so you can make a large batch and it will keep in the refrigerator for two months, tightly wrapped. MAKES 4 TO 6 SERVINGS

SPICE MIX

1 tbsp ground cardamom

1 tbsp ground cumin

1 tbsp freshly ground black pepper

1 tbsp ground cinnamon

CAKE

1 lb pitted dates, roughly chopped

½ cup pomegranate molasses

¼ cup honey

3 tbsp Spice Mix (see above)

1 lb whole almonds, peeled and lightly toasted

1. To make the spice mix: Toast the spices in a sauté pan over medium heat for 2 minutes, combine in a spice grinder, and grind for 1 minute.

2. To make the cake: Combine the dates, pomegranate molasses, honey, and spice mix in a small saucepan. Slowly cook over very low heat until the dates are soft. Immediately place the mixture in a food processor and process until smooth; the mixture will be extremely dense, so it is easier to work with if it is still warm.

3. Return the date mixture to the pan and, using a wooden spoon, fold in the almonds. Remove the mixture from the pan, place on a greased sheet pan, and, working quickly, form it into a log approximately 2 inches in diameter. Place the log on a piece of plastic wrap and roll it up tightly, leaving enough plastic wrap free on either end to grab at both ends. Holding the ends of the plastic wrap in each hand, have someone else twist it in one direction until it tightens up completely. If no one is available, just roll the log on the countertop in one direction to compact it.

4. Let the log cool to room temperature, then refrigerate it until you're ready to serve. Cut the log into small pieces to serve.

TORTILLA DE PAPAS

Tortilla de papas is also known as a Spanish omelet. It is an egg dish made with fried potatoes and, despite the name, only shares the shape of Mexican-style flour or corn tortillas: In Mexico a tortilla is a flat, round style of bread, while in Spain, a tortilla is a flat, round omelet of sorts. Traditionally, it may be eaten at any time of day and makes a great tapas dish when served in small pieces. It does not have to be served hot; it is just as delicious at room temperature.

MAKES 5 TO 10 SMALL-BITE SERVINGS, DEPENDING ON SIZE

1 lb 4 oz russet potatoes, peeled

½ cup olive oil

1¾ cups small-dice Spanish onion

¾ cup small-dice green bell pepper

10 large eggs, beaten

1 tbsp salt, plus as needed

2 tbsp chopped flat-leaf parsley

1. Preheat the oven to 325°F.

2. Boil the potatoes until tender in salted water and allow to cool until they can be handled. Slice the potatoes into ¼-inch-thick slices.

3. Heat the olive oil over medium heat in an oven-safe, large skillet or sauté pan. Add the onions and bell peppers and sweat until tender, about 5 minutes.

4. Stir in the potatoes, cover, and cook over low heat for 3 minutes.

5. Meanwhile, stir together the eggs, salt, and parsley in a bowl.

6. Add the egg mixture to the potato mixture and lower the heat.

7. Cook the omelet slowly on the stovetop, shaking the pan, until the egg starts to set up. Finish cooking the omelet in the oven for 5 to 7 minutes; the tortilla should be set like a custard.

8. Flip the omelet out of the pan and cut it into wedges or squares.

FATTOUSH

Fattoush is a broad term for Middle Eastern bread salads that use leftover pita bread. If you don't have any leftover pita, don't worry, just rip up some fresh pita and toast it to replicate the stale pita in the traditional version.

MAKES 6 TO 8 SMALL-BITE SERVINGS

4 pieces store-bought pita bread or leftover homemade Whole Wheat Pita (page 203), cut into small wedges

¼ cup extra-virgin olive oil

2 tsp salt

½ tsp freshly ground black pepper

½ tsp za'atar (see Chef's Note)

DRESSING

1 tbsp freshly squeezed lemon juice

¼ cup red wine vinegar

2 garlic cloves, finely chopped

¾ cup extra-virgin olive oil

1 tsp salt

¼ tsp freshly ground black pepper

2 tbsp chopped thyme

½ tsp cayenne

1 tbsp sugar

SALAD

1 bunch scallions, chopped

1 cup chopped flat-leaf parsley

6 plum tomatoes, seeded and diced

1 hothouse cucumber, peeled, seeded, and diced

1 cup sliced radishes

1 yellow bell pepper, seeded and diced

1 red bell pepper, seeded and diced

1 head romaine lettuce, chopped

1. Preheat the oven to 350°F.

2. Toss the pita wedges with the olive oil, salt, pepper, and za'atar to coat. Arrange in a single layer on a sheet pan and bake in the oven until the pitas are crisp but not crumbly, about 15 minutes, turning halfway through the baking. Reserve.

3. To make the dressing: In a bowl, stir together all the ingredients for the dressing.

4. To assemble the salad: Combine all the vegetables with the dressing and toss to coat. Add the reserved pita bread and toss to coat. Taste and adjust the seasoning, if necessary.

Chef's Note *Za'atar is a spice blend that is popular in Middle Eastern cuisine. There are many different regional recipes for it. You can buy it online, but it is simple to make it at home. Place ¼ cup imported sumac, 2 tablespoons dried thyme, 1 tablespoon toasted sesame seeds, 2 tablespoons dried marjoram, 2 tablespoons dried oregano, and 1 teaspoon coarse salt in a spice grinder and pulse to combine.*

STUFFED GRAPE LEAVES

After grapes are picked for the crush, there are lots of leaves still on the vines. Although many wineries compost this by-product, the leaves can be put to a delicious use. Generally you can find stuffed grape leaves anywhere you find vineyards, but the fillings vary by region. Some fillings are strictly vegetables and rice, while others contain meat or fish. Grape leaves are most often purchased already cooked or pickled in jars. If you choose to use fresh grape leaves for this dish, briefly plunge them into boiling salted water and, using a skimmer, immediately transfer them to a bowl of ice water to stop the cooking. I find it easier to stuff the leaves if you shingle several of them together so that the leaf is not too thin around the filling. MAKES ABOUT 10 SMALL-BITE SERVINGS

STUFFED GRAPE LEAVES

¼ cup long-grain rice

2 cups plus 2 qt water

¼ cup plus 2 teaspoons salt

60 grape leaves, stems trimmed off

2 scallions, finely chopped

½ cup trimmed and finely chopped fennel bulb

1½ cups finely chopped onion

½ cup chopped dill

½ cup chopped mint

1 cup olive oil

Juice of 2 lemons

¼ tsp freshly ground black pepper

GARNISH

1 lemon, cut into wedges

1 cup plain Greek-style yogurt

1. To prepare the grape leaves: Put the rice in a sieve and rinse under cold running water until the water runs clear. In a sauce pot, bring the 2 cups water and 1 teaspoon of the salt to a boil over high heat. Add the rice and continue to boil until the rice is tender, about 7 minutes. Drain the rice and reserve.

2. In a pot, bring the 2 quarts water and ¼ cup salt to a boil over high heat. Add the grape leaves in batches to avoid overcrowding the pot. Blanch each batch of leaves for 45 seconds to 1 minute. Drain and immediately rinse under cold running water. Drain again and reserve.

3. To make the filling: Mix the cooked rice, scallions, fennel, onion, dill, mint, ½ cup of the olive oil, lemon juice, remaining teaspoon salt, and pepper to combine well.

4. Lay one grape leaf flat on a work surface. Place 2 tablespoons of the filling on top of the leaf. Roll the leaf over once to enclose the filling. Fold the sides of the leaf in and finish rolling the leaf. Roll the filled leaf in one more grape leaf using the same rolling technique. Repeat with the remaining leaves.

5. Tightly pack the rolled grape leaves, seam side down, in a single layer in a high-sided pan. Pour in the remaining ½ cup olive oil and just enough water to cover the grape leaves. Cover the pan with a lid and cook at a gentle simmer over low to medium heat. After 15 minutes, check the water level and add more water to cover, if necessary. Cook until the leaves are tender, about 30 minutes total. Carefully remove the grape leaves from the pan and drain the cooking liquid.

6. Serve at room temperature with Greek-style yogurt and lemon wedges on the side.

Chef's Note *If the heat is too high during cooking, the grape leaves could explode—be sure to keep the heat at low to medium.*

KIBBEH

Kibbeh is a favorite in the Levant area of the Middle East. It is traditionally ground lamb mixed with green wheat, mint, and various spices that is formed into little patties. It can be made in a cake form or breaded and fried. I like to pan roast the little patties and eat them with a yogurt and mint sauce. You can purchase ras el hanout online or in specialty shops. MAKES 5 TO 6 SMALL-BITE SERVINGS

FILLING

2 cups water

½ cup bulgur wheat

1 tbsp olive oil

4 oz ground lamb

2 tbsp finely chopped onion

1 tsp finely chopped garlic

1½ tsp ras el hanout

½ cup beef, lamb, *or* veal broth

¼ cup pine nuts, toasted and chopped

1 tbsp chopped mint

Salt, to taste

Freshly ground black pepper, to taste

KIBBEH

2 cups water

1 cup bulgur wheat

½ tbsp olive oil

¼ cup chopped onion

2 garlic cloves, finely chopped

¾ tsp ras el hanout

¾ cup ground lamb

3 tbsp all-purpose flour

Salt, to taste

Freshly ground black pepper, to taste

Vegetable oil, as needed for frying

1. To make the filling: Bring the water to a boil. In a bowl, cover the bulgur with the boiling water and allow to soak for 20 minutes. Drain the bulgur well and reserve.

2. In a large sauté pan over medium heat, heat the olive oil, add the lamb, and sauté until cooked through, about 8 minutes. Add the onion and garlic and cook until soft and translucent, about 4 minutes.

3. Add the ras el hanout and cook until aromatic, about 2 minutes. Add the broth and simmer gently until the liquid thickens enough to coat the back of spoon, about 8 minutes.

4. In a bowl, combine the lamb mixture with the pine nuts, mint, salt, and pepper.

5. To make the kibbeh: Bring the water to a boil. In a bowl, cover the bulgur with the boiling water and allow to soak for 20 minutes. Drain the bulgur well and reserve.

6. In a large sauté pan over medium heat, heat the olive oil, add the onion, and sauté until soft and translucent, about 4 minutes. Add the garlic and ras el hanout and continue cooking until aromatic, about 2 minutes. Remove from the heat and allow to cool.

7. Place the lamb, flour, bulgur, and cooled onion mixture in a food processor and pulse until well incorporated. Season with salt and pepper.

8. Portion the mixture into walnut-size balls. Roll each ball into an oval (torpedo) shape, dipping your hands in cold water, as necessary, to facilitate rolling. Using your index finger or the back of a spoon, make a cavity in the center of each oval. Fill each cavity with filling, packing it in gently. Seal the filling inside by crimping the kibbeh mixture around it at the ends. Remold each piece into the oval shape as necessary. Refrigerate for 1 hour.

9. In a high-sided pan, heat ¼ inch of oil over medium-high heat. When the oil reaches 350°F, add the kibbeh. Cook on both sides until each piece is golden brown on the outside and fully warmed through, about 2 minutes per side. Remove from the oil and drain briefly on paper towels. Serve immediately.

SHRIMP AND GARLIC

This recipe can be found in any coastal area where shrimp is abundant. It also is made with prawns or langoustine in some areas. For the home cook, shrimp is widely available and easy to prepare. Be sure that your shrimp is nice and fresh with no discernible "fishy" smell. Serve this with some crusty bread to dip in the sauce. MAKES 4 TO 5 SMALL-BITE SERVINGS

¾ cup extra-virgin olive oil

1 tsp red pepper flakes

10 garlic cloves, very thinly sliced

20 (31/35 count) shrimp, peeled and deveined

1 tsp salt

⅔ cup white wine

¾ cup freshly squeezed lemon juice

½ cup roughly chopped flat-leaf parsley

1. Heat the olive oil in a large sauté pan over high heat.

2. Add half the red pepper flakes, garlic, and shrimp and season with half the salt. Remove the shrimp from the pan when just cooked through, 2 to 3 minutes. Reserve on a platter or in a bowl.

3. Add half the wine and lemon juice to the pan and reduce by three-quarters. When the oil and the liquid are at an even volume, you will be able to shake and emulsify it like a glaze. Finish the glaze with half of the chopped parsley and pour over the shrimp.

4. Repeat steps 1 through 3 with the remaining ingredients, but be sure to serve the first batch warm.

Chef's Note *Try combining the shrimp and garlic with pasta for a new dish.*

GRAPPA MUSSELS

My restaurant in Atlanta was called Grappa. We needed a few signature dishes and these Grappa Mussels were one of our best sellers. If you don't have any grappa, just use more dry white wine. The combination of garlic, shallots, fennel, and saffron is one of my favorites. MAKES 12 SMALL-BITE SERVINGS

¼ cup extra-virgin olive oil

2 fennel bulbs, trimmed and thinly sliced

4 shallots, sliced

1 head garlic, cloves peeled and crushed

Finely grated zest of 2 lemons

¼ tsp saffron threads

1 cup grappa

1 750-mL bottle white wine

1 qt fish broth

Salt, to taste

Freshly ground black pepper, to taste

3 lb Prince Edward Island *or* rope-cultured mussels, cleaned and debearded

1 cup unsalted butter, cubed

1 cup chopped flat-leaf parsley

1. Heat the olive oil in a large pot over medium heat. Add the fennel, shallots, garlic, and lemon zest and cook until the shallots and fennel are tender and translucent with no color, about 5 minutes. Add the saffron, grappa, and wine. Continue cooking until the liquid has reduced by half. Add the broth and continue cooking until the liquid has reduced by half. Season with salt and pepper.

2. Add the mussels, cover the pan, and allow to steam until the shells open, 3 to 4 minutes. Discard any unopened mussels. Remove the mussels from the pan and hold in a covered bowl with a small amount of the cooking liquid to keep them moist. Continue cooking the liquid over medium heat until it has reduced by half. Remove the pan from the heat and whisk in the butter until completely emulsified.

3. To serve, portion about ¼ pound of mussels per bowl and cover with the cooking liquid. Sprinkle each portion with the parsley. Serve immediately.

CATAPLANA CLAMS

A *cataplana* is a hammered copper, hinged pot of Portuguese origin that resembles a clam shell. It is used to steam shellfish and can be used on the stovetop or in the oven. Besides being fun to cook in and a bit unusual, it also looks great hanging on a kitchen wall. I bought my cataplana in Portugal in 1986 after eating numerous versions of cataplana clams. MAKES 5 SMALL-BITE SERVINGS

6 large garlic cloves, peeled and crushed

1 tbsp pimentón (smoked Spanish paprika)

1 tsp red pepper flakes

1 cup olive oil

8 oz pancetta

1 medium yellow onion, diced

2 cups dry white wine

20 Manila or other small clams

½ cup chopped flat-leaf parsley

Salt, to taste

1. In the bowl of a food processor fitted with the metal blade, process the garlic, pimentón, red pepper flakes, and ½ cup of the olive oil until it forms a paste.

2. In a bowl, pour the paste over the pancetta and allow it marinate for at least 1 hour; you can marinate it overnight, if you wish.

3. Heat the remaining ½ cup olive oil in a large sauté pan over medium heat. Add the onion and cook until tender and translucent, about 4 minutes. Add the marinated pancetta, cover, and continue cooking for 10 minutes more. Remove the lid and add the white wine. Replace the lid and continue cooking until the liquid has reduced by half. Add the clams and cook, covered, until all the clams have opened, 4 to 5 minutes. Discard any unopened clams. Sprinkle with the parsley and season with salt. Serve in warmed bowls with lots of crusty bread.

TABBOULEH

Tabbouleh is very popular in the Levant area of the Middle East. In Lebanon, it is soaked bulgur wheat mixed with parsley, mint, tomato, and scallions. I love the Lebanese version because it contains more herbs than grain and is particularly refreshing on hot summer days. MAKES 10 SMALL-BITE SERVINGS

½ cup bulgur wheat

2 cups chopped flat-leaf parsley

½ cup chopped mint leaves

1 cup diced tomato

1 cup peeled and diced cucumber

¼ cup good-quality olive oil

½ cup good-quality red wine vinegar *or* lemon juice

½ cup chopped scallions

Salt, to taste

Freshly ground black pepper, to taste

Soak the bulgur in warm water for 30 minutes and drain. Combine the drained bulgur with the remaining ingredients and season with salt and pepper. Chill the salad for at least 30 minutes in the refrigerator before serving.

Chef's Note *For a slightly different flavor, replace the red wine vinegar with a combination of freshly squeezed lemon and orange juice and some finely grated zest.*

SPICY CARROT SALAD

This carrot salad is easy to make and has a cooling effect on the body in the summertime. Use the same ingredients, but slice the carrots, then cook briefly and you have an excellent side dish in the winter as well. MAKES 5 SMALL-BITE SERVINGS

3 cups carrots, finely grated

½ tbsp sugar

½ tsp cumin seeds, toasted

Juice of 1 lemon

½ tbsp extra-virgin olive oil

3 tbsp chopped cilantro

Salt, to taste

Freshly ground black pepper, to taste

1. Combine the carrots, sugar, cumin seeds, and lemon juice in a bowl.

2. Add the olive oil and cilantro, stirring to combine. Season with salt and pepper. Serve immediately or reserve in the refrigerator for up to 2 days.

SPICED ROASTED ALMONDS

Almonds are thought to have originated in Central Asia centuries ago. They got to Europe and the Mediterranean via the spice trade and became a staple product because they grew well in the climate. Almonds are loaded in nutrients and so have been an important staple in the diet of the Mediterranean basin. They make an amazing addition to a tapas or cocktail party. MAKES 2 CUPS

2 cups whole raw almonds
1 tbsp unsalted butter, melted
1½ tsp curry powder
⅛ tsp garlic powder
⅛ tsp onion powder
Cayenne, to taste
Salt, to taste

1. Preheat the oven to 350°F.

2. Toss the nuts in the melted butter until evenly coated.

3. Combine the curry powder, garlic powder, onion powder, cayenne, and salt. Toss the nuts in the spices until evenly coated.

4. Place the nuts in a single layer on a sheet pan and bake until golden brown and slightly aromatic, 8 to 10 minutes.

5. Remove from the oven and allow the nuts to cool completely before serving. The nuts can be stored in an airtight container for up to 10 days.

Chef's Note *Make this recipe with olive oil instead of butter if you are watching your cholesterol.*

Variation
PIMENTÓN ALMONDS: *Replace the melted butter with 1 tablespoon olive oil and replace the spices above with 2 teaspoons pimentón (Spanish paprika). Smoked and sweet paprika both work well in this dish.*

SCALLOP CARPACCIO WITH VERJUS

In French, *verjus* literally means "green juice." It is juice squeezed from unripe grapes, and its use has been documented as far back as ancient Rome. It is usually squeezed from the grapes that need to be picked to thin out the crop, so it is a natural outgrowth of many wine-making regions. It is commonly used in Middle Eastern countries and is a delicious substitute for, or addition to, citrus juice. Verjus can be purchased in both green and red varieties and should be refrigerated after opening. If not refrigerated, it will ferment and you will end up with a bottle of vinegar before too long. MAKES 6 SMALL-BITE SERVINGS

6 dry-packed fresh sea scallops, muscle tabs removed (see Chef's Note)

2 tbsp extra-virgin olive oil

¼ cup verjus

½ cup finely chopped chives

1 cup green grapes, thinly sliced

1 cup red grapes, thinly sliced

1 shallot, finely chopped

Freshly ground black pepper, to taste

Sea salt, to taste (see Chef's Note)

¾ cup frisée lettuce

1. Slice each scallop horizontally into 6 thin rounds. Arrange the rounds from each scallop in a circle on an individual piece of plastic wrap and cover with another piece of plastic wrap. Using a light, flat mallet, lightly pound the scallops until they are all a uniform thickness of about ⅛ inch. Refrigerate until ready to serve.

2. Combine the olive oil, verjus, and chives and toss the grape slices in the mixture to coat. Marinate in the refrigerator for 10 minutes to allow the flavors to meld. Meanwhile, chill six flat plates in the refrigerator.

3. When ready to serve, peel the top layer of plastic wrap off the scallops, invert each portion of scallop rounds onto a chilled plate, and peel off the remaining piece of plastic wrap. Evenly distribute the finely chopped shallot among the six plates, sprinkling it on top of the scallops. Grind some pepper on top and sprinkle with sea salt.

4. Place about ½ cup of frisée in the center of the plate. Divide the grape mixture evenly among the plates, arranging it in the center of the frisée. Drizzle the remaining verjus "dressing" over the plates and serve immediately.

Chef's Notes *This recipe requires no cooking, so the freshness of the ingredients is absolutely critical.*

Try to find U-10–size sea scallops, meaning 10 scallops to the pound. Use only dry-packed fresh scallops, not the ones that come packed in brine.

This dish lends itself to some of the fancy finishing salts available. They add flavor, color, and a really nice crunch; it can be fun to experiment with the different flavors and textures. You may want to just use fleur de sel, from the Brittany coast in France, or try the red Hawaiian sea salt, which adds a very earthy, almost claylike taste to the dish. Pink Himalayan sea salt comes in flakes, which add texture contrast to the dish. The best way to decide which one to use is to experiment. There are small samplers that you can buy at Artisansalt.com.

FALAFEL WITH TAHINI

The place you are from in the Middle East will dictate whether you use chickpeas, fava beans, or a combination of both for this dish. Since dried legumes are easily transportable and last forever, falafel was a constant, convenient staple food for nomadic tribes. Today, it remains a tasty and inexpensive source of protein. If you don't have time to soak your beans, you might try canned, but they will require some prep. Canned legumes have a much moister texture, so you may want to add some chickpea flour to the mixture. Be sure to rinse, drain, and dry canned chickpeas or favas well on paper towels before using. MAKES 4 SMALL-BITE SERVINGS

SAUCE

2 tbsp tahini

2 tbsp plain Greek-style yogurt

2 tbsp freshly squeezed lemon juice

¼ cup water

1 tbsp honey

1 tsp salt

¼ tsp freshly ground black pepper

FALAFEL

1 cup dried chickpeas *or* fava beans

2 tbsp chopped flat-leaf parsley

¼ cup finely chopped scallions

3 garlic cloves

2 tsp salt

¼ tsp cayenne

1 tsp ground cumin

1 tsp ground coriander

1 tsp baking powder

1 cup olive oil, or as needed for frying

1. To make the sauce: Whisk all the ingredients together until smooth; the mixture will be slightly runny.

2. To make the falafel: Place the beans in a large container and cover with cold water by at least 2 inches. If using chickpeas, soak for 48 hours; if using fava beans, soak for 24 hours.

3. Drain the beans and mix thoroughly with the remaining ingredients except for the olive oil.

4. Run the beans once through a grinder fitted with the coarse die, and then run the mixture twice through the grinder fitted with the fine die. Make sure all the wet paste comes out of the grinder. If you don't have a meat grinder, just use your food processor; it works just as well.

5. Mix thoroughly to combine; the paste should resemble very wet coarse sand.

6. Form the mixture into tight 1½-inch disks that are about ½ inch thick and reserve.

7. Heat the olive oil over medium heat in a large, flat-sided sauté pan. When the oil is hot, working in batches, add the falafel and cook until they are golden brown on both sides, about 4 minutes per side.

8. Drain on a baking rack and serve hot with the dipping sauce.

CHEESE AND POTATO CIGARS

These crispy little bites are attractive on a meze table and excellent as a passed hors d'oeuvre. We suggest using egg roll wrappers for ease of assembly, but feel free to use phyllo dough instead. It is a bit harder to work with, but once you get used to it, it's a breeze. MAKES ABOUT 20 SMALL-BITE SERVINGS

FILLING

1 lb 8 oz russet potatoes, peeled and diced

Salt, to taste

4 large eggs

1 lb feta, crumbled

4 tsp ground turmeric

Freshly ground black pepper, to taste

Freshly grated nutmeg, to taste

EGG WASH

1 large egg

2 tbsp whole milk

CIGARS

20 egg roll wrappers

Vegetable oil, as needed for frying

1. To make the filling: Place the potatoes in a medium sauce pot with enough cold water to cover and sprinkle with salt. Bring to a boil over high heat, reduce the heat to establish a simmer, and cook until fork-tender. Drain, allow the potatoes to dry, and set aside until cool enough to handle. Mash the potatoes or, if desired, run them through a ricer.

2. Whisk the eggs in a bowl and add the mashed potatoes, cheese, and turmeric. Season with salt, pepper, and nutmeg. Mix by hand until the mixture is well combined.

3. To make the egg wash: Whisk the egg together with the milk to combine.

4. To make the cigars: Lay an egg roll wrapper out on a clean work surface. Add 2 tablespoons of the filling. Roll the wrapper over once, enclosing the filling. Fold the sides inward and finish rolling the wrapper. Brush the edges with the egg wash to seal.

5. In a deep fryer or a large, heavy-bottomed pot over medium heat, heat the oil to 350°F. Line a plate with paper towels. Working in batches so as not to overcrowd the pot, fry the cigars until golden brown, 1 to 2 minutes per batch. Using tongs or a skimmer, remove the fried cigars from the oil and transfer to the plate to drain briefly. Serve immediately.

Chef's Note *When frying, it is important to always use a thermometer to regulate the oil's temperature. To avoid getting burned, always use extreme caution when adding and removing items from the oil.*

PROSCIUTTO WITH PEACHES AND BALSAMIC VINEGAR

Of course the classic combination is melon and prosciutto, but peaches are my favorite fruit. In the middle of peach season, this fresh approach to an old standard will blow you away. If your peaches are not perfectly ripe, or it is not peach season, try it with mangos for something different. MAKES 8 SMALL-BITE SERVINGS

16 slices prosciutto, very thinly sliced

16 chives

2 perfectly ripe peaches, peeled and cut into 8 wedges per peach

Freshly ground black pepper, to taste

Extra-virgin olive oil, as needed

2 tbsp good-quality aged balsamic vinegar

1. Preheat the oven to 325°F.

2. Wrap 8 pieces of the prosciutto around the bottom of the wells of an inverted standard muffin pan and bake until crispy. Remove the prosciutto from the muffin wells and break into large shards. Reserve until needed for the final plate.

3. Lay the remaining slices of prosciutto out flat on a serving plate and then put a crispy piece at the end of each piece of prosciutto.

4. Finely chop the chives and mix with the peaches. Grind some pepper onto the prosciutto. Arrange the seasoned peaches on the piece of prosciutto on a platter and drizzle with the olive oil and balsamic vinegar. Serve at room temperature.

ORANGE AND ONION SALAD

This salad is simple and refreshing. It is all about the ingredients. The most important step is to soak the onions in salted ice water to remove any trace of sulfur. Also be sure to use a good-quality olive oil. For a twist, you can add some shaved fennel to the onions and dress the salad an hour before serving.

MAKES 5 SMALL-BITE SERVINGS

2 oranges, peeled, pith removed, and sliced crosswise into ⅛-inch slices

½ red onion, sliced paper thin and reserved in 2 cups of ice water with 1 tbsp salt

1½ cups black Kalamata or Niçoise olives

Extra-virgin olive oil, as needed

Cayenne, to taste

Combine the oranges, onions, and olives in a bowl and toss with the olive oil to coat. Season with cayenne. Serve at room temperature.

PANISSE

In this classic dish of southwestern France, chickpea flour is cooked like polenta and poured into a dish to firm up. You can then slice and sauté it like crispy polenta. It makes a great hors d'oeuvre or side dish for an entrée. In this recipe, I have introduced onions, cumin, and cayenne to give it a fresh, earthy flavor. Experiment by adding some fresh basil or your favorite herb to make it even more interesting. MAKES ABOUT 15 SMALL-BITE SERVINGS

1 tbsp extra-virgin olive oil

3 medium yellow onions, finely chopped

1 tsp ground cumin, toasted

¼ tsp cayenne, toasted

1 qt hot water

Salt, to taste

2 cups chickpea flour, sifted

Olive oil, as needed for frying

1. Heat the extra-virgin olive oil in a large pot over medium heat. Add the onions, cumin, and cayenne and cook until the onions are tender and translucent, about 4 minutes. Add the hot water and season with salt. Increase the heat and bring the mixture to a full boil. Reduce the heat to low and whisk in the chickpea flour. Cook the porridge for 15 minutes, stirring constantly with a wooden spoon.

2. Line a sheet pan with plastic wrap. Pour the porridge into the pan and spread it out into an even layer. Cover with another sheet of plastic wrap and refrigerate until it is firm enough to cut into pieces, about 30 minutes.

3. Transfer the panisse from the sheet pan to a cutting board and cut it into 1-inch squares.

4. In a deep fryer or large, heavy-bottomed pot over medium-high heat, heat the olive oil to 350°F. Working in batches to avoid overcrowding, pan fry the pieces until golden brown, about 5 minutes for each batch, flipping them halfway through the cooking time. Serve immediately.

GOAT CHEESE AND SWEET ONION TOASTS

Ingredients you may have lying around your kitchen can be turned into delicious little antipasti or hors d'oeuvre. A day-old baguette, sliced and toasted; some sliced onions slowly caramelized…yes, you might have to go out and purchase some goat cheese…but you get the picture. MAKES 5 SMALL-BITE SERVINGS

½ baguette

⅓ cup unsalted butter, at room temperature

1 whole garlic clove, plus 1 finely chopped garlic clove

1 sweet onion, diced

1½ tbsp olive oil

¼ cup chopped sun-dried tomatoes

2½ tsp sugar

1 tbsp red wine vinegar

1 tsp salt

¼ tsp freshly ground black pepper

¾ cup goat cheese

1. Preheat the oven to 400°F.

2. Slice the baguette on the diagonal into fifteen ⅛-inch-thick slices. Brush each slice with the butter and toast in the oven until crisp and lightly browned around the edges, 8 to 10 minutes. Remove the toast from the oven and immediately rub each piece with the whole garlic clove. Reduce the oven temperature to 350°F.

3. Toss the onion in 1 tablespoon of the olive oil. Place on a sheet pan and roast in the oven, stirring every 10 minutes to prevent burning, until tender and translucent, 1½ to 2 hours. Cool and reserve.

4. In a sauté pan over low to medium heat, cook the sun-dried tomatoes in the remaining 1½ teaspoons olive oil until slightly tender, about 10 minutes. Gently stir the mixture with a wooden spoon to prevent breaking up the ingredients. Add the finely chopped garlic and reserved onions and continue to cook over low heat until the ingredients are warm and the flavors have blended together, 12 to 15 minutes. Add the sugar and vinegar and season with the salt and pepper.

5. Spread ¼ ounce of the goat cheese on each slice of toast, top with 1½ teaspoons of the relish, and serve.

CHEESE AND ONION TART

Who doesn't love a flaky pastry crust with creamy custard baked in it? This is much like a quiche, if you will. Cheese and onion is a favorite combination of mine. Gruyère is a classic ingredient, but try substituting some of your favorite cheeses for variety. Add some lightly caramelized apples and you will be in heaven. MAKES ONE 10-INCH TART

TART DOUGH

2²/₃ cups all-purpose flour

¹/₈ tsp salt

7 tbsp unsalted butter, cubed and chilled

7 tbsp ice water

FILLING

1 qt water

3 thick slices bacon

¼ cup unsalted butter

5 cups finely sliced onions

Salt, to taste

Freshly ground black pepper, to taste

Freshly grated nutmeg, to taste

2 tbsp all-purpose flour

1 cup Gruyère, diced

½ cup heavy cream

½ cup whole milk

1 large egg, lightly beaten

1. Preheat the oven to 400°F.

2. To make the dough: Place the flour and salt in a mixing bowl and work the cold butter into the flour until the mixture resembles fine crumbs. Add the cold water and mix just until the dough forms a ball; do not knead or overwork the dough. Wrap the dough in plastic wrap and refrigerate for at least 30 minutes.

3. On a board or work surface lightly dusted with flour, roll out the dough into 12-inch circle with a thickness of ⅛ inch. Line a 10-inch tart pan with the dough and chill the tart shell for at least 30 minutes in the refrigerator.

4. Prick the bottom and sides of the tart shell with the tines of a fork and then line with parchment paper or aluminum foil. Weight down the paper with some dried beans, lentils, or rice to keep the dough from puffing up as it bakes.

5. Blind bake the tart shell until the dough sets and the edges look dry, 10 to 12 minutes. Remove the paper or foil and the beans and set the shell aside to cool. Reduce the oven temperature to 350°F.

6. To make the filling: Bring the water to a boil in a pot over high heat. Add the bacon slices and blanch for about 10 seconds. Remove the bacon from the water and allow to drain completely. When cool, cut into a ¼-inch dice.

7. In a sauté pan over low to medium heat, melt the butter. Add the onions and season with salt, pepper, and nutmeg. Cook until the onions are a rich golden brown and smell sweet, about 50 minutes. Do not hurry this process; the onions should cook slowly to attain a rich golden color.

8. Sprinkle the flour onto the onions and cook for another 5 to 7 minutes, stirring to avoid burning the onions. Remove from the heat and allow the mixture to cool.

9. To fill the tart: Place the onion mixture and cheese on the bottom of the prebaked and cooled tart shell. In a bowl, whisk together the cream, milk, and egg. Pour the milk mixture into the tart shell. Sprinkle the pieces of blanched bacon on top.

10. Place the tart on a sheet pan on the lowest shelf of the oven and bake until the crust is golden brown and the filling is completely set, about 25 minutes.

Chef's Note *To facilitate removing the finished tart from the pan, line the bottom of the tart pan with parchment paper and grease with butter before lining with the dough.*

GNOCCHI FRITTI

My favorite type of gnocchi are made with potatoes, but they are not the only game in town. Make this simple dough with "00" flour and fry the gnocchi for a wonderful little snack. You can make a sauce to dip them in or just simply sprinkle with sea salt. They are easy and delicious. Keep the dough covered and refrigerated. After you make the gnocchi, you should also let the dough rest before attempting to roll it out. You don't want to overwork it because they will be tough.

MAKES 5 SMALL-BITE SERVINGS

1½ cups "00" flour

½ tsp salt

¼ tsp baking soda

1 tbsp olive oil, plus more as needed for frying

7 tbsp whole milk, warmed

¼ cup water

1. In a mixing bowl, combine the flour, salt, and baking soda. Add the olive oil and mix to incorporate. Add the milk and water and mix until incorporated. Knead until the mixture forms a dough; be careful not to overwork. Form the dough into a ball, wrap in plastic wrap, and allow to rest at room temperature for 1 hour. If you are not using the dough the same day, refrigerate or freeze it until ready to use.

2. When the dough has rested, roll it into logs ¼ inch in diameter. Cut the logs on the diagonal into ½-inch-thick slices.

3. In a deep fryer or large, heavy-bottomed pot, heat the olive oil to 350°F. Line a plate with paper towels. Fry the dough pieces, in batches to avoid overcrowding, until golden brown, 2 to 3 minutes. Transfer the gnocchi to the paper towel–lined plate to drain briefly. Serve immediately.

Chef's Note *A drizzle of reduced balsamic vinegar or a simple marinara sauce for dipping is the perfect accompaniment to this dish.*

BRANDADE WITH RED PEPPER COULIS

Salt cod is found in some form or another in almost every culture that borders the sea. Because it is so well preserved, you must soak it several times before using it. I recommend dicing the cod before soaking. When you are done soaking it, simmer it in a mixture of half milk and half water. The lactic acid in the milk will take that salt bite out of the cod. My ex-husband is also a chef and, hailing from the south of France, he made the very best brandade croquettes with red pepper coulis. MAKES 4 TO 6 SMALL-BITE SERVINGS OF BRANDADE; 1 PINT COULIS

COD
2 oz salt cod

SACHET
1 garlic clove
4 parsley stems
1 tsp black peppercorns
1 bay leaf
1 thyme sprig

BRANDADE
1 qt whole milk
8 oz russet potatoes
4 garlic cloves
½ cup extra-virgin olive oil
½ cup heavy cream
Salt, to taste
Freshly ground black pepper, to taste
1 cup vegetable oil, as needed for sautéing
2 cups all-purpose flour, or as needed

COULIS
1 lb red bell peppers, seeded and diced
¼ cup finely chopped shallots
2 tbsp olive oil
⅓ cup dry white wine
⅓ cup Vegetable Broth (page 4) *or* Chicken Broth (page 6)
1 tsp salt, or to taste
Freshly ground black pepper, to taste

1. Soak the cod in water for 2 days, changing the water twice per day.

2. To make the sachet: Cut a piece of cheesecloth large enough to hold all the sachet ingredients. Place the garlic, parsley, peppercorns, bay leaf, and thyme into the cheesecloth, gather it into a bundle, and tie it securely closed with a piece of kitchen twine.

3. To prepare the brandade: In a high-sided pan, heat the milk and sachet to 165°F to 180°F. Drain the salt cod and rinse it well. Add the cod and poach until the fish is opaque and tender but firm to the touch, about 10 minutes. Be watchful to keep the milk at the proper temperature. Using a spatula, carefully remove the cod, discard the sachet, and reserve the cooking liquid.

4. Place the cod in the bowl of a food processor fitted with a metal blade and pulse until it reaches the consistency of a coarse paste. If necessary, use some of the reserved cooking liquid to adjust the consistency.

5. In a medium sauce pot over medium heat, simmer the potatoes and garlic in just enough water to cover. Cook until the potatoes are fork-tender, about 8 minutes. Drain the potatoes in a colander and allow to dry by placing them back in the pot over low heat for 1 to 2 minutes. Process the potatoes through a food mill or ricer to make a purée and reserve.

6. Blend the olive oil into the cream until a homogenous texture has formed. Taste the mixture as you go and season with salt and pepper, if necessary. Fold in the potato purée and cod paste just until combined. Form tablespoonfuls of the mixture into little round cakes with straight sides as you would form a crab cake.

7. In a large sauté pan over medium heat, heat a small amount of oil. Lightly flour the cakes and shake off any excess flour. Carefully add the floured cakes to the oil. It is best to work in batches to avoid overcrowding the pan. Cook until golden brown on both sides and warm throughout, about 10 minutes.

8. To make the coulis: In a covered sauté pan over medium heat, cook the bell peppers and shallots in the olive oil until tender, 15 to 20 minutes. Deglaze the pan with the white wine and continue cooking until the wine has bubbled and cooked out. Increase the heat to medium-high. Add the broth and continue cooking until the liquid has reduced to half of its original volume, 10 to 15 minutes.

9. Place the mixture in a food processor fitted with a metal blade and blend until smooth. Season with the salt and pepper. If not serving immediately, store in the refrigerator and rewarm before serving.

10. Serve the brandade cakes warm on a pool of the red pepper coulis.

FRIED CALAMARI

Any place where squid swim you will find a different version of fried calamari. Be sure to rinse and dry the squid thoroughly before seasoning it. You can use both the tubes and the tentacles, but you may want to fry them separately. Sprinkle with sea salt and chopped parsley and serve with lemon wedges. Keep it simple and let the calamari speak for itself. MAKES 6 SMALL-BITE SERVINGS

2 lb squid, cleaned and cut crosswise into rings

6 large egg whites, beaten

Salt, to taste

½ cup cornstarch

½ cup all-purpose flour

5 cups olive oil for frying

1 lemon, cut into 8 wedges

1. Soak the squid in the egg whites and ¼ teaspoon of salt for 10 minutes. Drain the squid in a colander.

2. Combine the cornstarch with the flour. Dust the squid with the mixture and shake off any excess. The squid rings should be fully, but lightly, covered.

3. In a deep fryer or large, heavy-bottomed pot over medium-high heat, heat the oil to 350°F. Line a plate with paper towels. Carefully place the squid into the oil and fry, in batches to avoid overcrowding the pot, until golden, about 1 minute. Transfer to the paper towel–lined plate to drain briefly.

4. Give the squid another light sprinkling of salt and serve immediately with the lemon wedges.

PANZAROTTI

Panzarotti are stuffed fried gnocchi. You can use leftover gnocchi dough or make the dough fresh. Think of them as miniature calzones and serve with a drizzle of olive oil or a simple marinara sauce for dipping.   MAKES 8 SMALL-BITE SERVINGS

FILLING

1 large egg

2 tsp salt

⅓ cup diced mozzarella

¼ cup ricotta

2 tbsp shaved Parmigiano-Reggiano

⅓ cup diced salami

Freshly ground black pepper, to taste

PANZAROTTI

14 oz Gnocchi Fritti dough (page 61)

5 cups olive oil for frying

1. To make the filling: Whisk the egg with the salt, add the cheeses and salami, and season with pepper. Combine well.

2. Roll the dough out into an even layer ⅛ inch in thickness and, using a 2-inch round cutter, cut into circles.

3. Place 1 teaspoon of filling in the center of each circle of dough. Fold one side of the circle over the filling to make a half-moon shape. Use your fingers to crimp the edges together, making certain that they are tightly sealed.

4. In a deep fryer or large, heavy-bottomed pot over medium-high heat, heat the olive oil to 350°F. Line a plate with paper towels. Carefully place the panzarotti into the oil and fry, in batches, until golden and crisp, 2 to 3 minutes per batch. Transfer to the paper towel–lined plate to drain briefly and serve immediately.

PIQUILLOS STUFFED WITH TUNA

Piquillo means "little beak" in Spanish. These flavorful little peppers are grown in northern Spain. They are roasted and packed in their own juices, and they are readily available canned. They are quite sweet and not at all spicy. Piquillos can be stuffed with numerous fillings, and the tuna in this particular filling is easily interchangeable with cooked salt cod. It makes a great tapas dish, drizzled with some good-quality olive oil. MAKES 5 SMALL-BITE SERVINGS

1 Yukon Gold potato

1 hard-boiled egg, chopped

4 scallions, thinly sliced

1 cup canned tuna, drained

12 green olives, pitted and chopped

3 anchovies, finely chopped

½ cup Aïoli (page 28)

1 tsp freshly squeezed lemon juice

Salt, to taste

Freshly ground black pepper, to taste

10 canned piquillo peppers

1. Preheat the oven to 350°F.

2. Place the potato in a medium sauce pot with enough water to cover it by 2 inches. Bring the water to a boil over medium heat, reduce the heat, and cook at a gentle simmer until the potato is tender enough that a skewer goes through it easily, about 10 minutes. Drain and set aside until cool enough to handle. Peel and dice.

3. In a mixing bowl, combine the potato, chopped egg, scallions, and tuna. Use a potato masher to mash the mixture until the texture is creamy with a few chunks. Fold in the olives and anchovies. Fold in the aioli and lemon juice. Season with salt and pepper.

4. Fill a pastry bag with the tuna salad and pipe about 2 tablespoons into each of the piquillo peppers.

5. Place the peppers on a parchment paper–lined sheet pan and bake in the oven until the filling is heated through, about 15 minutes. Serve immediately.

GRAINS, LEGUMES, AND PASTA

Throughout the Mediterranean basin, wheat, grapes, and olives, known as the "Mediterranean Trinity," have always been a vital part of the cuisine and culture. Prior to the discovery of the New World, there was no corn in Europe, so wheat was the most important grain of that time. Other cereals, such as farro, known as the ancient grain of Roman warriors, and Kamut, also known as "camel's tooth," are high in protein and easy to transport, which made them perfect for both the Nomadic tribes and Roman armies. They were also relatively easy to grow, which made them perfect for poor farmers, provided they had enough irrigation. In the past decade or so, many of these ancient heirloom grains have reemerged on the market and are gaining in popularity.

GRAINS AND LEGUMES

Most grains and legumes have relatively subtle flavors, making them eminently useful as palate cleansers and heat tamers. Since they carry other flavors well, they are often paired with small amounts of intensely flavored foods to bring them into balance. They absorb flavors as they cook, responding well to an array of aromatics and seasonings, and they reward you with soothing, soul-satisfying sustenance.

Selecting Grains

No longer are we preparing only white rice; commonly available now are starchy round-grained Arborio rice for risottos; long-grain and fragrant rices, such as basmati, jasmine, and pecan rice for steaming or for pilafs; and black, brown, red, and wild rices for adding robust flavor and color. Pearl barley, cracked wheat and bulgur, kasha, quinoa, millet, and teff are also turning up on menus and are readily available on supermarket shelves. One of the best ways to make an ethnic meal taste authentic is to include an appropriate grain. Even if you typically stick to one cooking style, substituting other grains for rice adds new flavors, textures, and colors to your meals.

When purchasing grains, look for stores with a high turnover of inventory, especially if you prefer to purchase in small quantities from bulk bins. Grains do have a long shelf life, but the older they are, the longer they take to cook and the more liquid they may require. And, as they age, their flavor can turn musty and stale. Keep whole grains in the refrigerator or freezer if you won't be using them within a few weeks of purchase, or else their natural oils may become rancid.

Most grains cook quickly, few requiring more than 30 minutes. Some, notably bulgur, cook in 10 minutes or less. See the chart below for ratios for cooking the grains as well as cooking times.

GRAINS

TYPE OF GRAIN	RATIO OF GRAIN TO LIQUID (IN CUPS)	APPROX. YIELD (IN CUPS)	COOKING TIME	PREPARATIONS	FLAVORING SUGGESTIONS
Pearl barley	1 : 2	4	35–45 minutes	Boiled or pilaf style	Herbs, mushrooms, sun-dried tomatoes, wilted greens
Barley groats	1 : 2½	4	50 minutes–1 hour	Pilaf style or boiled	Mushrooms, herbs, sautéed vegetables
Buckwheat groats	1 : 1½ –2	2	12–20 minutes	Boiled or pilaf style	Mushrooms, carrots, onions, garlic
Couscous*	1 cup; 2 cups if pilaf style	2–3	Steamed over simmering water or stock 3 times for 20 minutes each time, fluffed between each steaming or cooked pilaf style	Steamed or pilaf style	Butter, herbs, diced precooked vegetables
Whole hominy**	1 : 4–6	3	2½–3 hours	Boiled or cooked in pressure cooker	Cooked onions, cooked garlic, cilantro, diced precooked vegetables
Hominy grits	1 : 4	3	25 minutes	Polenta method	Cheddar cheese, cooked onions, garlic
Millet	1 : 2	3	30–35 minutes	Boiled or pilaf style	Onions, garlic, mushrooms
Oat groats	1 : 2	2	45 minutes–1 hour	Boiled	Can be savory or sweet: vegetables such as carrots, onions, and garlic; or cinnamon and dried fruits
Polenta	1 : 4	3–4	35–45 minutes	Simmered on stove top or covered and baked in the oven	Cheese, butter, cream, onions, garlic, sun-dried tomatoes, chopped olives, herbs
Arborio rice (for risotto)	1 : 3–4	3	20–30 minutes	Simmered	Herbs, cheese, garlic, onions, mushrooms, asparagus, sun-dried tomatoes
Basmati rice	1 : 1½	3	25 minutes	Simmered, boiled, pilaf style	Herbs, diced precooked vegetables such as carrots, dried fruits such as currants and apricots, coconut, curry spices
Converted rice	1 : 1¾	4	25–30 minutes	Boiled, pilaf style, or steamed	Adapts to almost any application of flavor
Long-grain brown rice	1 : 3	4	40 minutes	Boiled, pilaf style, or steamed	Earthy flavors are best, although this rice can be used for a hearty rice pudding

TYPE OF GRAIN	RATIO OF GRAIN TO LIQUID (IN CUPS)	APPROX. YIELD (IN CUPS)	COOKING TIME	PREPARATIONS	FLAVORING SUGGESTIONS
Long-grain white rice	1 : 1½–1¾	3	18–20 minutes	Boiled, pilaf style, or steamed	Adapts to almost any application of flavor
Short-grain white rice	1 : 1–1½	3	20–30 minutes	Boiled or steamed	Usually starchy or sticky. Using flavored liquids to cook the rice does the best job of imparting flavors. Garnishes should be kept simple to avoid overworking the rice
Wild rice	1 : 3	4	30–45 minutes		Toasted nuts such as pecans and pine nuts, mushrooms, herbs such as savory, rosemary, thyme, and bay leaf
Wheat berries**	1 : 3	2	1 hour or more	Boiled or steamed	Herbs, tomatoes, wilted greens, mushrooms, vinaigrettes, dried fruits such as cherries, cranberries, and apricots, toasted nuts such as pecans, walnuts, pine nuts, and almonds
Bulgur***	1 : 4	2	2 hours		Herbs, mushrooms, tomatoes, cucumbers, dried fruits, vinaigrettes
Cracked wheat	1 : 2	3	20 minutes	Pilaf style or covered with boiling water and soaked for 2 hours	Herbs, tomatoes, wilted greens, mushrooms, vinaigrettes, dried fruits such as cherries, cranberries, and apricots, toasted nuts such as pecans, walnuts, pine nuts, and almonds

*From 1 cup of uncooked grain
**Grain should be briefly soaked in warm water, then drained before it is cooked
***Grain should be soaked overnight in cold water, then drained before it is cooked
Note: All long and medium grain rice varieties as well as all whole or cracked grains can also be cooked in a rice steamer.

Selecting Legumes

At one time, dried beans, lentils, and peas had all but disappeared from many kitchens across our nation. Beans have come back into their own, and there are even heirloom varieties available that can be sourced on the Internet. As with grains, choose dried legumes from a store with a high turnover. Beans, lentils, and dried peas can be stored in plastic bags or other airtight storage containers for a few months and don't require refrigeration.

Preparing Legumes

Although it is certainly fine to substitute one bean for another in many recipes, there is a noticeable difference in taste between, for example, favas and limas, black beans and kidney beans, and navy beans and black-eyed peas. Different types of beans require different cooking times (see chart below). Lentils and split peas cook in 30 to 45 minutes, whereas chickpeas and lima beans can take up to 2 hours. If time is limited, use canned beans instead of cooking dried beans from scratch. Drain the beans and rinse them well to remove the flavor and starch of the canning liquid. This will also help reduce the sodium level, allowing you to season the dish to suit your own taste.

DRIED LEGUMES

TYPE OF LEGUME	SOAKING TIME	COOKING TIME
Black beans	4 hours	1½ hours
Black-eyed peas*	—	1 hour
Chickpeas	4 hours	2–2½ hours
Fava beans	12 hours	3 hours
Great Northern/cannellini/ white beans	4 hours	1 hour
Kidney beans (red or white)	4 hours	1 hour
Lentils	—	30–45 minutes
Lima beans	4 hours	1–1½ hours
Navy beans	4 hours	2 hours
Split peas	—	30–45 minutes
Whole peas	4 hours	40 minutes
Pigeon peas	—	30 minutes
Pink beans	4 hours	1 hour
Pinto beans	4 hours	1–1½ hours
Soybeans	12 hours	3–3½ hours

*Soaking is not necessary.

CHELOW

The first time I made *chelow,* it was a bit of a curiosity to me. It combines cooking methods, which is unusual for a rice dish. The crispy bottom layer is called the *tah dig.* The nicest piece is usually reserved for the guest of honor. Be sure to use basmati rice to showcase the true flavor of this dish. MAKES 4 TO 6 SERVINGS

1 qt water

1½ tbsp salt, plus more as needed

1¼ cups basmati rice

1 tbsp extra-virgin olive oil

3 tbsp plain Greek-style yogurt

⅛ tsp ground saffron, dissolved in 2 tbsp warm water

¼ tsp freshly ground black pepper

1. In a pot over high heat, bring the water and salt to a boil. Add the rice and reduce the heat to establish a simmer. Cook the rice until tender, about 7 minutes. Drain and reserve.

2. In a bowl, stir together one-third of the cooked rice, the olive oil, the yogurt, 1 tablespoon of the saffron water, the pepper, and salt, if needed. Season the mixture prior to cooking in order to avoid breaking the final product.

3. Using a large shallow pot as a guide, trace and cut out a circle of parchment paper. Lightly oil the parchment paper on both sides and place it in the bottom of the pot. Place the pot over medium-high heat, place the rice-yogurt mixture on top of the paper, and press until flat but not spilling over the paper.

4. Gently add the remaining rice on top of the rice-yogurt mixture to form a mound. Using the handle of a wooden spoon, poke a few holes into the rice mound. Pour half of the remaining saffron water on top of the rice mixture and into the holes.

5. Lightly oil the bottom of a large piece of parchment paper. Cover the pot with the parchment paper to trap the steam and cook the rice.

6. Reduce the heat and steam the rice, adding the remaining saffron water as needed to retain the steam. Cook the rice until the bottom layer is golden brown, about 15 minutes. Lift the parchment paper up slightly to check the color.

7. The rice is ready when it is steamed on top and crispy and golden brown on the bottom. To serve, place a plate on top of the pot and invert the rice mixture onto the plate; the golden brown rice should be on the top.

TOP ROW LEFT TO RIGHT:

Place the rice-yogurt mixture into the pan lined with oiled parchment paper to form a base.

Add the remaining rice on top to form a mound.

BOTTOM ROW LEFT TO RIGHT:

Using the handle of a wooden spoon, poke a few holes in the mound of rice and pour saffron water into the holes.

Spoon the steamed rice into a serving dish, then invert the crispy brown part from the pan onto serving dish of rice so that the crispy side is now on top.

BULGUR PILAF WITH SCALLIONS

Pilaf is a method of preparing grains that professional chefs employ. Of course, rice pilaf is the most common, but you can make other grains using the same method, and the result is a lot more flavorful than simply boiling. The pilaf method involves cooking aromatics, such as onions and or garlic, in oil or butter; then the grain is added and cooked until it is "thirsty," which means it will readily accept the addition of liquid. Broth or water is added and brought to a simmer, and then the cooking is finished in the oven. Be sure to add enough salt to the grain so that it seems almost too salty; since starch absorbs salt, the dish will not taste as good if you season it only after it cooks. MAKES 8 SERVINGS

8 oz bulgur wheat

Pinch of salt, plus more to taste

2 lb tomatoes, diced

2 lb cucumbers, diced (peeled, if desired)

4 bunches scallions, thinly sliced

4 cups coarsely chopped flat-leaf parsley

½ cup coarsely chopped mint

Extra-virgin olive oil, to taste

Freshly squeezed lemon juice, to taste

1. Rinse the bulgur in cold water and place it in a bowl.

2. Pour hot water over the bulgur to cover by about 1 inch. Add a pinch of salt and allow the bulgur to sit, covered, until tender, about 20 minutes.

3. Drain the excess water from the bowl, if necessary, but *do not stir*. Mix the drained bulgur with a large fork and chill in the refrigerator until cold.

4. In a bowl, combine the chilled bulgur, the tomatoes, cucumbers, scallions, parsley, and mint.

5. Season with the olive oil, lemon juice, and salt, to taste.

6. Cover the bowl and chill in the refrigerator for a few hours.

GREEN LENTILS WITH CHARD AND LEMON

This is delicious served cold as a salad or warm as a pilaf if you make a few adjustments. Because of the protein content in the lentils, you can leave meat out of the mix and still have a nice lunch. Make it as a pilaf and serve it as a side dish at dinner. MAKES 6 TO 8 SERVINGS

1 lb dried green lentils
(lentilles du Puy)

3 tbsp finely chopped garlic

½ cup extra-virgin olive oil

¾ cup chopped cilantro

Salt, to taste

10 large Swiss chard leaves,
stemmed and cut into
chiffonade (see Chef's Note)

2 tbsp freshly squeezed lemon
juice

¼ cup pomegranate molasses

1. Rinse the lentils.

2. In a medium sauce pot, sweat the garlic in 2 tablespoons of the olive oil over medium heat. Add the lentils and stir to coat with the olive oil. Toast the lentils briefly and add the cilantro. Add enough water to cover the lentils by 2 inches and season the water with salt.

3. Bring the water to a boil, reduce the heat to establish a simmer, and cook the lentils until tender, 20 to 25 minutes. Remove the pot from the heat and drain off any excess liquid. Reserve and keep warm.

4. Meanwhile, prepare the Swiss chard. Heat 2 tablespoons of the olive oil in a large sauté pan over medium-high heat. Add the Swiss chard and cook until the leaves have wilted. Reserve until needed.

5. Add the chard, lemon juice, and pomegranate molasses to the drained, reserved lentils. Cover and keep warm until ready to serve.

6. Just prior to serving, taste and adjust the seasoning and drizzle with the remaining ¼ cup olive oil.

Chef's Note *To cut leaves into chiffonade, strip the leaves off their stems. Stack the leaves, roll up, and cut crosswise into thin ribbons.*

FARRO SALAD

Farro is known as the grain of the ancient Romans. It was sent along with Roman armies as a compact source of protein. The grain has survived and is now a delicious staple of a healthy diet. Eaten cold or at room temperature as a salad, or hot as a side dish, it is satisfying and delicious and amazingly easy to prepare.

MAKES 6 TO 8 SERVINGS

3 cups water

1 tbsp salt

1 cup farro

1 cup oil-cured olives

½ cup diced red onion

½ cup diced carrot

½ cup diced celery

½ cup diced trimmed fennel

½ cup peeled, seeded and diced cucumber

1 cup sliced plum tomatoes

2 tbsp capers

2 tsp finely chopped garlic

¼ cup extra-virgin olive oil

¼ cup red wine vinegar

2 tbsp chopped flat-leaf parsley

2 tbsp chopped basil

2 tbsp chopped mint

½ tsp freshly ground black pepper

1. In a 2-quart pot over medium heat, bring the water and 2 teaspoons of the salt to a boil. Pour in the farro and simmer until tender, about 20 minutes.

2. Strain the farro and immediately return it to the warm pot. Pan steam it by covering the pot and letting the steam finish cooking the farro, about 10 minutes.

3. Mix the cooked farro with the olives, onion, carrot, celery, fennel, cucumber, tomatoes, capers, and garlic. Add the olive oil, vinegar, and herbs. Season with the remaining 1 teaspoon salt and the pepper.

MUJADARA

There are different versions and spellings of this delicious lentil and rice dish throughout the Middle East, but the main thing to focus on is the caramelized onions. Don't skimp on the quantity and don't try to hurry them. This dish is good served with some Greek-style yogurt and a simple cucumber salad. MAKES 5 SERVINGS

LENTIL AND RICE FILLING

1 cup dried chickpeas

1 qt Vegetable Broth (page 4)

2 tbsp extra-virgin olive oil

1¼ cups diced onion

1 tsp finely chopped garlic

3 tbsp peeled and finely chopped ginger

½ tbsp tomato paste

¼ tsp ground allspice

⅛ tsp cayenne

¾ cup dried lentils

1 tbsp salt, plus more as needed

½ cup brown rice

Freshly ground black pepper, to taste

CRISPY SHALLOTS

¾ cup sliced shallots

3 cups olive oil

Salt, to taste

5 pita breads, split in half

Extra-virgin olive oil, as needed

Freshly ground black pepper, to taste

1 cup plain Greek-style yogurt, drained

1. To prepare the filling: Put the chickpeas in a large bowl and add enough cold water to cover them by 2 inches. Immediately discard any chickpeas that float to the surface. Soak the chickpeas overnight.

2. The following day, drain the soaked chickpeas. In a medium pot, combine the water with the drained chickpeas and bring the liquid to a boil. Reduce the heat to establish a simmer and cover the pot. Cook the chickpeas until tender, 45 minutes to 1 hour. Drain the chickpeas and reserve.

3. Bring the broth to a simmer in a sauce pot over medium heat.

4. In a small pot, heat the olive oil over low to medium heat. Add the onions and caramelize until they are a deep golden brown color, about 30 minutes. Add the garlic and cook for 1 minute. Add the ginger, tomato paste, allspice, and cayenne. Stir the mixture well.

5. Add the lentils and stir until fully coated with the oil in the pot. Add 2 cups of the simmering broth and bring to a boil. Reserve the remaining broth in the pot. Reduce the heat to establish a simmer, season with salt, cover, and cook until tender, about 20 minutes. Drain the lentils and reserve.

6. Bring the remaining 2 cups broth back to a boil. Add the rice and reduce the heat to establish a simmer. Cover the pot and cook until the rice is tender, about 30 minutes. Drain the rice and combine with the lentil mixture. Season with salt and pepper and set aside in a warm spot.

7. To prepare the crispy shallots: Preheat the oven to 200°F. While the rice and lentils are cooking, bring the shallots and olive oil to 250°F over medium-high heat in a saucepan. Cook the shallots until they are crispy and golden brown, about 10 minutes. Using a skimmer, remove the shallots from the oil and transfer to paper towels. Sprinkle lightly with salt. Reserve the shallot oil for cooking the chickpeas.

8. In a large sauté pan, pan fry the chickpeas in batches in some of the shallot oil over medium heat until the skins bloom. Each batch will take 2 to 3 minutes. Transfer the chickpeas to paper towels and season lightly with salt.

9. Lightly brush each pita bread with extra-virgin olive oil and season with salt and pepper. Warm the breads in the oven, about 10 minutes.

10. To serve, place 3 ounces of the lentil rice filling into each pita half. Garnish each with some fried chickpeas, crispy shallots, and 2 tablespoons of yogurt per pita.

COUSCOUS

Couscous is somewhat of a mystery to many people. To clarify, couscous is actually steamed semolina that is separated and dried, and thus precooked. The final method for serving is just soaking it in warm water, draining, and steaming so that the couscous takes on the flavor of the stew it is cooking over. Traditional couscous made in a couscousière can be steamed several times. MAKES 3 CUPS

1 cup plus 1½ tbsp water

2⅛ tsp salt

1 cup couscous

3 tbsp melted unsalted butter *or* olive oil

⅛ tsp ground turmeric

⅛ tsp freshly ground black pepper

1. Combine 1 cup of the water with 2 teaspoons of the salt and stir until the salt is dissolved. Soak the couscous in the salted cold water for 1 hour.

2. Place the couscous in the top of the couscousière and steam for 15 minutes.

3. Transfer the couscous to a glass baking dish or metal sheet pan and stir with a fork to separate the pasta.

4. Add 1½ teaspoons of water and mix together by hand. Let the couscous rest for 15 minutes.

5. Return the couscous to the couscousière for the final 15 minutes of steaming.

6. Repeat step 4.

7. Steam a third time for 10 minutes.

8. Repeat step 4 and then stir in the melted butter, turmeric, the remaining salt, and the pepper.

Chef's Note *If you do not have a couscousière, you can improvise one by lining a strainer basket that fits inside the top of your stew pot with cheesecloth. Soak the couscous and then steam it over the stew in the lined strainer for the second half of the cooking process. The steam from the stew will finish the couscous. Then you can butter and season it before serving.*

LAMB AND PUMPKIN COUSCOUS

This is a lamb and pumpkin stew served on a bed of couscous. If you want to change it up a little bit, make the dish with Israeli couscous in the style of risotto. It will be creamy and delicious, if not exactly traditional. MAKES 5 SERVINGS

8 oz dried chickpeas

2 tbsp extra-virgin olive oil, plus more as needed

3½ cups diced onions

1½ lb lamb shoulder or leg, cut into 1-inch cubes

1 tsp salt, plus more as needed

½ tsp freshly ground black pepper, plus more as needed

1 tsp peeled and finely chopped ginger

½ tsp ground turmeric

¼ tsp saffron threads

1 qt Chicken Broth (page 6), or as needed

6 cups water

1 onion

1 bay leaf

3 whole cloves

3 bunches baby turnips, cleaned and trimmed

2 cups oblique-cut carrots

2 cups peeled and trimmed diced pumpkin

2½ cups cooked Couscous (page 79)

¼ cup chopped cilantro

1. Put the chickpeas in a large bowl and add enough cold water to cover them by 2 inches. Immediately discard any chickpeas that float to the surface. Soak the chickpeas overnight.

2. The following day, in a large, wide, heavy-bottomed pot or enameled casserole, heat the olive oil and sweat the onions until they are soft and sweet, about 10 minutes. Season the lamb with salt and pepper. Add the lamb to the pot and cook the meat to allow the juices to concentrate and caramelize, about 10 minutes.

3. Add the ginger, turmeric, and saffron to the pot and toast briefly. Add enough broth to the pot to just cover the meat. Cover the pot and braise the lamb over medium heat, maintaining a simmer and cook until the meat is fork-tender, about 1 hour and 10 minutes. Meanwhile, drain the chickpeas from their soaking water.

4. Cut a slit in the onion wide enough and deep enough to securely hold the bay leaf. Place the bay leaf in the slit and stud the onion with the cloves to make an onion piqué.

5. Fill a pot with the water, add the drained chickpeas and onion piqué, and bring to a simmer. Add additional water, as needed, to keep the liquid simmering. Cook the chickpeas until they are creamy on the inside, about 1 hour and 45 minutes. Remove the onion piqué from the pot and drain the chickpeas, reserving the chickpea cooking liquid.

6. Once the lamb is almost tender, add the turnips and carrots and continue cooking until they are tender, about 20 minutes. Add the pumpkin to the braise and return to a simmer, cover, and cook until the pumpkin is tender, about 15 minutes. By the time all the vegetables are tender, the lamb should be fork-tender.

7. Add the cooked chickpeas to the lamb and vegetable mixture. Adjust the consistency of the braise by adding up to 1½ cups of the reserved chickpea cooking liquid. The consistency should be that of a stew, not too watery but not too dry.

8. Place ½ cup of the couscous in the center of each of five plates. Using a ladle or a spoon, divide the lamb and vegetable stew between the plates and top each dish with the chopped cilantro.

WILD BOAR STEW WITH POLENTA

This dish can be made with pork, but if you are able to get your hands on some wild boar, the meat is darker and more flavorful. Wild boar can be found in specialty shops or Italian markets or you may be able to special-order it through your local butcher. Although the traditional preparation is described in this recipe, this dish would also be well suited to preparation in a slow cooker. MAKES 8 SERVINGS

2 medium onions, cut into small dice

4 celery stalks, cut into small dice

6 garlic cloves, finely chopped

2½ tbsp finely chopped sage

2½ tbsp finely chopped rosemary

⅓ cup finely chopped flat-leaf parsley

2 tbsp olive oil

3 lb wild boar, cut into ½ inch cubes

Salt, to taste

Freshly ground black pepper, to taste

Beef broth, as needed

4 bay leaves

1 cup green olives, pitted and rinsed

1½ cups red wine

½ cup tomato paste

2 to 3 cups soft polenta or Buckwheat and Parmesan Polenta (page 83)

1. Heat a large, wide, heavy-bottomed pot or rondeau over medium heat. Add the onions, celery, garlic, sage, rosemary, and parsley and sauté for 5 minutes. Remove the vegetables from the pot, add the olive oil, and reserve.

2. Dry the meat with paper towels and season it with salt and pepper. Heat the oil in the pot until almost smoking, add the meat, and sear until brown. Return the vegetables to the pot and season with salt and pepper.

3. Deglaze pot with beef broth and add enough to almost cover the meat-vegetable mixture. Bring to a simmer and cook for 30 minutes.

4. Add the bay leaves and olives to the simmering mixture and stir to mix in.

5. Mix the red wine with the tomato paste and add to the simmering stew.

6. Cover the pot and simmer the stew gently for 1½ hours, or until the meat is fork-tender. Remove and discard the bay leaf.

7. Serve the stew with soft polenta or Buckwheat and Parmesan Polenta.

BUCKWHEAT AND PARMESAN POLENTA

Polenta can be prepared in two different ways. Soft polenta is somewhat like cream of wheat; really comforting and filling in cold weather. In warmer weather, when you might not want something creamy and filling, use the hard polenta recipe. After cooking and chilling, it firms up. You can then cut it, dust it with flour, and sauté in olive oil until the edges are crispy. Either way, it's delicious. MAKES 4 CUPS

8 cups water for soft polenta or 6 cups water for hard polenta (see Chef's Note)

3 tbsp salt

2 cups buckwheat polenta

¼ cup grated Parmigiano-Reggiano

1. Preheat the oven to 325°F.

2. Bring the water to a boil in a large oven-safe pot over medium-high heat and add the salt. Stream the dry polenta into the water, stirring constantly to incorporate and prevent lumps from forming. Adjust the heat to establish a simmer.

3. Cover the pot and place it in the oven, or continue to cook over low heat on the stovetop, about 30 minutes. Stir in the cheese.

4. Spoon the soft polenta onto warmed plates and serve.

Chef's Note *For hard polenta, use 6 cups of water instead of 8 cups. When the polenta is cooked, pour it into a buttered baking dish and let cool. Refrigerate until set and then cut into squares. Dust the squares with flour and sauté until crispy on both sides. Transfer to paper towels to drain excess oil and sprinkle with salt. Crispy polenta can be served as a side dish or as a component of a plate. Try adding crispy polenta to a roasted leg of lamb and some roasted tomatoes.*

CHICKPEA POTATO PURÉE

This purée is a delicious and unusual side dish. You certainly can use canned chickpeas instead of soaking and cooking dried chickpeas, but be sure to drain and rinse them. Serve this purée piping hot, drizzled with some good-quality olive oil and a sprinkle of pimentón dulce—sweet Spanish paprika. MAKES 4 TO 6 SERVINGS

1 lb dried chickpeas, soaked in water overnight, or substitute one 36-oz can chickpeas, rinsed and drained

2 heads garlic

½ cup good-quality olive oil

1 tbsp salt, plus more as needed

⅛ tsp freshly ground white pepper, plus more as needed

1 lb russet potatoes

½ tsp ground cumin

1. In a large pot, cover the chickpeas with cold water and bring to a simmer. Cook, covered, until they are tender, about 3 hours. Once the chickpeas are tender on the inside, drain and reserve ½ cup of the cooking liquid.

2. Preheat the oven to 350°F.

3. Cut off the tops of each head of garlic to expose the cloves inside. Drizzle each head with olive oil and season with salt and pepper. Place the garlic heads on a small sheet pan or wrap loosely with aluminum foil and roast in the oven until golden brown and tender, about 45 minutes. Once the garlic is roasted, remove the pulp from the papery skin by squeezing the head of garlic. Leave the oven on at 350°F.

4. In a blender, purée the drained, cooked chickpeas with the roasted garlic cloves. Set the mixture aside.

5. Peel and roughly chop the potatoes. Place in a pot and cover with cold water. Bring the potatoes to a boil and cook until tender, about 20 minutes. Remove the potatoes and place on a sheet pan in the oven to dry until all excess water has evaporated, about 10 minutes. Pass the dried potatoes through a food mill or ricer.

6. In a bowl, combine the warm potatoes with the chickpea purée. Add the reserved chickpea cooking liquid, as needed, to make a smooth mixture and achieve the desired consistency. (If using canned chickpeas, use water instead of the reserved cooking liquid. Season with salt, pepper, and cumin.

SAFFRON RISOTTO AND VEGETABLES

Making risotto is all about the rice. Traditionally it is made with short-grain, starchy rice, and there are two varieties readily available in the United States. The more traditional Arborio rice is a bit tricky to work with because the grains have a tendency to stick together. Today many cooks are using Carnaroli rice instead because it doesn't clump and is easier to work with. It is very starchy and results in a sublime risotto that, when made properly, looks like rice in a cream sauce. The finished risotto should be very loose and spread across the plate when served. MAKES 6 SERVINGS

3 qt water

3 tbsp salt

¾ cup asparagus, peeled and cut into 1-inch pieces

½ cup carrots, peeled and sliced ¼-inch thick

½ cup sugar snap peas, cut into thirds

½ cup snow peas, cut into thirds

¾ cup spring onions, green parts only sliced thin, white parts quartered

⅓ cup unsalted butter

3 tbsp vegetable oil

3 tbsp finely chopped shallots

½ tsp crumbled saffron

2 cups Arborio or Carnaroli rice

½ cup white wine

2 qt Chicken Broth (page 6), warmed

1 tbsp salt

½ tsp freshly ground white pepper

5 tbsp grated Parmigiano-Reggiano

1. Prepare an ice bath. In a large pot, bring the water and salt to a boil over high heat. Add the asparagus and cook just until tender, about 20 seconds. Immediately remove the asparagus from the pot and shock in the ice bath. Drain the asparagus and reserve. Repeat the blanching process with the carrots, sugar snap peas, snow peas, and onions; the peas and onions will take a little less time to cook, about 10 seconds.

2. In a 2-quart sauce pot, heat 3 tablespoons of the butter and the oil over medium heat. Add the shallots and saffron and sweat until translucent, about 3 minutes.

3. Add the rice and stir to coat with the butter, oil, saffron, and shallots. Toast the rice without coloring, 1 to 2 minutes.

4. Add the wine and cook the rice until the wine is absorbed, about 3 minutes.

5. Add the broth in increments, using just enough to cover the rice, about 1 cup at a time; this process is referred to as veiling. Continue adding broth and veiling the rice until all the liquid has been absorbed and the consistency of the rice is *all'onda* (wavelike), meaning that the risotto has a creamy texture, but the individual grains are slightly firm, or al dente. The whole process of adding wine and broth should take roughly 30 minutes. It is important not to rush this process.

6. Once the broth has been absorbed, finish the dish with the remaining butter, season with the salt and pepper, and add the cheese. Fold the precooked vegetables into the risotto and serve once the vegetables are heated through.

Chef's Note *If the specific vegetables listed are not available, simply substitute 3 cups of your favorite cooked seasonal vegetables. In the spring, think peas, favas, and asparagus, and in the winter, try roasted root vegetables. For a vegetarian version, substitute Vegetable Broth (page 4) for the chicken broth.*

RISOTTO WITH WINTER SQUASH AND SWEET SAUSAGE

This particular risotto recipe is a bit different because the rice is finished with a squash purée. The result is a beautiful orange rice with some roasted squash and grilled sausage on top. It is a hearty dish that is a complete meal, so the only other thing you might think about serving with it is a light side salad. MAKES 4 TO 6 SERVINGS

1 small winter squash, such as acorn or butternut

½ cup plus 1½ tbsp extra-virgin olive oil, or as needed

Salt, to taste

Freshly ground black pepper, to taste

2 tbsp chopped marjoram

5 cups Chicken Broth (page 6)

1½ lb sweet sausage, sliced into ½-inch disks

1 cup diced onion

2 garlic cloves, thinly sliced

1½ cups Carnaroli rice

⅓ cup white wine

2 cups thinly sliced parsnips

2 cups olive oil, plus as needed

¾ cup unsalted butter, cubed

2 cups grated Parmigiano-Reggiano

3 tbsp chopped chives

1. Preheat the oven to 425°F.

2. Cut the squash in half lengthwise, peel, and remove the stem. Scoop the seeds and fiber from the squash and then cut into large dice.

3. Line a sheet pan with aluminum foil and lightly brush the foil with 1½ teaspoons of the olive oil. Place the squash on the sheet pan, season with salt and pepper, and scatter the marjoram on top. Pour the ½ cup olive oil over the squash. Cover with another sheet foil and bake until soft, about 50 minutes. Reserve until needed.

4. In a medium saucepan, heat the broth over medium heat and keep at a gentle simmer until ready to use.

5. In a medium saucepan over medium-high heat, heat 1½ teaspoons of the extra-virgin olive oil. Add the sausage and brown on all sides, 10 to 15 minutes. If necessary, cook in batches to avoid overcrowding the pan. Remove the sausage and all but 1 table-spoon of the oil from the pan.

6. Heat the remaining extra-virgin 1½ teaspoons olive oil in the pan over medium heat, add the onion and garlic, and sauté until soft and translucent, about 10 minutes. Add the rice and stir until it is fully coated with the oil. Return the sausage to the pan.

7. Add the wine and simmer over medium heat, stirring occasionally. When the wine has bubbled completely away, add 2 or 3 ladlefuls of hot broth, or just enough to cover the rice. Simmer, stirring, until the rice has absorbed nearly all the liquid.

8. Continue to add more broth, 2 to 3 ladlefuls at a time, once the previous addition has been absorbed. After 18 to 22 minutes, each grain will have a creamy coating, but remain al dente.

9. While the rice is cooking, fry the parsnips. In a medium sauce pot, cover the parsnips with the 2 cups olive oil and bring to a simmer over medium heat. Add the parsnips and cook until they turn golden brown, about 2 minutes. Remove the parsnips and transfer to paper towels to drain, then sprinkle with salt.

10. Add the butter, squash, and 1¾ cups of the cheese to the rice and stir quickly to incorporate. Heat until the squash is warmed through.

11. Taste and adjust the seasoning, if necessary. Garnish with the fried parsnips, sausage, the remaining ¼ cup cheese, and the chives and serve.

SPINACH TAGLIATELLE WITH BOLOGNESE SAUCE

Tagliatelle is a fresh pasta cut that is shaped much like fettuccine. Because it is fresh it is porous, so it's perfect for holding on to thick sauces like Bolognese. In Bologna, where Bolognese sauce originated, there is also a classical Lasagna Bolognese, made with spinach pasta. We have simplified the idea by serving the Bolognese sauce with just the pasta, but if you wish to make a classic Lasagna Bolognese, be sure to thinly layer the Bolognese and some homemade béchamel sauce between seven layers of pasta. Why seven? It is the number of perfection in many Mediterranean religions and cultures. MAKES 5 SERVINGS

BOLOGNESE SAUCE

⅓ cup finely chopped pancetta

1 tbsp olive oil

1 tbsp unsalted butter

1 cup finely chopped onion

½ cup finely chopped carrot

⅓ cup finely chopped celery

8 oz lean ground beef

8 oz lean ground pork

4 oz chicken livers, cleaned and finely chopped

1 cup white wine

3 tbsp tomato paste

1 tsp salt

⅛ tsp freshly ground black pepper

⅛ tsp freshly grated nutmeg

2 cups Chicken Broth (page 6)

3 cups chopped tomatoes

1 cup heavy cream

PASTA DOUGH

2 large eggs

¼ tsp salt

4 oz spinach, stemmed (about 5 cups, packed)

1 lb all-purpose flour (about 3 cups)

¼ cup grated Parmigiano-Reggiano

1. To make the sauce: In a saucepan over medium-low heat, render the pancetta gently in the olive oil and butter until golden brown, about 10 minutes.

2. Add the onion, carrot, and celery and cook until lightly browned, about 8 minutes.

3. Add the beef and pork and cook just until the red color is gone, 3 to 5 minutes.

4. Add the chicken livers and cook just until barely done, brown on the outside and slightly rosy on the inside, about 1 minute.

5. Add the wine and cook until it has reduced by half, about 8 minutes.

6. Add the tomato paste, salt, pepper, and nutmeg, mix well, and cook for 2 to 3 minutes. Add the broth and the tomatoes and bring to a simmer.

7. Cover and simmer for 2 hours, adding more broth, if necessary, so that the sauce does not dry out.

8. Meanwhile, make the pasta dough: In a blender (not a food processor), purée the eggs with the salt and spinach until smooth.

9. Add the egg-spinach mixture to the flour and knead into a smooth dough. Rest the dough for 1 hour at room temperature. If making the dough ahead of time, shape the dough into a ball and place on a piece of plastic wrap. Wrap in the plastic and flatten the ball and refrigerate. Be sure to remove the dough from the refrigerator 30 minutes before rolling and allow it to come to room temperature.

10. After the dough has rested for 1 hour, divide it into 4 equal pieces, pressing each piece out until it will fit comfortably through the pasta machine. Keep the remaining dough covered while you work with each individual piece. Roll each piece through the machine, starting at the widest setting and moving down until the dough is about ⅛ inch thick. Repeat this process with each piece of dough until they are all rolled to a thickness of ⅛ inch.

11. Change the attachment to the fettuccine cutter and cut out all of the rolled dough. Place the pasta on a parchment paper–lined sheet pan that has been lightly floured and cover it with plastic wrap.

12. After the sauce has simmered for 2 hours, remove the lid and simmer, uncovered, if necessary, to reduce if too runny. Stir in the cream.

13. Bring a large pot of salted water to a boil. Add the pasta and cook until al dente, 3 to 5 minutes. Drain the pasta and toss it with the Bolognese sauce. Transfer the pasta to a platter and sprinkle with the cheese.

Variation *Substitute an equal amount of pappardelle for the spinach tagliatelle to make Pappardelle Bolognese (as pictured below).*

GNOCCHI WITH DUCK RAGOÛT

This recipe is a favorite of our students in our Cuisines of the Mediterranean class at The Culinary Institute of America. The main ingredient in the dish is the gnocchi, served with a perfectly made duck ragoût to accent those fluffy little pillows. I make the pillowlike gnocchi just as my mother and grandmother did. You can roll them on a fork or use a gnocchi board. Either way, these are really easy to make. MAKES 4 TO 6 SERVINGS

GNOCCHI

2 medium russet potatoes

2 cups bread flour, plus more for dusting

4 large eggs

⅛ tsp salt

⅛ tsp freshly ground black pepper

⅛ tsp freshly grated nutmeg

2 gal water

5 tbsp salt

RAGOÛT

1 rosemary sprig

1 thyme sprig

1 bay leaf

1½ tbsp chopped flat-leaf parsley

6 juniper berries, crushed

2 black peppercorns, crushed

2 tbsp olive oil

4 duck legs, cut into drumstick and thigh pieces

¼ cup finely chopped pancetta

½ cup finely chopped red onion

¼ cup finely chopped carrot

¼ cup finely chopped celery

1½ tsp finely chopped garlic

1 tbsp tomato paste

2 tbsp white wine

2 tbsp brandy

3 cups brown veal stock

Salt, to taste

Freshly ground black pepper, to taste

2 tbsp unsalted butter

1. Preheat the oven to 400°F.

2. To make the gnocchi: Bake the potatoes until soft, about 1 hour. Peel and, while still hot, purée through the large holes of a food mill. Spread out the purée on a plastic wrap–lined sheet pan and cool. Lower the oven temperature to 350°F.

3. In a large bowl, combine the cooled potato purée with the flour, eggs, salt, pepper, and nutmeg. Dust a work surface with bread flour so that the dough will not stick. Turn the dough out onto the work surface and knead quickly, adding more flour, if necessary, to achieve a pliable dough.

4. Using a bench scraper, cut the dough into 5 portions. Roll each portion into a log roughly ¾ inch in diameter. Using the bench scraper, cut the log into ½-inch pieces. Run each gnocchi piece along a gnocchi board or the back of a fork to create a seam, or press your thumb into the piece to create a pillow. Place the gnocchi on a parchment paper–lined sheet pan that has been lightly floured. Cover the gnocchi with plastic wrap and store the gnocchi in the refrigerator or freezer until the ragoût is done.

5. To make the ragoût: Combine the rosemary, thyme, bay leaf, parsley, juniper berries, and peppercorns and wrap in cheesecloth to make a sachet.

6. In a large, wide, heavy-bottomed pot or rondeau, heat the olive oil over medium heat. Add the duck legs and the pancetta and brown slowly, rendering the excess fat. Once the duck legs have browned, gradually increase the heat to medium-high. Add the onion, carrot, celery, and garlic and sauté until browned, 15 to 20 minutes.

7. Add the tomato paste and cook over medium heat, stirring frequently, until it turns a rusty color and smells sweet, 3 to 4 minutes. Deglaze the pan with the wine and brandy. Reduce the liquid by half, then add the broth and sachet; the broth should cover the meat by 1 inch. Taste the liquid and season with salt and pepper.

8. Braise the duck and vegetables in the oven, keeping the liquid at a slow simmer, for 1 hour or until the duck meat is fork-tender. Cool and skim the fat; it will rise to the top and turn bright orange, making it easy to skim.

continued

GARNISH

¼ cup grated Parmigiano-Reggiano

2 tbsp chopped flat-leaf parsley

9. Remove the duck legs from the braising liquid and shred the meat. Return the meat to the ragoût and reduce over medium-high heat until it lightly coats the back of a spoon.

10. Bring the water and salt to a boil. Add the gnocchi to the water, cooking in batches, if necessary, to avoid overcrowding the pot. Cook the gnocchi until they float to the surface, then remove with a skimmer and transfer to a colander to drain.

11. Stir the butter into the sauce in the pot. Combine the gnocchi with the sauce in the pot and reheat. To serve, the sauce should be just thick enough to coat the back of a wooden spoon. Serve topped with the cheese and parsley.

FROM LEFT TO RIGHT:

Once the gnocchi dough is portioned into ½-inch pieces, press your thumb into the center of each piece to create a pillow shape.

Add enough broth to cover the seared duck by 1 inch.

When the dish is properly cooked, the duck meat should be tender enough to easily fall off the bone and shred. Combine the gnocchi with the sauce in the pot and reheat. To serve, the sauce should be just thick enough to coat the back of a wooden spoon. Serve topped with grated Parmigiano-Reggiano and chopped parsley.

FARRO WITH BRUSSELS SPROUTS AND BALSAMIC VINEGAR

This dish of farro and Brussels sprouts is so satisfying that you may not need anything else for dinner. Eat it warm, and if you have any leftovers, dress it with a vinaigrette to turn it into a nice salad for the next day. MAKES 5 SERVINGS

2 qt water

5 tbsp salt

1 cup farro

1 pint Brussels sprouts

¼ cup olive oil

2 shallots, thinly sliced

1 garlic clove, sliced or pressed

Salt, to taste

Freshly ground black pepper, to taste

1 rosemary sprig

1 cup balsamic vinegar

1. Bring the water and salt to a boil. Stir in the farro, reduce the heat, and establish a simmer. Simmer until the farro is tender but still has a little bite to it; this may take as long as 40 minutes. When it is tender, drain the farro and reserve in a bowl.

2. Trim the Brussels sprouts, remove the tough outer leaves, and cut them in half lengthwise.

3. Preheat the oven to 400°F.

4. Place a baking dish or roasting pan in the oven and heat the pan for about 5 minutes.

5. Pour the olive oil into the roasting pan and then add the Brussels sprouts, shallots, and garlic. Season with salt and pepper and add the rosemary.

6. Roast the Brussels sprouts, turning occasionally, until they are caramelized and tender, 15 to 20 minutes.

7. Meanwhile, reduce the balsamic vinegar slowly on the stovetop over medium-low heat to ½ cup.

8. When the Brussels sprouts have caramelized, add the cooked farro and reheat thoroughly in the oven, about 15 minutes.

9. Remove from the oven and transfer to a serving dish. Drizzle with the reduced balsamic vinegar and serve.

RED PEPPER TORTELLI WITH CELERY ROOT FILLING AND SAGE BROWN BUTTER

Tortelli are stuffed ravioli-like pasta. They can be round, square, or triangular and are usually made by putting a large spoonful of filling on a piece of pasta and sealing it in. Depending on the region or family, they may take different shapes. Why not come up with your own shape and make it your family favorite? MAKES 5 SERVINGS

PASTA DOUGH

1 lb "00" flour

2 large eggs

4 oz red bell pepper purée (see Chef's Note)

FILLING

12 oz celery root

2 tbsp unsalted butter

2 tbsp olive oil

2 shallots, finely chopped

1 garlic clove, thinly sliced

2 cups ricotta cheese

2 large egg yolks

¼ cup chopped flat-leaf parsley

1 tbsp chopped sage

Salt, to taste

Freshly ground black pepper, to taste

CRISPY SAGE BUTTER SAUCE

½ cup extra-virgin olive oil

8 sage leaves (about 1 oz)

Salt, to taste

3 tbsp unsalted butter

Reserved pasta water, as needed

Grated Parmigiano-Reggiano, as needed

1. To make the pasta: Place all the ingredients for the dough in a food processor and pulse until it forms a ball. Mix until the dough is smooth and elastic, about 1 minute.

2. Shape the dough into a ball and place it on a piece of plastic wrap. Wrap in the plastic and flatten the ball. Let it rest for at least 30 minutes before rolling. You can make it a day in advance, if necessary and store in the refrigerator. Be sure to remove the dough from the refrigerator 30 minutes before rolling and allow it to come to room temperature.

3. To make the filling: Peel and cut the celery root into large dice and place in water acidulated with lemon juice to keep it from turning brown.

4. In a small sauce pot, melt the butter and olive oil over low heat. Add the drained, diced celery root, shallots, and garlic and cook slowly until soft, 15 to 20 minutes. Be careful not to get too much color on the vegetables. If they start to brown, add 1 tablespoon of water to slow down the cooking.

5. When the vegetables are soft, 15 to 20 minutes, put them in the bowl of a food processor fitted with the metal blade and blend until they are smooth, about 2 minutes. Scrape down the side of the bowl, as necessary, and then cool the purée.

6. Add the ricotta, egg yolks, parsley, and sage to the purée. Pulse a few times and season with salt and pepper. Remove from the processor bowl and reserve in the refrigerator.

7. Cut the pasta dough into four pieces and keep the other three wrapped while you roll out the first one. Roll out the pasta into long rectangles at least 3 inches wide. Set them on a parchment paper–lined sheet pan that has been lightly floured. Repeat with the other three pieces, being careful not to overlap the pasta.

8. When all the sheets have been rolled out, cut out 3-inch rounds from the dough and return them to the sheet pan. Keep the rounds covered with plastic wrap so that they don't dry out.

9. Working with one round at a time, brush the perimeter of the dough lightly with water.

10. Spoon 1 to 2 teaspoons of the filling in the middle of a round and fold it in half so that the two edges meet. Press the edges together. Take the straight edge of the half-moon and pull the two ends toward each other until they meet. Pinch the edges together.

11. Bring a large pot of salted water to a rolling boil.

12. To make the sage butter sauce: In a sauté pan large enough to accommodate the pasta, heat the olive oil to approximately 300°F and slowly crisp the sage leaves in the oil, 3 to 4 minutes. When they are crispy, transfer them to paper towels to drain and salt lightly.

13. Cool the cooking oil slightly so that the butter won't burn, then add the butter to the oil in the pan.

14. Since this is fresh pasta, it will take barely any time to cook, so have your sauce almost ready before you start to cook the tortelli so that they can go from the water directly into the sauté pan. Pasta cooking water is important when finishing a pasta dish. It is always advisable to reserve some of the pasta cooking water. Since the water holds much of the starch from the pasta, it is very helpful in achieving correct consistency in a sauce.

15. Plunge the tortelli into the boiling salted water all at once and cook until tender. This may only take 2 to 3 minutes. The tortelli will sink and then start to float. Once they float, they need only a few more minutes to cook.

16. Meanwhile, place the sage butter sauce over medium heat and cook until it starts to brown lightly. At this point remove it from the heat or, if the pasta is ready, transfer the pasta into the sauté pan with the sauce. Increase the heat to medium high and ladle in just enough pasta water to bind the oil and butter; it may only take about ½ cup.

17. Transfer the pasta to a serving bowl and sprinkle liberally with the Parmigiano. Garnish with the crispy sage leaves and serve.

Chef's Note *To make roasted pepper purée: Roast red bell peppers in a 350°F oven until the skins blister and the flesh is soft. Place the peppers in a bowl, cover with plastic wrap, and allow the peppers to steam, which will loosen the skins. Once the peppers are cool enough to handle, peel off the skins and remove the stems and seeds. Purée the roasted peppers in a blender. Alternatively, you can purchase fire-roasted peppers and drain and purée them.*

CAVATELLI WITH MUSHROOMS AND RAMPS

There are a few different variations of cavatelli. Growing up I knew it as a torpedo-shaped ricotta pasta. But it can also be a simple semolina and water dough, rolled and then shaped like a little hot dog bun. This recipe is for the simple semolina type. If I had my druthers, the mushrooms in this recipe would be chanterelles, but they can be expensive and are typically only available in the spring. A good substitution would be shiitake mushrooms. As for the ramps—wild, leafy, scallionlike vegetables—they are seasonal and you might actually find them in your backyard. If you can't find them, just use small scallions for this dish. MAKES 5 SERVINGS

PASTA DOUGH
1 lb semolina flour

1 tbsp olive oil

1 cup water, warmed to 95°F

MUSHROOMS AND RAMPS
Olive oil, as needed

2 cups mushrooms, washed, dried, and sliced ¼ inch thick

2 cups ramps *or* scallions, cut into 1-inch lengths

1 thyme sprig

1 cup water, Vegetable Broth (page 4), or Chicken Broth (page 6)

Salt, to taste

Freshly ground black pepper, to taste

1 cup shaved Parmigiano-Reggiano or Pecorino Romano

1. To make the pasta dough: Combine all the ingredients for the dough in the bowl of an electric mixer fitted with the paddle attachment and mix on medium speed for about 10 minutes, or until thoroughly incorporated. Cover the bowl with plastic wrap and let the dough rest for 20 minutes.

2. Pinch off a marble-size piece of dough and roll it out with a pencil-size wooden dowel. It should ultimately be curled up on both sides and be shaped like a little hot dog bun.

3. Place the rolled cavatelli on a parchment paper–lined sheet pan that has been lightly floured and cover them with plastic wrap. At this point you, can freeze the cavatelli or cook them. To freeze, place them on a sheet pan and freeze until solid, then transfer them to zipper-lock bags; they won't stick together.

4. To make the mushrooms and ramps: In a large sauté pan, heat the olive oil, add the mushrooms, and sauté on high heat until lightly browned, 4 to 5 minutes.

5. Add the ramps and thyme and brown lightly, 2 to 3 minutes. Add the water or broth and cook until tender, 2 to 3 minutes more. Season with salt and pepper.

6. Bring a large pot of salted water to a boil. Cook the pasta until al dente, 8 to 10 minutes. Skim the pasta and add to the pan of hot mushrooms and ramps. Add just enough pasta water to make a light, slightly thin sauce.

7. Remove the thyme sprig and transfer the pasta to a serving bowl. Add the cheese, toss lightly, and serve immediately.

Chef's Note *If using scallions instead of ramps, cut them in half lengthwise before cooking.*

FLAGEOLETS WITH GARLIC SAUSAGE AND DUCK CONFIT

This is a version of the classic cassoulet from the Toulouse region of France. The ingredients vary, depending on which region you are in, but the main three ingredients in cassoulet are legumes, sausage, and confit of duck. MAKES 5 SERVINGS

2 cups dried flageolet beans

3 tbsp extra-virgin olive oil

12 oz lamb shoulder meat, cut into 2-inch cubes

1¾ tsp salt

¼ tsp freshly ground black pepper

1 cup diced yellow onion

⅓ cup diced carrots

⅓ cup diced celery

1 garlic clove, sliced, finely chopped, and worked into a paste with ¼ tsp kosher salt (see Chef's Note)

½ cup tomato purée

¼ cup white wine

3½ cups beef broth

2 bay leaves

2 duck legs confit, meat shredded with skin included

1 lb garlic sausage, diced

1½ tsp finely chopped chives

1½ tsp finely chopped thyme leaves

½ cup bread crumbs

1 tbsp melted duck fat, reserved from the duck confit

1. Soak the beans overnight in a large container, covered by at least 2 inches of cold water.

2. The following day, add the olive oil to a large, wide, heavy-bottomed pot or rondeau and place the pan over medium-high heat. Season the lamb meat with the salt and pepper. When the oil is almost smoking, add the lamb and brown thoroughly on all sides, about 7 minutes.

3. Remove the meat from the pan and reserve. Add the onions, carrots, celery, and garlic to the pan and, stirring constantly, cook until the carrots start to brown on the edges, about 5 minutes.

4. Add the tomato purée and stir constantly until the purée darkens and starts to thicken, about 3 minutes. Quickly deglaze the pan with the wine, scraping the bottom of the pan to remove the brown bits.

5. When the wine has evaporated, return the meat to the pan and barely cover with the broth, about 2 cups. Add the bay leaves, bring to a simmer, cover, and reduce the heat to low.

6. After the mixture has cooked for 15 minutes, drain the soaked beans and add them to the pan. Continue to simmer over low heat, covered, until the beans are tender, about 2½ hours. If the mixture starts to dry out, add more broth, ¼ cup at a time.

7. When the beans are tender, add any of the remaining broth. The stew should resemble thick baked beans at this point. Stir in the duck confit and sausage and cook until heated through, about 1 minute.

8. Remove the cassoulet from the pot and transfer to a 13 by 9-inch baking dish. Cover with plastic wrap and place in the refrigerator overnight.

9. The following day, preheat the oven to 350°F. Remove and discard the bay leaves.

10. Place the cassoulet into the oven and bake until the mixture starts to bubble and is hot, about 20 minutes. Combine the chives, thyme, and bread crumbs and add the duck fat. Remove the cassoulet from the oven and cover with the bread crumb mixture. Increase the oven temperature to 450°F and return the dish to the oven until the bread crumbs brown, about 15 minutes. Serve piping hot.

Chef's Note *To mash the garlic into a paste, slice the clove thinly, sprinkle with salt, finely chop, then press into the cutting board by dragging your knife across it several times until a homogenous paste is formed.*

POTATOES ANNA

Thought to have been invented during the reign of Napoleon, the story is that this potato dish was named for a great beauty of the time. The dish contains copious amounts of butter, but please don't let that scare you off. If you are worried about the cholesterol factor, simply substitute a good-quality olive oil or other healthy oil for the butter. Don't just try to use less fat because, in this case, the fat is really what makes the dish. And whatever you do, don't rinse the potato slices! Immediately after slicing the potatoes, put them into a bowl and toss with some clarified butter. This will help prevent them from turning brown while you are constructing the potato cake.

You can still buy a special pan for this dish: a *cocotte à pommes Anna*. The classic design is a two-piece pan, frequently copper, specially made to cleanly flip the cake over during cooking. You can, however, make this dish with very few ingredients and little special equipment. Rather than using a special pan, I usually use a straight-sided sauté pan on the stovetop and finish the cake in the oven. I flip it only when the potatoes are fully cooked to a crisp on the bottom.

MAKES 10 SERVINGS

4 lb russet potatoes

½ cup clarified unsalted butter, or as needed

1 tbsp salt, plus more as needed

Pinch of freshly ground black pepper, or as needed

1. Preheat the oven to 400°F.

2. Scrub, peel, and trim the potatoes into uniform cylinders. Using a mandoline or an electric slicer, slice the cylinders very thinly so that they are almost translucent. They should actually be so thin that they will bend. Put them in a bowl with the clarified butter and season with the salt and a pinch of pepper.

3. Liberally brush an oven-safe sauté pan with butter. Arrange the potato slices in the pan in concentric rings. Lightly drizzle each layer with butter and season with additional salt and pepper.

4. Cover the potatoes and cook them on the stovetop over medium heat until the bottom layer is brown, about 8 minutes.

5. Place the pan in the oven, cover with aluminum foil, and cook the potatoes until tender, 30 to 35 minutes. Flip the cake over and continue to cook until the second side is brown.

6. Spoon off the excess butter and invert the potato cake onto a platter. Let it rest for 5 minutes before slicing. Slice and serve immediately, or set aside and reheat in the oven at serving time.

FRIED FINGERLING POTATOES WITH GARLIC AND HERBS

Fingerling potatoes are small and shaped like a crooked finger. Different varieties have different colors. They cook quickly and crisp up nicely. If you are unable to find them, use small white creamer potatoes or small red potatoes instead. I like to roast the whole head of garlic until soft, and then squeeze the pulp out of the papery skins. The potatoes, when combined with the herbs and some good-quality olive oil, make an amazingly simple dish with a big flavor. MAKES 4 SERVINGS

1 whole head garlic

1 tsp olive oil

1 lb fingerling potatoes

2 cups extra-virgin olive oil

1 rosemary sprig

1 basil sprig

1 thyme sprig

1 tbsp chopped rosemary

½ tsp chopped thyme

1 tbsp chopped basil

2 tbsp chopped flat-leaf parsley

Salt, to taste

Freshly ground black pepper, to taste

1. Preheat the oven to 350°F.

2. Rub the head of garlic with the olive oil and wrap in aluminum foil. Roast in the oven until soft, about 30 minutes.

3. Cool the garlic until you are able to handle it, then cut it in half, exposing the cloves. Squeeze out the pulp from the papery skin and reserve in a serving bowl.

4. Wash and dry the fingerling potatoes. Cut in half lengthwise, if desired.

5. In a heavy-bottomed pot, heat the extra-virgin olive oil to 300°F. Add the potatoes and herb sprigs and cook until the potatoes are tender, about 20 minutes. Test by inserting a knife into the potato. When it pierces the flesh easily, the potatoes are done; if in doubt, taste one. During the frying, if the herb stems start to brown, remove and discard them.

6. When the potatoes are tender, increase the heat and fry until crispy on the outside, about 10 minutes. Using a skimmer, transfer the crispy hot potatoes to the serving bowl with the roasted garlic. Add the chopped herbs, season with salt and pepper, and toss gently to combine. Spoon some of the hot cooking oil over the potatoes and serve.

FAVA BEANS WITH BRAISED CIPOLLINI ONIONS AND PANCETTA

Cipollini onions are small and somewhat flat. They are perfect for braising since they don't roll around in the pan. You can get both sides equally browned, which gives the final dish a really nice flavor and color. The combination of pancetta, onions, and favas is one of my favorites. This recipe works with dried favas, but is really special when made with fresh. If you have leftovers, add some freshly squeezed lemon juice and a splash of red wine vinegar and you have a great lunch salad. MAKES 6 SERVINGS

2 lb fresh fava beans or 1 lb dried fava beans

4 oz pancetta, finely chopped

¼ cup olive oil

1 lb cipollini onions

2 celery stalks, peeled and cut into small dice

2 small carrots cut into small dice

1 thyme sprig

1 bay leaf

2 cups Chicken Broth (page 6)

Salt, to taste

Freshly ground black pepper, to taste

1. Preheat the oven to 350°F.

2. If using fresh fava beans, shell, blanch, and peel them as described on page 35. If using dried fava beans, soak them overnight in cold water, then simmer them for 1 hour in fresh water. Either way you cook them, they should be slightly al dente. Reserve until needed.

3. Render the pancetta in a large sauté pan over medium heat until almost crispy, about 5 minutes. Add the olive oil to the pan.

4. Add the onions and brown on both sides, about 8 minutes.

5. Add the celery, carrots, thyme, and bay leaf and sauté for several minutes until they start to brown. Deglaze the pan with the broth and bring to a simmer.

6. Cover the pan, place in the oven, and cook for about 20 minutes. Remove the cover, add the favas, and continue to cook until hot and tender. Season with salt and pepper.

KAMUT WITH FRESH CORN AND PEAS

Khorasan wheat, also known as "camel's tooth," is distributed under its trade-marked name, Kamut. It is an ancient wheat rumored to have been found in Egyptian tombs and was said to have been the pharaohs' wheat. Another legend suggests it was the wheat used aboard Noah's ark. Kamut is always organic. It is a great base for many dishes, as it is hearty and light at the same time. I find that it is easier to cook if you soak it first for an hour or so in cold water. When combined with fresh corn and peas, it is delicious as a side dish. MAKES 6 TO 8 SERVINGS

2 cups Kamut

4 ears fresh corn

1 gal water or Vegetable Broth (page 4), plus more as needed

3 tbsp salt

1 bay leaf

1 thyme sprig

¼ cup olive oil, plus more as needed

1 small onion, peeled and cut into small dice

1 cup frozen peas, thawed

1 cup snow peas, blanched, shocked, and cut on the diagonal into ½-inch pieces

Salt, to taste

Freshly ground black pepper, to taste

¼ cup finely chopped chives (optional)

¼ cup chopped mint (optional)

1. In a large bowl, soak the Kamut in cold water for 1 to 2 hours.

2. Cut the corn kernels off the cob and reserve the kernels and cobs separately.

3. Bring the water or vegetable broth and salt to a boil in a pot on the stovetop with the corn cobs. The corn cobs will give the cooking liquid a sweet flavor and, by using the cobs, no flavor is wasted. Remove and discard the cobs once the water comes to a boil.

4. Drain the Kamut and add it to the pot with the bay leaf and thyme. Simmer until tender but still slightly al dente, about 45 minutes. Drain and discard the bay leaf and thyme sprig.

5. In a sauté pan, heat the olive oil over medium heat, add the onion, and sauté lightly until aromatic, 4 to 5 minutes.

6. Add the reserved corn kernels, increase the heat to high, and sauté until lightly caramelized, 4 to 5 minutes.

7. Add the cooked Kamut and heat through. Add the peas and snow peas and cook until warmed through, about 5 minutes more. Add a few drops of broth, as necessary, to moisten. Season with salt and pepper.

8. Stir in the herbs, if using, drizzle some olive oil over the Kamut, and serve.

ORECCHIETTE WITH LAMB AND MINT STEW

In the southern part of Italy where my grandfather was born, the simple cuisine of ordinary people was called *cucina povera,* "the cuisine of poverty." This dish is a great example of that cuisine, although traditionally there likely was more pasta and less meat. Add plenty of chopped mint as well as some chopped tomato. This recipe makes enough stew for about a pound of orecchiette. Don't rinse the pasta after you cook it, just mix it in with the stew. The starch on the pasta will help thicken the sauce. MAKES 5 TO 6 SERVINGS

1 lb 8 oz lamb shoulder, cut into 1-inch cubes

1 tsp salt

¼ tsp freshly ground black pepper

2 tbsp olive oil

1 cup small-dice yellow onion

1 tsp finely chopped rosemary

1 tsp finely chopped mint

½ cup finely chopped prosciutto

2 tbsp tomato paste

⅓ cup red wine

¼ tsp red pepper flakes

2½ cups Chicken Broth (page 6), hot

⅔ cup coarsely chopped mint

⅔ cup tomato concassé (see page 122)

1⅓ cups baby spinach leaves

1 lb cooked orecchiette (see Chef's Note)

1. Preheat the oven to 350°F.

2. Dry the lamb cubes and season with the salt and pepper. In a large, heavy-bottomed pot, heat the olive oil, add the lamb, and brown over medium-high heat, about 5 minutes. Remove the lamb from the pot and reserve.

3. Add the onion, rosemary, finely chopped mint, and prosciutto. Cook over medium-high heat until the onion is lightly caramelized, about 5 minutes.

4. Add the tomato paste and cook until it has caramelized and become a dark, rusty red color, 2 to 3 minutes. Deglaze the pan with the wine and reduce to nearly a dry consistency, about 5 minutes, stirring often. Add the red pepper flakes and return the lamb to the pot.

5. Add enough hot broth to come halfway up the lamb. Bring to a simmer. Skim off any scum that rises to the surface. Cover and braise in the oven until the lamb is tender, about 40 minutes.

6. When the lamb is fork-tender, remove it from the pot and set aside. Reduce the sauce until it coats the back of a wooden spoon. Add the coarsely chopped mint and tomato concassé and stir to combine. Stir in the spinach and cook just until wilted. Return the lamb to the pot, toss with the orecchiette, and serve.

Chef's Note *Start with 8 ounces of dried pasta to yield 1 pound cooked orecchiette.*

ISRAELI COUSCOUS RISOTTO WITH PUMPKIN AND CHANTERELLE MUSHROOMS

Israeli couscous is a large, round and smooth pasta that is sometimes called "Ben Gurion rice" in Israel. It is good in soups and there is even a recipe that bakes it in a pie. My favorite way to cook it is in a risotto-type preparation. MAKES 5 SERVINGS

VEGETABLES

2 shallots, finely chopped

¼ cup olive oil

2 cups chanterelle mushrooms, washed, dried, and diced

Salt, to taste

Freshly ground black pepper to taste

2 cups fresh pumpkin, peeled and diced

COUSCOUS RISOTTO

1 tbsp unsalted butter

1 shallot, finely chopped

2 cups Israeli couscous

1 qt Chicken Broth (page 6) *or* Vegetable Broth (page 4)

6 sage leaves, finely chopped

1 thyme sprig, finely chopped

1 tbsp kosher salt

Freshly ground black pepper, to taste

¼ cup shaved Parmigiano-Reggiano

1. To prepare the vegetables: Preheat the oven to 350°F.

2. In a large sauté pan, sauté 1 of the shallots in 2 tablespoons of the olive oil over medium heat until translucent. Add the mushrooms and cook until they are caramelized, 8 to 10 minutes. Season with salt and pepper.

3. On a sheet pan, toss together the remaining shallot, the remaining olive oil, and the diced pumpkin and roast in the oven until caramelized and tender, about 15 minutes.

4. To make the couscous: Melt the butter in a small sauce pot over moderate heat, add the shallot, and cook until aromatic, 1 to 2 minutes.

5. Add the couscous and cook gently for a few minutes until it is "parched" and smells lightly toasted. (Parching is a method that makes the product absorb the liquid more easily.) Add the broth in small additions and stir until it has evaporated and the couscous looks a bit dry. Turn off the heat.

5. Stir in the pumpkin, mushrooms, sage, and thyme. Just before serving, season with salt and pepper. Top with the cheese and serve.

LOBSTER RAVIOLI WITH CORN SAUCE

This dish was a favorite at my restaurant in Atlanta. We served two very large ravioli with corn sauce and wilted spinach. It was served as an entrée, but the recipe could easily be divided between two people and served as an appetizer. You might want to make the ravioli smaller.

Striping the pasta is really fun, but also takes some time. You may want to batch it out and save some of the dough for later. I suggest that when you make this, you make extra ravioli and freeze them. The sauce will also freeze well if you don't add the heavy cream until reheating and serving. The sauce should taste like a buttered ear of corn. MAKES 5 TO 6 SERVINGS

SAFFRON PASTA DOUGH

1 lb "00" *or* all-purpose flour

2 tbsp water

½ tsp saffron threads

3 large eggs

1 large egg yolk

SQUID INK PASTA DOUGH

8 oz "00" *or* all-purpose flour

2 large eggs

1 tsp squid ink *or* squid ink powder

LOBSTER FILLING

1 lobster

2 tbsp unsalted butter

3 shallots, finely chopped

2 cups corn kernels, fresh or frozen

Salt, to taste

Freshly ground black pepper, to taste

1 cup ricotta cheese

1 large egg

1. To make the saffron pasta: Put the flour in the bowl of a food processor fitted with the metal blade.

2. Warm the water and saffron threads in the microwave for 5 to 10 seconds and let sit for 5 minutes until bright orange.

3. Add the eggs, egg yolk, and saffron water to the flour all at once. Pulse the mixture in the processor until it forms a ball.

4. Place the dough on a lightly floured work surface and knead it into a ball. Cover it with plastic wrap and rest in the refrigerator for 20 minutes before rolling.

5. To make the squid ink pasta: Place the flour in the bowl of a food processor fitted with the metal blade. Add the eggs and squid ink all at once. Pulse the mixture until it forms a ball.

6. Place the dough on a work surface and knead it into a ball. Cover it with plastic wrap and rest in the refrigerator for 20 minutes before rolling.

7. To make the lobster filling: Cook the lobster in a large pot of simmering water for 5 minutes. Let it cool and then remove the claw and knuckles and the tail. Crack the shells with a lobster cracker and remove the meat from the shell. (You could also buy a precooked lobster from your fishmonger.) After removing the meat from the shell, cut it into medium dice.

8. In a sauté pan, melt the butter, add the shallots, and cook slowly over low heat until translucent.

9. Add the corn and cook until soft, about 10 minutes. Remove from the heat and add the diced lobster; season with salt and pepper. Cool the mixture.

10. In a bowl, fold the lobster-corn mixture into the ricotta. Mix in the egg and chill until ready to use.

continued

CORN SAUCE

2 tbsp unsalted butter

2 shallots, sliced

2 cups corn kernels, fresh or frozen

2 cups Vegetable Broth (page 4) *or* Chicken Broth (page 6), warmed

Salt, to taste

Freshly ground black pepper, to taste

1 cup heavy cream

11. Roll out the saffron pasta into a large rectangle with a thickness of approximately ⅛ inch. Roll out the squid ink pasta in the same manner.

12. Run the squid ink pasta through a fettuccine cutter so that you have long thin strips of pasta. The strips and the saffron sheet should be the same length. You may have to do this several times until you use up all of the pasta.

13. Brush the squid ink pasta with a little water and lay the strips on top of the saffron pasta approximately the same width apart as the strips are wide. You will now have evenly stripped pasta with raised black strips. Increase the number on the pasta roller to two settings thicker than you originally rolled out the pasta. Roll through so that the strips flatten out into the saffron base; this usually takes an additional two rolls.

14. Roll out the striped pasta to the desired thickness. Cut the dough in half so that you have two pieces of pasta that are equal in length. Place 1 tablespoon of filling at 2½-inch intervals down one piece of pasta. Brush the exposed pasta lightly with water. Place the second piece of pasta over the piece with the filling, making sure to line up the edges.

15. Press down gently around the mounds of filling to seal the pasta around the filling. Cut out the ravioli using a 2-inch cutter, making sure that the filling is in the center of the ravioli. Place the ravioli on a parchment paper-lined sheet pan and reserve the ravioli, covered with plastic wrap, until needed.

16. To make the corn sauce: Melt the butter over moderate heat in a 2-quart saucepan, add the shallots, and cook slowly until aromatic, about 2 minutes.

17. Add the corn and cook slowly until it starts to soften, about 4 minutes. Add the broth and bring to a simmer. Skim off the foam that rises to the surface and continue to simmer until the corn is soft, about 5 minutes.

18. Place the corn mixture in a blender and blend until very smooth. Pass through a fine-mesh sieve to remove the corn skins. Adjust the seasoning with salt and pepper. Reserve warm until needed.

19. Bring a large pot of salted water to a boil, add the ravioli, and cook until al dente. Drain the pasta and finish the sauce.

20. Lightly whip the cream to soft peaks. Whisk the whipped cream into the corn sauce, toss with the pasta, and serve immediately.

LEFT TO RIGHT:

Use a very small amount of water to adhere the strips of squid ink pasta onto the saffron pasta sheet, making sure that the strips are straight and even.

Once the strips are adhered, run the pasta through a pasta roller until the strips are the same thickness as the sheets.

To make the ravioli, place a small scoop of the filling mixture at an even interval on top of a 2-inch-wide strip of pasta. Lightly brush the non-striped side of another 2-inch strip of pasta with water and place it on top of the filling with the strip side up. Use a round cutter to press the pasta together around the filling, but not enough to cut through, then use a slightly larger round cutter to cut out each of the ravioli.

CAPELLINI WITH CLAMS, BOTTARGA, AND PRESERVED MEYER LEMONS

This capellini and clam dish is just a little different than the usual spaghetti with clam sauce. Bottarga is smoked, dry-cured tuna roe and it adds a delicious new twist to this dish. The preserved Meyer lemons add a little aromatic acidity to balance the clams and bottarga. If you can't find bottarga in a gourmet grocery, look for it online. Should you use only part of the bottarga, just freeze the rest. Wrap it tightly in plastic wrap and put it in a zipper-lock bag. It will last indefinitely.

MAKES 5 SERVINGS

PRESERVED LEMON ZEST
4 Meyer lemons

2 tbsp salt

CLAM BROTH
2 tbsp olive oil

2 shallots, halved and thinly sliced

1 garlic clove, finely chopped

2 cups clam juice

1 cup dry white wine

Juice of 1 lemon

Salt, to taste

Freshly ground black pepper, to taste

PASTA
1 cup panko bread crumbs (optional)

2 tbsp unsalted butter, melted (optional)

1 gal water

6 tbsp kosher salt

1 lb dried capellini

2 lb Manila clams

1 oz shaved bottarga

¼ cup chopped flat-leaf parsley

1. To make the preserved lemon: Peel the yellow zest off the outside of the lemons with a vegetable peeler and cut into julienne, or remove in strips using a zester. Place the zest in a nonreactive bowl.

2. Sprinkle the zest with the salt and add the juice of 2 of the lemons. Let sit for 6 to 8 hours. Rinse before using.

3. To make the clam broth: In a large sauté pan, heat the olive oil over moderate heat, add the shallots and garlic, and sauté slowly until aromatic.

4. Add the clam juice and reduce by half. Add the white wine and reduce by half. Add the lemon juice, salt, and pepper. The broth is now ready to steam the clams in.

5. To make the pasta: You will need to have the rest of the ingredients for the preparation ready so that when the pasta is cooked you will be able to assemble it quickly. Combine the breadcrumbs, if using, with the melted butter and stir to thoroughly coat.

6. Add the clams to the broth and steam open over medium heat, 5 to 10 minutes, depending on the size of the clams. Discard any clams that do not open. Remove three-quarters of the clams from the shells and discard the shells; return the clam meat to the broth. Reserve the remaining clams in their shells for garnish.

7. Meanwhile, bring the water and salt to a boil in a large pot. Boil the capellini according to the package directions. When the pasta is al dente, drain it, and place the pasta directly into the hot broth with the clams.

8. Add the rinsed preserved lemons, bottarga, and parsley. Transfer the pasta to a serving bowl and pour the broth over it. Garnish with the clams in their shells. Sprinkle with buttered bread crumbs, if desired.

BUCATINI AMATRICIANA

Bucatini are long, tubular pasta that look like straws. You can almost drink with them. Bucatini has always been one of my favorite fun pasta cuts. You can make this recipe with regular spaghetti, but the hollow bucatini fills up with some of the sauce, making it that much more delicious. MAKES 4 SERVINGS

8 oz dried bucatini

1 tbsp extra-virgin olive oil

¼ cup diced pancetta

½ small onion, finely chopped

1 tbsp red pepper flakes

¼ cup chopped ripe or canned plum tomatoes

¼ cup roughly chopped flat-leaf parsley

½ cup grated Pecorino Romano

1. Cook the pasta in a large pot of salted boiling water until al dente, 6 to 8 minutes.

2. While the pasta is cooking, heat the olive oil in a large sauté pan over medium heat. Add the pancetta and cook until it browns, about 3 minutes. Drain the pancetta on paper towels.

3. Add the onion and red pepper flakes to the pan. Cook the onion over medium heat until it is soft and lightly caramelized, about 3 minutes.

4. Add the tomatoes and continue to cook over medium heat until the flavors are fully combined and the tomatoes are hot, about 5 minutes. Return the diced pancetta to the pan.

5. Drain the pasta and reserve about ¼ cup of the pasta water. Add the pasta to the sauté pan and toss to coat with the sauce. If necessary, adjust the consistency of the dish with the reserved pasta water. Finish with the parsley. Serve in a warmed soup plate or pasta bowl and sprinkle with the cheese.

PATATAS BRAVAS

Patatas bravas, or "fierce potatoes" (which refers to their spiciness), can be any shape you like. Use a melon baller for smaller pieces, or cut the potatoes into large steak fries. Either way they are delicious. This variation calls for the potatoes to be cooked slowly in olive oil and then rolled in a spice mixture before refrying in hotter oil. Some versions will actually make a sauce out of the spice blend, but the potatoes in this recipe are really tasty and a lot easier to prepare.

MAKES 5 TO 6 SERVINGS

4 russet potatoes

Olive oil, as needed for blanching and frying

1 tsp salt

1 tsp pimentón (Spanish paprika)

1 tsp red pepper flakes

¼ tsp ground cardamom

¼ tsp garlic powder

2 tbsp sherry vinegar

1. Cut the potatoes as desired and hold in cold water to prevent oxidation.

2. In a 3-quart sauce pot or large sauté pan, blanch the potatoes in the olive oil over low heat, about 275°F, until tender. Using a skimmer or spider, remove the potatoes from the oil.

3. In a bowl, stir together the salt, pimentón, red pepper flakes, cardamom, and garlic powder, and roll the potatoes in the spice mixture until the potatoes are well coated.

4. Bring the oil to 375°F, add the coated potatoes, and fry until golden brown. Using a skimmer or spider, remove from the oil. Toss the potatoes in the spice mixture and sprinkle with the vinegar just before serving.

CURRIED BLACK RICE WITH VEGETABLES

We served a variation of this rice at my restaurant, Grappa. The cooking methods are decidedly French but reflect the influx of Asian culture in the south of France after the Vietnam War. We served this with pan-roasted halibut, a reduction of the aromatic broth, and finished the dish with crème fraîche. It was delicious, and kept our customers coming back for more. MAKES 4 TO 6 SERVINGS

AROMATIC STOCK

¼ cup unsalted butter

4 shallots

1 cup diced well-washed leeks

1 cup diced carrots

2 tbsp peeled and finely chopped ginger

4 kaffir lime leaves

2 tbsp finely chopped lemongrass

1 tbsp curry powder

1 tsp saffron threads

2 tbsp ground turmeric

1 cup Quady Electra Orange Muscat wine

½ cup mirin

3 cups Chicken Broth (page 6)

1 cup coconut milk

FORBIDDEN RICE PILAF

1 cup forbidden rice (black rice)

Salt, as needed

1 cup small-dice onion

½ cup diced carrot

½ cup diced celery

1 oz peeled and finely chopped ginger

¼ cup unsalted butter

3 cups hot aromatic stock (see above)

Freshly ground black pepper, as needed

1 stalk lemongrass, crushed and tied into a bundle

2 kaffir lime leaves

GARNISH

½ cup carrots, cut into fine dice and blanched

½ cup celery, peeled, cut into fine dice, and blanched

½ cup leeks, well washed and cut into fine dice and blanched

½ cup tomato concassé (see page 122), cut into fine dice

¼ bunch chives, chopped

1. To make the stock: In a large sauce pot, melt the butter. Add the shallots, leeks, and carrots and sweat over medium heat until tender and aromatic, 6 to 8 minutes. Add the ginger, lime leaves, and lemongrass. Add the curry powder, saffron, and turmeric.

2. Add the wine, mirin, and broth and slowly reduce by half.

3. Add the coconut milk and slowly reduce by half.

4. Strain through a fine-mesh sieve and reserve the stock for cooking the rice.

5. To make the rice: Preheat the oven to 350°F.

6. Blanch the rice in about 4 cups of boiling salted water for 5 minutes; this will reduce the cooking time. Drain and cool.

7. In a large sauce pot, sweat the onion, carrot, celery, and ginger in the butter over medium heat, making sure they do not color.

8. Add the rice and parch for 1 minute in the pot. Add the hot aromatic stock and butter and season. Add the lemongrass and lime leaves and establish a simmer. Cover and place in the oven for about 1 hour or until all the liquid has been absorbed.

9. Remove from the oven and let sit for 10 minutes. Add the vegetable garnish and the seasoning. Serve warm.

PAELLA WITH QUAIL, CLAMS, AND CHORIZO

There are many different versions of paella depending on where you are in Spain. Proximity to the sea will dictate more seafood; farther inland, you might find more poultry and less seafood, or even no seafood at all. Using real Calasparra rice is critical to great paella. Be sure to get a nice crust on the bottom of the pan, and if you don't have a paella pan, just use a large sauté pan. Once the liquid has been added, don't stir anymore. MAKES 4 TO 6 SERVINGS

6 cups Chicken Broth (page 6)

¼ tbsp saffron

8 quail, bones removed

1 tsp salt

¼ tsp freshly ground black pepper

2 cups all-purpose flour (optional)

⅓ cup extra-virgin olive oil

2 cups chorizo, cut into ½-inch cubes

2 cups squid, cleaned and cut into rings

2 cups diced onions

1½ garlic cloves, finely chopped

1 cup medium-dice tomatoes

1½ tsp pimentón (Spanish paprika)

1½ tsp thyme leaves

1 cup Calasparra rice

12 Manila clams

2 cups cooked peas

¼ cup unsalted butter, cubed

1. In a large sauce pot, heat the broth and saffron until simmering.

2. Season the quail with the salt and pepper. Dredge the quail in the flour, if using, and shake off any excess flour. Set aside.

3. To a large, wide, heavy-bottomed pot or rondeau over high heat, add the olive oil. When the oil is hot, add the quail and lightly brown, 1 to 2 minutes per side. This may need to be done in batches to avoid overcrowding the pan. Remove from the pan and reserve.

4. Reduce the heat to medium-high, add the chorizo, and cook until brown, about 4 minutes. Remove the chorizo from the pot and reserve. Add the squid and sauté until browned and dry, about 2 minutes. Remove from the pot and reserve.

5. Reduce the heat to medium-low heat, add the onions and garlic, and cook until the onions are transparent, about 5 minutes. Add the tomatoes and cook until they have softened. Add the pimentón and thyme and cook for 1 minute. This mixture is now what is referred to as a *sofrito*.

6. Add the rice to the pan and toast slightly, about 1 minute, until fully coated.

7. Add the chorizo, squid, and 2 cups of the hot saffron–chicken broth. Place the quail on top and cook, covered, over medium heat. *Do not stir the rice mixture!*

8. When most of the liquid has been absorbed, about 15 minutes, add the clams and 1 cup of the broth. Cook until the clams partially open. Add the peas and cook until the clams are completely open and the liquid has been absorbed, about 10 minutes. Discard any unopened clams.

9. While the paella is cooking, reduce the remaining 3 cups broth by half. Stir in the butter and keep warm.

10. For each serving, to an entrée-size bowl, add some of the rice mixture and top with 2 pieces of quail and 2 clams. Spoon ¼ cup of sauce into each bowl around the rice mixture, if desired.

Chef's Note *The sauce is completely optional. It is not traditional, but it adds moisture and texture to the dish.*

CRISPY BUCKWHEAT POLENTA WITH CARAMELIZED SHALLOTS

If you can't find buckwheat polenta, regular corn polenta can be used. Polenta is basically cornmeal, but when it's labeled "polenta," the grind is usually a bit finer.

MAKES 5 TO 6 SERVINGS

POLENTA

6 cups water

1 tbsp salt

2 cups buckwheat polenta

All-purpose flour, as needed for dusting

Olive oil, as needed for frying

CARAMELIZED SHALLOTS

8 shallots

¼ cup olive oil

1 cup finely chopped pancetta

1 thyme sprig

1 bay leaf

1 cup Chicken Broth (page 6)

¼ cup sherry vinegar

1 marjoram sprig

Salt, to taste

Freshly ground black pepper, to taste

½ cup shaved Parmigiano-Reggiano

1. To make the polenta: Preheat the oven to 350°F. Grease an 8-inch cake pan or standard 12-cup muffin pans.

2. In an oven-safe, large, wide, heavy-bottomed pot or enameled casserole, bring the water to a boil and add the salt. Stream in the polenta slowly and stir constantly with a wooden spoon to incorporate and prevent lumps from forming. Bring to a simmer, cover, and place in the oven for 30 minutes or until soft.

3. Pour the cooked polenta into the prepared cake pan or muffin pans and let cool. Refrigerate until solid. If using a cake pan, cut the polenta into 6 wedges.

4. Just before serving, lightly dust the polenta with flour. Sauté in olive oil in a sauté pan over medium-high heat until crispy, about 3 minutes per side. Keep warm.

5. To prepare the caramelized shallots: Preheat a roasting pan in the oven for 10 minutes.

6. Roll the shallots in 2 tablespoons of the olive oil and place them in the hot pan with the pancetta, thyme sprig, and bay leaf.

7. Roast until the shallots are golden brown and soft, about 15 minutes. Every so often, add a little of the broth. When the shallots are brown and soft, about 5 minutes, remove them from the pan.

8. Deglaze the pan with the vinegar and reduce by half. Swirl in the remaining 2 tablespoons olive oil and the chopped marjoram. Return the shallots to the pan, season with salt and pepper, and heat through.

9. Serve the shallots over the warm polenta and garnish with the cheese.

VEGETABLES
AND GREENS

In the Mediterranean basin, vegetables have always been an important part of the diet. The ancient Egyptians learned how to divert water, turning their arid environment into what we now know as the Fertile Crescent.

There are so many possibilities when it comes to the preparation of vegetables and greens that it is almost staggering. Select your vegetables with care for the best results. Freshness is key when it comes to a good vegetable dish. So, if at all possible, purchase your produce from a local farm or farmers' market. The nutrient content is much greater when plants are grown in the right way, and one of the most obvious advantages of local, sustainably grown produce is the superior flavor.

MAKING TOMATO CONCASSÉ

To prepare tomato concassé, blanch your tomatoes, shock them in an ice bath, and remove the skins. After removing the skins, quarter the tomatoes and remove the seeds. What remains is the tomato flesh. The strict definition of a concassé calls for a rough chop, but the peeled and seeded tomatoes can be cut into precise squares or strips, or as desired. Use only as many tomatoes as you need at one time; once peeled and chopped, tomatoes begin to lose their flavor and texture.

1. Score an X into the bottom of each tomato, but be sure not to cut too deeply. Remove the stem core.

2. Prepare an ice bath. Bring a pot of water to a rolling boil. Drop the tomatoes into the boiling water. Blanch the tomatoes for 10 to 15 seconds, depending on their ripeness, re-move them, and shock them in the ice bath to top the cooking process.

3. Using a paring knife, peel away the skin. If the tomatoes were properly blanched, none of the flesh will be removed with the skins.

4. Halve the tomatoes crosswise at their widest point. (Cut plum tomatoes lengthwise in order to seed them more easily.) Gently cut or squeeze out the seeds. For precise cuts, quarter the tomatoes and cut away the seeds. For a rough concassé, simply squeeze out the seeds and chop. The seeds and juices of the tomato may be reserved for other preparations.

SAUTÉED SPINACH WITH APPLE AND RAISINS

I love fresh spinach and usually just sauté it with shallots and butter. This recipe is a nice change because it has a bit more depth of flavor. The earthiness of the spinach combined with the sweetness of the raisins and apples and the nuttiness of the pine nuts results in something nicely balanced and more complex, though easy to make. It goes really well with Chickpea Potato Purée (page 84).

MAKES ABOUT 4 SERVINGS

¼ cup extra-virgin olive oil

2 Golden Delicious apples, peeled, cored, and cut into small cubes

2 shallots, finely chopped

¼ cup raisins

Salt, to taste

Freshly ground black pepper, to taste

One 8-oz bag spinach, stemmed and washed

¼ cup pine nuts, toasted

1. In a large sauté pan, heat the olive oil over high heat. Add the apples and shallots and sauté until lightly browned, less than 1 minute.

2. Add the raisins, season with salt and pepper, and stir to combine.

3. Add the spinach, stir, and sauté very quickly until it starts to wilt. Remove the pan from the heat and set aside; the spinach will continue to wilt off the heat.

4. Add the toasted pine nuts just before serving. Serve immediately.

GRILLED RADICCHIO WITH PARMESAN CRISPS AND BALSAMIC REDUCTION

Radicchio is one of my favorite leafy vegetables. Radicchio's lesser known cousin *treviso* is a comparable substitution, but you probably won't find it as readily available as standard radicchio. Since radicchio has a somewhat bitter, albeit delightful, flavor, the balsamic reduction adds a necessary sweetness. Add in the saltiness of the Parmesan and the aroma of fresh herbs and you will find this dish really well balanced while still simple to prepare. MAKES 4 SERVINGS

DRESSING

1 tbsp olive oil

1 tbsp balsamic vinegar

1 tsp chopped oregano

1 tsp chopped basil

Salt, to taste

Freshly ground black pepper, to taste

RADICCHIO

2 heads radicchio, outside leaves removed, halved through the core and then quartered

PARMESAN CRISPS

½ cup grated Parmigiano-Reggiano

GARNISH

1 bunch chives, trimmed

1 cup balsamic vinegar, reduced to ⅓ cup

Shaved Parmigiano-Reggiano, as needed

1. To make the dressing: Whisk together the olive oil, vinegar, herbs, salt, and pepper.

2. To make the radicchio: Lightly salt the radicchio quarters and brush generously with the dressing. Reserve the remaining dressing. Cover the radicchio with plastic wrap and set aside at room temperature for 1 hour.

3. Preheat a grill pan over medium-high heat. Grill the radicchio quarters on each side for 4 minutes per side. Reserve until ready to serve.

4. To make the Parmesan crisps: Sprinkle 2 tablespoons of the grated cheese into a 6-inch nonstick frying pan. Heat the pan until the cheese starts to bubble and turns golden brown. Remove the pan from the heat and allow the cheese to cool just until you are able to pick it up out of the pan. While it is still warm, shape it over a bottle or rolling pin and let cool until crisp. Remove from the bottle or rolling pin and repeat the process with the remaining cheese. Reserve the crisps in an airtight container at room temperature.

5. To serve, place a Parmesan crisp on each plate and lean 2 radicchio quarters, cut side up, against it. Garnish each plate with a few chives, a drizzle of balsamic vinegar reduction, and some shaved cheese.

GRILLED ASPARAGUS WITH PICKLED RED ONIONS AND ORANGE WATER

This is a really nice summer dish and can be eaten warm or cold. Be sure to blanch the asparagus before grilling so that it doesn't dry out. It is a dense vegetable and needs a little moisture to grill successfully. MAKES 5 SERVINGS

PICKLED RED ONION

½ cup red wine vinegar

½ cup sugar

1 red onion, sliced

Zest of 1 orange, white pith removed, orange reserved

Reserved orange, cut into segments

2 tbsp orange flower water

ASPARAGUS

1 bunch asparagus

¼ cup olive oil

Salt, to taste

Freshly ground black pepper, to taste

1. To pickle the red onion: Combine the vinegar and sugar in a pot over high heat and bring to a boil. Boil until the sugar dissolves, about 1 minute. Remove from the heat and add the onion, orange zest, and orange water. Allow to cool, then refrigerate in a nonreactive container. Use within 1 week.

2. To prepare the asparagus: Cut ¼ inch off the end of the asparagus and peel the stalks up to just below the tip.

3. Prepare an ice bath. Bring a large pot of salted water to a boil. Blanch the asparagus in the boiling water. After 1 minute, remove them using tongs and plunge them into the ice bath to stop the cooking process.

4. Line up the blanched asparagus, side by side, on a cutting board. Skewer the asparagus with two bamboo skewers so that you have an asparagus "raft"; this will facilitate turning the asparagus during grilling. Brush the asparagus raft with olive oil and season with salt and pepper.

5. Preheat a grill pan. Place the asparagus raft on the hot pan and grill on both sides until tender, about 3 minutes per side. The asparagus may also be grilled on a traditional charcoal or gas grill.

6. Transfer the asparagus to a platter and remove the skewers. Garnish with the pickled red onion and orange segments and drizzle with the pickling liquid.

Chef's Note *Crumbled feta or mild goat cheese is a great addition to this salad.*

ROASTED SQUASH WITH PANCETTA

The earthiness and sweetness of the squash combined with the saltiness of the pancetta makes for a nicely balanced side dish. It is easy to make and really delicious. When you are pressed for time, make it a day in advance and reheat it.

MAKES 4 TO 5 SERVINGS

2 acorn squash, each cut into 6 wedges, seeds and fiber removed

4 oz pancetta, finely chopped

2 shallots, sliced

1 tbsp unsalted butter, melted

1 tbsp olive oil

¼ cup Sauternes *or* Riesling

Salt, to taste

Freshly ground black pepper to taste

1. Preheat the oven to 350°F.

2. In a bowl, toss the squash wedges with the pancetta, shallots, butter, olive oil, and wine and season with salt and pepper.

3. Transfer the squash mixture to a roasting pan, cover with aluminum foil, and roast for 30 minutes.

4. Remove the foil from the pan and continue roasting until the squash starts to turn golden brown, about 10 minutes.

5. To serve, place the wedges on a serving platter and spoon the shallot and pancetta mixture over the squash.

CELERY ROOT PURÉE

The first time I ate celery root purée, I was working for Guenter Seeger at the Ritz-Carlton Hotel in Atlanta. He was serving it with venison and, honestly, I had never tasted anything so good. It has become a staple in my repertoire, and for those of you trying to watch your carbs, substitute this for potato purée. MAKES 5 SERVINGS

1 celery root knob, peeled and cut into large dice (about 1 lb 8 oz)

2 tbsp unsalted butter

½ cup heavy cream, warmed

Salt, to taste

Freshly ground white pepper, to taste

1. In a pot, cover the diced celery root with salted water by 1 inch and bring to a boil over high heat. Boil until tender.

2. Drain the celery root well and mash with a potato masher until it is the consistency of mashed potatoes.

3. Place the mashed celery root, butter, and half of the cream in a blender. Process for a few seconds and then add the remaining cream. Process again until the mixture is smooth. Season with salt and pepper.

Chef's Note *If you make this purée in advance and need to reheat it before serving, add a little more warm cream, if needed, to loosen the mixture.*

FRISÉE SALAD WITH OLIVE OIL–POACHED EGG AND LARDONS

This is a classic bistro salad that you will love from the first bite. The slightly bitter frisée pairs really well with the smoky, salty bacon, and the crunchy texture of both components is set off by the unctuous soft yolk of the olive oil–poached egg. The egg can be cooked to your liking, but the salad is at its best when the yolk is runny. MAKES 6 SERVINGS

6 oz pancetta or smoked bacon, cut into lardons (about ¼ inch by ¼ inch by 2 inches)

3 shallots, thinly sliced

2 tbsp champagne vinegar

½ cup olive oil

6 large eggs

3 heads frisée, washed and thoroughly dried

Salt, to taste

Freshly ground black pepper, to taste

½ cup tomato concassé (see page 122)

1 tbsp finely chopped chives

1. In a small sauté pan over medium heat, cook the pancetta until crispy, about 3 minutes. Transfer the pancetta to paper towels to drain and reserve.

2. Add the shallots to the pan and cook until translucent and tender, about 4 minutes. Remove the shallots and reserve.

3. Add the vinegar to the pan and increase the heat to high. Bring the vinegar to a boil and immediately remove the pan from the heat. Add the shallots back to the pan of hot vinegar.

4. In another sauté pan, heat the olive oil over medium heat until hot but not smoking. Break one egg into the oil and constantly spoon the hot oil over the top of the egg to poach it. Cook each egg until the white is opaque but the yolk is still soft, about 2 minutes. Reserve the cooking oil and hold the eggs in warm water while you dress the salad.

5. Place the frisée in a bowl and toss with the shallot-vinegar mixture. Add the lardons and season with salt and pepper.

6. Divide the salad among six plates, top each with a warm egg, and drizzle with some of the warm cooking oil. Sprinkle some tomatoes and chives on top.

SALADE NIÇOISE

Summer in Provence can be dry and sweltering. Enjoying a *salade niçoise* with a very cold bottle of French rosé is a great way to keep cool. You can make the salad using the Olive Oil–Poached Tuna Provençal on page 188 or any good-quality canned tuna in oil. If you can't find haricots verts, use thin, regular green beans.

MAKES 6 SERVINGS

POTATOES

2 cups fingerling potatoes

1½ tsp olive oil

VINAIGRETTE

2 tbsp white wine vinegar *or* lemon juice

½ cup extra-virgin olive oil

1½ tsp finely chopped shallots

1 tbsp prepared Dijon mustard

Salt, to taste

Freshly ground black pepper, to taste

SALAD

1 head Bibb lettuce, leaves separated, washed, and dried

1 cup plum tomato concassé (see page 122), cut into quarters

1 yellow bell pepper, seeded and thinly sliced into strips

3 radishes, thinly sliced

½ cup tuna canned in olive oil, drained

6 hard-boiled eggs, quartered

2 cups haricots verts *or* green beans, ends trimmed, blanched

12 anchovy fillets

¼ cup finely chopped chives

36 Niçoise olives, pitted, if desired

Salt, to taste

Freshly ground black pepper, to taste

1. To prepare the potatoes: Put the potatoes in a medium pot with enough salted water to cover and bring to a boil over high heat. Reduce the heat to establish a simmer and cook until tender, about 8 minutes. Drain the potatoes and set aside until cool enough to handle. Peel the potatoes and slice them lengthwise in half (or quarter them, depending on the size). Reserve in the olive oil.

2. To make the vinaigrette: Whisk together the vinegar or lemon juice, olive oil, shallots, and mustard until the mixture is well combined. Season with salt and pepper.

3. To compose the salad: Dress the lettuce leaves very lightly with the vinaigrette. Reserve the leftover vinaigrette. Line a salad platter with the dressed lettuce leaves.

4. Arrange the tomatoes, bell pepper, radishes, tuna, eggs, haricots verts or green beans, potatoes, anchovies, chives, and olives in rows on top of the lettuce. Dress with a drizzle of the remaining vinaigrette and season with salt and pepper.

HARICOTS VERTS WITH OIL-CURED OLIVES

I love this recipe because it tastes like tapenade, that Provençal olive paste we love to spread on crusty French bread. Haricots verts are readily available in gourmet grocery stores and are simply a thin variety of green beans. A good substitute, if you can find them, are Nickel Filet beans, a domestic version of haricots verts. If you cannot find them, use thin, regular green beans. MAKES 5 SERVINGS

1 lb haricots verts

2 tbsp olive oil

1 garlic clove, finely chopped

1 anchovy, packed in oil or vinegar, finely chopped

2 tbsp water

½ cup oil-cured olives, pitted and lightly chopped

Salt, as needed

Cracked black pepper, as needed

¼ cup chopped flat-leaf parsley

1. Prepare an ice bath. Bring a pot of salted water to a boil. Blanch the haricots verts for 3 minutes. Remove from the boiling water and plunge into the ice bath to stop the cooking process. Drain and reserve.

2. Heat the olive oil in a large sauté pan, add the garlic, and sauté lightly until aromatic, about 2 minutes.

3. Add the anchovy and cook briefly until it melts. Add the blanched haricots verts and the water and cook until the water has evaporated.

4. Continue to cook until the haricots verts start to brown lightly, about 10 minutes. Add the olives and cook until heated through.

5. Season with salt and pepper. Toss with the parsley and serve warm.

ARTICHOKE AND POTATO HASH

Artichokes grow really well in climates that are hot during the day with a cool evening mist coming off the sea. In the United States, they are grown inland from Monterey in California; overseas they grow really well in Provence and in many areas of Italy. After visiting Ocean Mist Farms in California's Salinas Valley, I can tell you that picking artichokes is not for wimps. So when you eat them, say a little thank-you to all the men and women who do all of that hard work for us.

MAKES 5 SERVINGS

6 artichokes

Juice of 1 lemon

½ cup olive oil

1 onion, peeled and cut into small dice

2 oz prosciutto, finely chopped

½ cup Chicken Broth (page 6)

4 Yukon Gold potatoes

4 sage leaves

Salt, to taste

Freshly ground black pepper, to taste

1. Lay the artichoke on its side and note where the leaves end and the bottom begins. Cut straight across the bottom of the leaves. Now you will have an artichoke bottom but the choke will need to be scraped out. The choke is the circular, fuzzy-looking matter. Scrape out the choke and peel the outside of the bottoms with a peeler, as the skin that covers the artichoke bottom is somewhat tough and fibrous. Dice the artichoke bottoms, sprinkling the lemon juice over the artichokes as you work to prevent discoloration. You can also use canned or frozen artichokes, but fresh artichokes will give the hash a better texture.

2. In a sauté pan, heat ¼ cup of the olive oil over medium heat. Add the onion and sauté until lightly browned, about 5 minutes.

3. Add the prosciutto and sauté until somewhat crisp, about 3 minutes.

4. Add the diced artichoke hearts to the pan and then the broth. Cook until all the broth has evaporated, about 10 minutes. Transfer the mixture to a plate.

5. Peel then cut the potatoes into ¼ inch dice and put them in a bowl of water as you work to prevent discoloration. Drain the potatoes and dry them on paper towels.

6. Heat the remaining ¼ cup olive oil in the sauté pan and, when very hot, add the potatoes. Cook until the potatoes are brown and soft in the middle. Add the sage leaves to the pan. Return the artichokes to the pan and heat through. Season the hash with salt and pepper and serve warm.

Chef's Note *This hash is excellent by itself, but add an olive oil–fried egg and some grilled focaccia and you'll have something really special.*

BRAISED BELGIAN ENDIVE WITH CARAMELIZED VEGETABLES

When I first started cooking in the late 1970s, Belgian endive only came from, well, Belgium. These days the entire West Coast and some of the Northeast are growing most of our endive. Richard Collins, the owner of California Vegetable Specialties, started growing endive back in the 1970s and found a way to perfect the growing process. All the endive is grown in the dark in a very large cool warehouse. Walking into his farm, you feel like you are walking on the moon. Endive has always been a favorite of mine, not raw but braised. Enjoy this dish with a nice bottle of wine, some crusty bread, and a little salad for a nice light dinner.

MAKES 4 SERVINGS

1 tbsp olive oil

4 Belgian endive, cut in half lengthwise

2 oz pancetta *or* smoked bacon, cut into small dice

2 shallots, finely chopped

1 carrot, cut into small dice

1 celery stalk, peeled and cut into small dice

1 bay leaf

1 thyme sprig

1 cup Chicken Broth (page 6), warmed

Salt, to taste

Freshly ground black pepper, to taste

2 tbsp unsalted butter, at room temperature

1 tbsp finely chopped chives

1 tbsp finely chopped parsley

1. Lightly heat the olive oil in a large sauté pan. Add the endive and brown on both sides, about 5 minutes. Transfer to a plate.

2. Render the pancetta or bacon in the same sauté pan over medium heat until crispy, about 10 minutes. Transfer the pancetta to the plate with the endive.

3. Sauté the shallots in the same pan in the remaining fat until aromatic, about 2 minutes. Add the carrot and cook until lightly browned, about 4 minutes, then add the celery. Return the endive to the pan and add the bay leaf and thyme.

4. Add the broth and bring to a simmer. Season with salt and pepper. Cover the pan with a lid or a piece of parchment paper and simmer until the liquid has evaporated and the endive is tender, about 4 minutes.

5. Remove the bay leaf and thyme sprig and transfer the endive to a serving platter. Swirl the butter and herbs into the pan and then pour over the endive. Serve warm.

ASPARAGUS WITH CHANTERELLES

This dish works well with either white or green asparagus. The time of year will determine which one you choose—it is in season in the spring. If you are lucky, you will find both in the store and you can prepare either. White asparagus is covered while it grows so that it does not develop any chlorophyll, which is what makes plants green. Germans are so crazy about white asparagus that they have *Spargel* festivals that revolve around it. In some parts of Italy and England you may even find purple asparagus—grab some and try it if you see it here in the United States. If you have any asparagus leftovers, they are great in panini sandwiches made with Fontina cheese. MAKES 5 SERVINGS

1 bunch asparagus

8 oz chanterelle or shiitake mushrooms

¼ cup olive oil

2 shallots, sliced

1 thyme sprig

Salt, to taste

Freshly ground black pepper, to taste

1 tbsp finely chopped chives

1. Cut ¼ inch off the end of the asparagus and peel the stalks up to just below the tip.

2. Prepare an ice bath. Bring a large pot of salted water to a boil. Plunge the asparagus into the boiling water. After 1 minute, remove them using tongs and plunge them into the ice bath to stop the cooking process.

3. Drain the asparagus and cut them in half on the diagonal. Reserve until needed.

4. Cut the end of the stems off the mushrooms and wash the mushrooms quickly in cold water. Be sure not to soak them; get them in and out of the water as quickly as possible.

5. Drain the mushrooms and spread them out on a paper towel–lined sheet pan to dry.

6. In a sauté pan, heat the olive oil over high heat. Add the mushrooms, the shallots, and the thyme sprig and sauté until the mushrooms are somewhat dry, about 10 minutes. Season the mixture with salt and pepper.

7. Add the asparagus to the pan and reduce the heat to medium. Cook until heated through, about 4 minutes. Transfer the asparagus to a serving platter and spoon the mushrooms over them. Sprinkle with the chives.

HEIRLOOM TOMATOES AND BREAD SALAD WITH GARLIC SCAPE PESTO

If you can find garlic scapes at your local farmers' market in the summer, you will have an amazing treat. This recipe takes tomatoes with pesto to another level. If you can't find fresh scapes, a good basil pesto always works as well: substitute 2 cups of tightly packed fresh basil leaves for the scapes. Be sure to select a seasonal heirloom variety of tomato that is aromatic and meaty. MAKES 4 SERVINGS

GARLIC SCAPE PESTO

2 cups chopped garlic scapes

½ cup grated Parmigiano-Reggiano

½ cup pine nuts

¼ cup chervil *or* fennel fronds

½ cup olive oil

Salt, to taste

Freshly ground black pepper, to taste

CRUSTY BREAD CROUTONS

2 cups diced crusty bread, cut in the size you prefer

SALAD

4 heirloom tomatoes, cut into medium dice and lightly salted

½ cup Garlic Scape Pesto (see above)

Juice of 1 lemon

Salt, to taste

Cracked black pepper, to taste

1. To make the pesto: Place all the ingredients for the pesto in the bowl of a food processor fitted with the metal blade and process until smooth. The pesto will keep indefinitely in the freezer.

2. To make the crusty bread croutons: Toast the bread in a 325°F oven until golden and crunchy.

3. To make the salad: Place the tomatoes and croutons in a bowl. Add ½ cup of the pesto and the lemon juice. Season with salt and pepper. Toss until the pesto is evenly distributed. Divide the salad evenly among six plates and serve.

SUMMER SQUASH GRATIN

This gratin is made with paper-thin slices of summer squash, shallots, and butter. It is like a squash version of the famous Gratin Dauphinois potatoes, made with potatoes and cream, but is lighter because of the squash. Be sure to make it ahead of time so that it has time to set up. You can actually make it a day in advance and reheat it. MAKES 6 SERVINGS

2 tbsp unsalted butter, plus more for greasing

4 oz shallots, thinly sliced (about 1½ cups)

1 cup panko bread crumbs (about 1¾ oz)

1 tsp finely chopped flat-leaf parsley

1 tsp finely chopped chives

1 lb 4 oz yellow squash, cut in half lengthwise, seeded, and sliced crosswise into ⅛-inch-thick half moons (about 5 cups)

¾ cup grated Gruyère, or as needed

2 tsp salt, or to taste

⅛ tsp freshly ground white pepper, or to taste

1 cup heavy cream, warmed

1. In a medium sauté pan, melt the butter over medium heat. Add the shallots and sweat until translucent, 3 to 5 minutes. Remove the shallots from the pan and reserve. Toss the bread crumbs with the remaining butter in the pan. Add the parsley and chives to the bread crumbs and reserve until needed.

2. Preheat the oven to 350°F. Grease an 8 by 8-inch baking pan lightly with butter. Reserve ¼ cup of the bread crumbs for the top of the gratin.

3. Alternate layers of the shallots, squash, the remaining ¾ cup bread crumbs, the cheese, salt, and pepper to make 4 even layers. Pour the cream over the gratin so that they are just covered. Cover with aluminum foil and bake until tender, about 30 minutes.

4. Remove the foil and top with the reserved ¼ cup bread crumbs. Turn on the broiler and broil the gratin until the bread crumbs are browned, about 2 minutes.

5. Allow the gratin to set, about 15 minutes before serving.

Chef's Note *The squash can also be sliced lengthwise to make even, wide layers.*

CARAMELIZED BUTTERNUT SQUASH, LEEKS, AND HAZELNUTS

This combination of roasted squash and hazelnuts is rich and buttery. Serve it hot or cold; it is delicious either way. This is a perfect accompaniment to any rich-flavored fowl such as duck or squab. Grill the birds and then serve this with the Sautéed Spinach with Apple and Raisins on page 128. MAKES 5 SERVINGS

Salt, to taste

1 butternut squash (about 2 lb), peeled, halved lengthwise, seeded, and sliced ¼ inch thick

2 leeks

¼ cup hazelnut oil

1 cup Chicken Broth (page 6)

Freshly ground black pepper, to taste

1 cup toasted, chopped hazelnuts

1. Preheat the oven to 350°F.

2. Lightly salt the squash and set aside until it starts to sweat.

3. Meanwhile, peel the first layer off the leeks, slice the leeks crosswise into ½-inch sections, wash thoroughly, and dry each section.

4. On a sheet pan, toss the squash with the hazelnut oil. Roast in the oven until the squash starts to brown, about 15 minutes. Add the broth and the leeks and continue to roast until the leeks are soft and the squash is golden brown, about 10 minutes.

5. When all the liquid has evaporated and the vegetables are tender, check the seasoning and add additional salt and pepper, if needed. Transfer the vegetables to a serving platter. Sprinkle with the hazelnuts and serve.

TOMATO CONFIT

A traditional *confit* is made with duck legs that are salted, cured, and then simmered in their own fat. What we call tomato "confit" takes license with the name and simply refers to tomatoes that are slow-cooked in a similar way in good-quality olive oil with fresh herbs, garlic, and salt. Once you have cooked the tomatoes in the oil, you can then use the oil for cooking, salad dressings, or even another batch of confit. MAKES 10 SERVINGS

10 ripe tomatoes

1 bunch rosemary

8 garlic cloves, sliced

1 tsp salt, or as needed

½ tsp freshly ground black pepper, or as needed

3 cups olive oil

1. Preheat the oven to 300°F.

2. Wash the tomatoes and cut them in half lengthwise.

3. Sprinkle a sheet pan with half of the rosemary, the garlic, salt, and pepper.

4. Arrange the tomato halves, cut side down, on the pan and sprinkle with the remaining rosemary, garlic, salt, and pepper. Drizzle with enough olive oil to almost submerge the tomatoes.

5. Cook slowly in the oven until you can pull the skins off and the tomatoes are soft, about 40 minutes.

RAINBOW SWISS CHARD WITH CHORIZO

This recipe can be made with plain old chard but, if you can find it, rainbow chard adds great color and a wonderful "visual flavor." Be sure to strip and rip the green: since the stem is so much denser than the greens, it is best to blanch them separately. The stem is somewhat like celery and should be peeled before blanching. I like to peel them and cut them on a diagonal, then blanch the stems. Just be sure to include the stems, or half the flavor and all the color will be lost.

MAKES 5 SERVINGS

1 bunch rainbow chard

¼ cup olive oil

2 shallots, sliced

1 cup dried Spanish chorizo

1 tsp pimentón dulce (sweet Spanish paprika)

1 cup Chicken Broth (page 6), Vegetable Broth (page 4), *or* water

1 bay leaf

Salt, to taste

Freshly ground black pepper, to taste

1. Prepare an ice bath. Strip the leaves off the chard stems and then cut or rip the leaves into smaller pieces. Peel the stems lightly with a peeler. Cook the leaves and the stems separately in boiling salted water until tender, about 2 minutes for the leaves and 4 minutes for the stems. Shock the leaves and stems in the ice bath to stop the cooking process. Drain and set aside.

2. Heat the olive oil in a sauté pan over medium heat, add the shallots, and sauté until tender, about 2 minutes.

3. Add the chorizo and pimentón dulce and sauté until the chorizo is a little crisp, about 4 minutes.

4. Add the cooked chard stems, the broth or water, and the bay leaf and cook until the broth has almost evaporated, about 4 minutes. Add the cooked leaves and season with salt and pepper. Remove and discard the bay leaf before serving.

BROCCOLI RABE WITH POMEGRANATE

I love broccoli rabe, but it does tend to be a little bitter. The pomegranate molasses in this recipe adds that touch of sweetness needed to cut down the bitterness. If you can't find fresh pomegranates, use a splash of pomegranate juice.

MAKES 5 SERVINGS

1 bunch broccoli rabe (about 8 oz)

2 tbsp olive oil

4 garlic cloves, sliced

2 tbsp water

Salt, to taste

Freshly ground black pepper, to taste

1 pomegranate, peeled, seeds removed and reserved

1 tbsp pomegranate molasses

1. Prepare an ice bath. Bring a large pot of salted water to a boil. Cut ¼ inch off the bottom of the broccoli rabe stems and lightly peel the stems. Plunge the broccoli rabe into the boiling salted water and cook until the stems are somewhat tender, about 3 minutes. Remove from the boiling water and plunge into the ice bath to stop the cooking process. Drain and reserve.

2. In a medium sauté pan, lightly heat the olive oil over medium heat. Add the garlic and cook until aromatic, about 2 minutes.

3. Add the reserved broccoli rabe to the pan. Add the water and cook until it has evaporated and the broccoli rabe is lightly browned, about 8 minutes.

4. Season with salt and pepper. Transfer to a serving platter, sprinkle with the fresh pomegranate seeds, and drizzle with the pomegranate molasses. Serve immediately.

ROASTED PEARS AND FENNEL WITH GORGONZOLA CHEESE

When summer vegetables are gone and fall produce is in season, these roasted pears and fennel with Gorgonzola cheese are perfect for a chilly autumn day. You might also consider grilling the pears. Should you decide to grill, just cut the pears in half lengthwise, lightly brush them with oil and, a pinch of salt and pepper and grill for about 3 minutes per side. It gives them a nice smoky flavor. Either way, this is a nice transition into fall. Serve this with grissini breadsticks or focaccia. MAKES 5 SERVINGS

4 red pears

¼ cup olive oil

2 shallots, thinly sliced

Salt, to taste

Freshly ground black pepper, to taste

1 fennel bulb, trimmed

4 oz young Gorgonzola (or any good blue cheese substitute)

1. Preheat the oven to 350°F. Preheat a sheet pan in the oven.

2. Cut the pears in half lengthwise and remove the core. Cut each half into thirds lengthwise. Toss the pears in half of the olive oil along with the shallots and season with salt and pepper.

3. Using a mandoline, shave the fennel as thinly as possible.

4. Place the oiled pears and shallots on the preheated sheet pan and roast for about 10 minutes. Add the sliced fennel. Continue to roast until the pears have a little color, about 10 minutes more.

5. Remove the pan from the oven and transfer the pears, shallots, and fennel to a serving platter. Let the pears cool slightly, then sprinkle with the cheese.

FRIED EGGPLANT, TOMATO CONFIT, MOZZARELLA, AND BASIL PESTO

My mother used to make fried eggplant for dinner. As fast as she fried it, I would eat it. There is something so inviting about that crispy outside and the soft, flavorful inside. These days, I like to bread my eggplant with panko bread crumbs; I think that they make the eggplant slices even crisper. This recipe combines a few of my favorite things: fried eggplant, tomato confit, fresh mozzarella, and pesto made from garden basil. Once assembled, this can be a side dish, or placed nestled in focaccia for the most sublime sandwich. MAKES 5 SERVINGS

10 eggplant rounds, sliced ¼ inch thick (about one 1-lb eggplant)

Salt, as needed

1 cup all-purpose flour

3 large eggs, whisked until smooth

2 cups panko bread crumbs

2 cups olive oil

Freshly ground black pepper, to taste

½ cup Pesto Genovese (page 245)

8 slices Fresh Mozzarella Cheese (page 227), sliced ¼ inch thick

8 halves Tomato Confit (page 141)

1. Salt the eggplant rounds and set aside until they start to sweat, about 15 minutes. Rinse them and pat them dry with paper towels.

2. Meanwhile, set up the flour, egg, and bread crumbs for dredging in three separate containers.

3. Dredge the eggplant rounds in the flour and shake off any excess. Place the rounds in the egg, making certain that they are fully coated. Place the coated rounds into the panko bread crumbs and press into the crumbs to coat thoroughly. The rounds are now ready to fry.

4. Preheat the oven to 350°F. Preheat the oil in a large skillet to about 325°F. Add the eggplant rounds, cooking in batches, and fry until golden brown, about 5 minutes. Remove the eggplant rounds from the pan and transfer to a wire rack set over a sheet pan. Sprinkle with salt and pepper.

5. Spread each eggplant round with a teaspoon of the pesto. Arrange a thin slice of mozzarella on top of each round and top with a tomato confit half.

6. Heat in the oven for 5 minutes until the mozzarella starts to melt. Serve hot.

CARAMELIZED SWEET POTATOES WITH PINE NUTS AND CURRANTS

When I was little, my mom, Amelia, made candied sweet potatoes. I always loved them and came up with this variation of the dish. The lemon juice adds notes of citrus while the currants add a little sweetness. The caramelization of the potatoes results in a delicious dish that conjures up memories of my childhood—different but just the same somehow. Thanks, Mom. MAKES 5 SERVINGS

2 sweet potatoes, peeled and diced into 1-inch cubes

1 shallot, thinly sliced

¼ cup olive oil

1 rosemary sprig

Juice of 2 lemons

2 tbsp brown sugar

½ cup dried currants

Salt, to taste

Freshly ground black pepper, to taste

½ cup pine nuts, toasted

2 tbsp finely chopped chives

1. Preheat the oven to 350°F.

2. In a roasting pan, toss the sweet potatoes and shallot with the olive oil and add the rosemary sprig.

3. Roast until the potatoes are somewhat tender, about 20 minutes.

4. Add the lemon juice and brown sugar and continue to roast until the potatoes are tender and golden brown, about 20 minutes more.

5. Remove the potatoes from the oven and toss with the currants. Season with salt and pepper. Remove and discard the rosemary sprig. Sprinkle with the toasted pine nuts and chives and serve.

ROASTED BEETS WITH FETA AND TANGERINES

If you like beets, which I do, this combination is truly wonderful. The natural sweetness of the beets and tangerines when combined with the saltiness of the feta is just amazing. This dish would be great on a meze table or served as a small tapas dish. MAKES 5 SERVINGS

BEETS

3 large beets

¼ cup red wine vinegar

1 tsp salt

2 shallots, diced

¼ cup olive oil

1 marjoram sprig

Salt, to taste

Freshly ground black pepper, to taste

VINAIGRETTE

4 tangerines *or* small oranges

1 shallot, thinly sliced

2 tbsp red wine vinegar

1 tbsp chopped marjoram

1 tbsp chopped flat-leaf parsley

3 tbsp extra-virgin olive oil

½ cup crumbled feta

2 tbsp finely chopped chives

1. To prepare the beets: In a pot, combine the beets with enough water to cover, along with the vinegar and salt. Bring to a simmer, cover, and cook for 15 minutes.

2. Remove the beets from the pot and set aside until cool enough to handle. Peel the beets and then quarter them.

3. Preheat the oven to 375°F.

4. In a roasting pan or on a sheet pan, toss the quartered beets with the shallots, olive oil, and marjoram and season with salt and pepper. Roast until the shallots are lightly browned, about 15 minutes.

5. Meanwhile, make the vinaigrette: Finely grate the zest of 3 of the tangerines or oranges and then peel and segment them. Juice the remaining tangerine. Combine the tangerine juice, zest, shallot, vinegar, marjoram, and parsley. Whisk in the olive oil and reserve ½ cup of the vinaigrette for garnish.

6. Remove the beets from the oven and toss with the remaining vinaigrette.

7. Arrange the dressed beets on a serving platter, sprinkle with the tangerine segments, sprinkle with the feta, and drizzle with the reserved ½ cup vinaigrette.

RATATOUILLE

Traditional ratatouille is simply a Provençal vegetable stew. In this straightforward dish, the key is to cook all the vegetables thoroughly. It is best to make ratatouille the day before you serve it to allow the flavors to fully develop. MAKES 4 SERVINGS

1½ tsp olive oil

1 cup medium-dice yellow onion

1 tbsp finely chopped garlic

1½ tbsp tomato paste

½ cup medium-dice green bell peppers

2½ cups medium-dice eggplant

1 cup medium-dice zucchini

½ cup finely chopped plum tomatoes

1½ tsp salt, plus more as needed

⅛ tsp freshly ground black pepper, plus more as needed

2 tbsp Chicken Broth (page 6) *or* Vegetable Broth (page 4)

2 tbsp chopped flat-leaf parsley

1. Heat the olive oil in a large, wide, heavy-bottomed pot or rondeau over medium heat. Add the onion and sauté until translucent, 4 to 5 minutes. Add the garlic and sauté until soft, about 1 minute.

2. Reduce the heat to medium-low. Add the tomato paste and cook until it completely coats the onions and deepens in color, 1 to 2 minutes.

3. Add the vegetables in the following sequence: bell peppers, eggplant, zucchini, and tomatoes. Cook each vegetable until it softens, 2 to 3 minutes each, before adding the next.

4. Add the salt, black pepper, and broth and reduce the heat to low. Allow the vegetables to stew; they should be moist but not soupy. Stew until the vegetables are tender and flavorful. Add the parsley, check the seasoning, and add additional salt and pepper, if needed. Serve immediately or cool and store in an airtight container in the refrigerator overnight.

Many areas of the Mediterranean are quite barren and arid. Meat is not necessarily in abundance, and the meat and poultry choices that are available are somewhat different than our standard American fare. Meat actually constitutes only a small percentage of the daily diet, and the typical portion size is generally smaller than in the United States.

Vegetables, fruits, grains, and legumes are very important in the Mediterranean diet, so complementary accompaniments are featured along with the protein in most of these dishes. I encourage you to break out of the box and prepare some new dishes using meats and poultry that you may never have tried before. Since meat is not the focus of the Mediterranean diet, many of these dishes are fairly simple.

There are several unusual methods of cooking meats in the Mediterranean. Depending on the area and the equipment, they can vary. There is a lamb dish called *méchoui,* in which you rub the lamb with soft butter and spices and let it marinate overnight in the butter rub. It is then roasted slowly to coax out the flavor and tenderness, not unlike our Leg of Lamb with Garlic and Savory (page 169). Many roasted or grilled meats are cooked at a low temperature for a long time for that very reason. Kebabs are a favorite for easy preparation. Another interesting version of a vertical sort of kebab is the gyro. It is usually a cylinder of lamb that is slow roasted vertically and then thinly sliced and served in sandwiches. The key is good ingredients and, if at all possible, try to get local meat or at least good-quality meat at a specialty shop.

CHICKEN PAILLARDS WITH FRISÉE, CAPERS, AND OLIVES

This is a quick dish that is packed with flavor. It is also easy to prepare, which makes it the perfect weeknight dinner. In the summer, I like to serve it out on the patio with a cold glass of rosé. MAKES 4 SERVINGS

1 garlic clove, finely chopped

Finely grated zest of 1 Meyer lemon (see Chef's Note)

1 tbsp chopped oregano

¼ cup olive oil

4 boneless, skinless chicken breasts, butterflied and pounded ¼ inch thick

Juice of 3 lemons

Salt, to taste

Freshly ground black pepper, to taste

3 cups frisée, washed and spun dry

1 shallot, finely chopped

3 tbsp capers

1 cup oil-cured olives, pitted

1 cup diced tomato

1. Combine the garlic, lemon zest, oregano, and 2 tablespoons of the olive oil and brush the mixture onto the chicken breasts. Squeeze the juice of 1 lemon over the chicken breasts and season with salt and pepper.

2. Preheat a grill or grill pan over medium heat. Place the chicken breasts on the grill and cook until each side has visible grill marks and the meat is cooked through, about 3 minutes per side. Remove from the grill and allow to rest for 5 minutes.

3. While the chicken is grilling, in a work bowl, toss the frisée with the juice of the remaining 2 lemons, the shallots, capers, olives, tomato, and the remaining 2 tablespoons olive oil. If necessary, season with salt and pepper.

4. Place the frisée in a serving bowl and arrange the grilled chicken on top. Spoon any olives, capers, and tomatoes that are leftover in the bottom of the work bowl onto the top of the chicken.

Chef's Note *If Meyer lemons are not available, simply substitute a regular lemon.*

CHICKEN TAGINE WITH APRICOTS AND GOLDEN RAISINS

A *tagine* is a North African dish of Berber origin and is a staple of Moroccan cuisine. This one combines the sweet of dried fruits and the sour of preserved lemons. It is important not to overcook the chicken so, if needed, take the chicken pieces out of the pot and reserve in a covered dish while you reduce the stew. The preserved lemons and dried limes add a lot of flavor, but if you can't find them, don't worry about it; the stew will be delicious just the same. MAKES 5 TO 6 SERVINGS

12 chicken thighs

Salt, to taste

Freshly ground black pepper, to taste

3 tbsp extra-virgin olive oil

12 cipollini onions, blanched for 10 seconds and peeled

3 tbsp peeled, sliced ginger

6 garlic cloves, thinly sliced

2 tsp toasted cumin seeds, ground

⅛ tsp crushed saffron threads

8 preserved lemon wedges, pith removed and rind thinly sliced

20 Picholine or pitted green olives

1½ cups golden raisins

8 oz dried apricots, diced

2 dried limes, soaked in hot water for 1 hour (see Chef's note)

6½ cups Chicken Broth (page 6), hot

¼ cup chopped flat-leaf parsley

¼ cup chopped cilantro

3 cups cooked couscous (page 79)

1. Season the chicken thighs with salt and pepper. In a large, oven-safe sauté pan over high heat, heat the olive oil, add the chicken thighs, skin side down, and cook until brown on each side, about 10 minutes. Work in batches when cooking the chicken thighs to avoid overcrowding the pan, which will cause them to steam instead of brown. Add the onions and cook until browned, about 4 minutes. Drain the grease from the pan. If working in batches, return all the chicken to the pan.

2. Add the ginger and garlic and cook until tender, about 2 minutes. Add the cumin, saffron, preserved lemons, olives, raisins, apricots, and dried limes. Stir in 1 cup of the broth to help combine all the ingredients. Add the remaining 5½ cups broth and cover the pan. Reduce the heat to medium to establish a simmer and begin the braising process. (See Chef's Note.) Braise until the chicken is fork-tender, about 50 minutes.

3. Continue cooking until the broth has reduced to a consistency thick enough to coat the back of a wooden spoon. If necessary, adjust the seasoning with salt and pepper. Garnish with the parsley and cilantro and serve with the couscous.

Chef's Notes *If dried limes are unavailable, preserved limes are a good substitute.*

You can braise this stew on the stovetop over medium heat as described above, or you can cook it in a 350° to 375°F oven in a large, oven-safe, heavy-bottomed pot or enameled casserole. Either way, a constant simmer must be maintained to achieve a proper braise.

TOP ROW LEFT TO RIGHT:

This dish is named for its traditional conical cooking vessel, but you can achieve the same result in a large sauté pan. It is best to brown the skin side of the chicken first, and to cook it in batches to avoid overcrowding the pan.

Before covering the pot to braise, add enough hot broth to cover the chicken.

BOTTOM ROW LEFT TO RIGHT:

Couscous (page 79) is traditionally cooked in a piece of special equipment called a couscousière. At home, you can steam couscous in the same manner by placing a mesh strainer lined with cheesecloth over a pot of water (see note on page 79).

Here, the dish was prepared in a sauté pan but served in the tagine for a more authentic presentation.

VINEGAR CHICKEN WITH CELERY ROOT PURÉE

Braising chicken in vinegar is a very popular cooking method in the Mediterranean. You will find numerous variations in different countries and regions, but this particular recipe is a version of the French *poulet sauté au vinaigre,* or vinegar chicken. The method calls for marinating the chicken in an Alsatian Riesling wine and then cooking it in the marinade with vinegar. The celery root purée is a great alternative to mashed potatoes and makes a perfect accompaniment to the chicken. MAKES 6 SERVINGS

CHICKEN

4 garlic cloves, finely chopped

4 shallots, finely chopped

1 cup Alsatian Riesling

6 chicken breasts, skin on, bone in

Extra-virgin olive oil, as needed

¼ cup tomato paste

1 cup apple cider vinegar

2 tbsp honey

1½ cups Chicken Broth (page 6)

2 tbsp fines herbes (see Chef's Note)

GLAZED CARROTS

2 tbsp unsalted butter

1¼ lb carrots, thinly sliced on the bias

¾ cup Vegetable Broth (page 4) or Chicken Broth (page 6), warmed

3 tbsp sugar

Salt, to taste

Freshly ground white pepper, to taste

1. To prepare the chicken: The day before, in a nonreactive bowl or container, combine the garlic, shallots, and wine to make a marinade. Add the chicken and allow to marinate in the refrigerator overnight.

2. On the following day, remove the chicken from the marinade and pat dry with paper towels. Strain the vegetables from the marinade and reserve both.

3. In a pan over medium heat, cook the chicken breasts in a small amount of olive oil until golden brown on both sides, about 10 minutes. If working in small batches to avoid overcrowding the pan, continue cooking until all the chicken breasts are browned. If excess fat accumulates in the pan or small solids in the bottom of the pan start to burn, drain the fat and add new olive oil, as needed, between batches.

4. In a clean pan over medium heat, cook the reserved garlic and shallots in a small amount of olive oil until tender, about 4 minutes. Stir in the tomato paste and allow it to cook for 3 minutes. Deglaze the pan with the vinegar and half of the reserved marinade. Add the honey and broth and continue cooking until the liquid has reduced by two-thirds. Add the chicken breasts and the remaining half of the marinade and cook until the juices from the chicken run clear, about 10 minutes. Transfer the chicken to a plate, cover lightly with aluminum foil, and allow the chicken to rest.

5. Strain the cooking liquid through a fine-mesh sieve and return the liquid to the pan. Cook over medium heat until the liquid has reduced to a consistency that coats the back of a wooden spoon. Stir in the fines herbes and reserve the vinegar sauce until needed.

6. To make the glazed carrots: Heat the butter in a pan over medium-low heat. Add the carrots, cover the pan, and cook for 2 minutes. Remove the cover, add the broth and sugar, and season with salt and pepper. Replace the cover and cook over low heat until the carrots are almost tender, about 5 minutes. Remove the cover and continue to simmer, uncovered, until the cooking liquid has reduced to a glaze and the carrots are tender, about 3 minutes.

7. To cook the cabbage: Prepare an ice bath. Bring a large pot of salted water to a boil. Add the sliced cabbage and blanch for 2 minutes. Remove from the pot and plunge into the ice bath, then drain.

SAVOY CABBAGE WITH PANCETTA AND SHALLOTS

½ head savoy cabbage, thinly sliced

¼ cup olive oil

½ cup finely chopped pancetta

3 shallots, thinly sliced

1 cup Chicken Broth (page 6)

1 tsp salt

Freshly ground black pepper, to taste

2 tbsp unsalted butter, at room temperature

3 cups Celery Root Purée (page 127)

8. Heat the olive oil in a sauté pan over medium heat, render the pancetta, and cook until almost crispy. Add the shallots and sauté until aromatic, about 2 minutes.

9. Add the blanched cabbage and broth and increase the heat. Season with the salt and pepper and cook until the broth has almost completely evaporated. Just before serving, swirl in the butter.

10. To serve: Place ½ cup celery root purée and ½ cup glazed carrots onto each of six serving plates. Arrange a chicken breast on top of the purée and nap with the vinegar sauce. Divide the cabbage evenly among the serving plates.

Chef's Note Fines herbes *is the French term for a combination of delicately flavored minced herbs that is frequently used in Mediterranean cooking. To make fines herbes, simply combine equal parts minced fresh parsley, chervil, tarragon, and chives.*

GRILLED QUAIL WITH MANGO AND ARUGULA

This is a really easy and refreshing little grilled dish. Prep the ingredients the night before and it will take you no time to prepare this for dinner. The combination of the grilled quail and the sweet-tart mango, citrus, ginger, and curry combination gives this dish complex flavor with simple preparation. MAKES 6 SERVINGS

6 quail, halved through the breastbone

¼ cup olive oil

Salt, to taste

Freshly ground black pepper, to taste

1 tsp curry powder

1 tsp grated, peeled, ginger

4 tarragon sprigs

2 mangoes, peeled, pitted, and thinly sliced, scraps diced and reserved

2 shallots, thinly sliced

Finely grated zest and juice of 1 orange

1 tsp sugar

3 cups arugula

1 tbsp finely chopped chives

½ cup mango, cut into julienne (see Chef's Note)

1. Preheat the oven to 250°F.

2. Rub the quail lightly with olive oil, then season with salt and pepper and rub with the curry powder and ginger. Place the quail in a pan, cut side down, on top of the sprigs of tarragon and add the mango slices so that they can absorb the flavor of the herbs and ginger. Set aside in the refrigerator for 30 minutes.

3. Preheat a grill or a grill pan over medium heat. Grill the mango slices until they have visible grill marks on each side, then arrange the slices on a serving platter.

4. Remove the quail from the spice rub and reserve any rub remaining in the pan. Place the quail halves on the grill or grill pan and grill until the skin has browned, about 3 minutes per side. Transfer the quail to the oven to keep warm.

5. While the quail is grilling, heat a pan over medium heat and scrape any of the remaining spice rub into the pan. Add the shallots and diced mango scraps to the pan and cook until slightly caramelized. Add the orange zest and juice and continue cooking until the juice has completely evaporated. Stir in the sugar. Add the arugula to the pan and cook until it has wilted.

6. Transfer the arugula to the serving platter with the mango slices. Arrange the grilled quail on top and sprinkle with the chives and mango julienne. Serve warm.

Chef's Note *A fine julienne is a matchstick-size cut. Cut your vegetable into slices that are approximately ¹⁄₁₆ inch thick and then cut them across ¹⁄₁₆ inch. They should not be any longer than 1½ inches so that they are not cumbersome to eat.*

DUCK BREAST WITH CARAMELIZED CAULIFLOWER AND PRUNES

This duck dish is reminiscent of Gascon cuisine. The combination of duck and prunes is a natural: In Gascony foie gras is king and Armagnac is queen. Armagnac is much like Cognac, but not as well known. It is distilled from wine made from a blend of Armagnac grapes grown in the region. Most Armagnac, unlike Cognac, is made by smaller producers and is not mass distributed. Along with abundant grape production in Gascony, there are many plum trees. Plums, when dried, become prunes and are the classic combination with foie gras. Most foie gras used to come from geese, but now comes from the moulard duck.

MAKES 4 SERVINGS

4 Pekin duck breasts or 2 moulard duck breasts (they will be twice the size of the Pekin breasts)

Salt, as needed

Freshly ground black pepper, to taste

2 tbsp olive oil

3 thyme sprigs

½ head cauliflower, sliced into ¼-inch pieces

2 shallots, diced

1 tbsp balsamic vinegar

1 cup Chicken Broth (page 6)

16 prunes

1. Preheat the oven to 200°F.

2. Place the duck breasts in a pan or baking dish and season with salt, pepper, and the olive oil. Add the thyme sprigs to the pan, place the duck breasts on top of the thyme, and set aside for 30 minutes at room temperature.

3. In a sauté pan over medium-low heat, place the duck breasts, skin side down, and cook so that the layer of fat directly under the skin renders out. Continue to sauté the duck breasts until the skin is golden brown, about 12 minutes, then turn the breasts over and add the thyme sprigs to the pan. Continue to cook the opposite side of the duck breasts until the internal temperature registers 135°F, about 4 minutes. Remove the thyme from the pan and reserve. Remove the duck from the pan, transfer to a sheet pan fitted with a rack, and place in the oven to keep warm.

4. Add the cauliflower to the pan with the duck fat and cook over medium heat until the cauliflower pieces are golden brown around the edges, about 5 minutes. Add the shallots to the pan and continue to cook until they are soft and a light golden brown, about 2 minutes. Remove the cauliflower from the pan and arrange on a serving platter.

5. Add the vinegar to the pan and cook over medium heat until the liquid has reduced to a syrupy consistency, about 3 minutes. Add the broth and prunes and continue cooking until the mixture has reduced to approximately ½ cup. Reserve the sauce over low heat until ready to serve.

6. Remove the duck breasts from the oven and allow them to rest at room temperature for 5 minutes so that the natural juices redistribute. Carve each duck breast into 6 to 8 slices slightly on the bias and arrange on the serving platter beside the cauliflower. Pour the sauce over the sliced duck and spoon the prunes on the side. Garnish the platter with the reserved thyme sprigs.

SQUAB WITH QUINCE PASTE AND PUMPKIN FARRO

Squab is one of my favorite birds, although I do prefer the breasts. Don't waste the legs, though. Make the sauce from them, and after they are cooked you can strip the meat off the bone and make a little squab salad, just like a chicken salad. Squab lends itself well to fruit and quince paste combined with the earthiness of farro and the herbaceousness of spinach, which makes this a really solid dish. MAKES 4 SERVINGS

FARRO

1 qt water

2 tbsp kosher salt, plus more as needed

1 cup farro

1 tbsp olive oil

½ cup diced trimmed fennel

1 shallot, chopped

2 cups diced pumpkin *or* butternut squash

1 cup spinach leaves

Freshly ground black pepper, to taste

SQUAB AND SAUCE

5 thyme sprigs

Finely grated zest and juice of 1 orange

Olive oil, as needed

Salt, to taste

Freshly ground black pepper, to taste

4 squab, bones removed and reserved, breasts and legs separated

1 carrot, diced

1 onion, diced

1 celery stalk, diced

1 fresh bay leaf

9 tbsp quince paste

2 cups Chicken Broth (page 6)

1. To prepare the farro: Bring the water and 2 tbsp salt to a boil in a pot over high heat. Slowly stream the farro into the boiling water, stir, and reduce the heat to establish a simmer. Continue to simmer until tender, about 30 minutes. Drain and reserve.

2. Heat the olive oil in a sauté pan over medium heat, add the fennel, shallot, and pumpkin and cook until tender and lightly caramelized. Add the spinach and cook until just wilted, about 1 minute. Add the reserved farro and stir in until well combined. Season the salad with salt and pepper and keep warm over low heat on the stovetop.

3. To prepare the squab: Combine 4 of the thyme sprigs, the orange zest, olive oil, salt, and pepper in a baking dish. Rub the squab breasts with the mixture and reserve.

4. Preheat the oven to 200°F.

5. Heat a small amount of olive oil in a sauce pot over medium heat. Put the legs and bones of the squab in the pot and cook until they are evenly browned, about 20 minutes. Remove the browned bones and legs and reserve. Add the carrot and onion to the pot and cook until the vegetables are caramelized, about 5 minutes. Stir in the celery, bay leaf, orange juice, and 1 tablespoon of the quince paste, then return the browned bones to the pot. Add the broth, bring to a simmer, and cook for 1 hour. Strain the liquid, return it to the pot, and reduce to 1 cup over medium heat.

6. Heat a small amount of olive oil in a sauté pan over medium heat and put the squab breasts, skin side down, in the hot oil. Cook for about 3 minutes to brown the skin, then add the remaining thyme sprig. Turn the breasts over and cook for 3 minutes more on the opposite side. Remove the breasts from the pan and reserve warm in the oven.

7. Pour the fat out of the pan and add the reduced sauce. Bring to a simmer over medium-high heat and allow it to reduce again by one-third. Whisk in ¼ cup of the quince paste.

8. To serve: Divide the warm farro salad evenly among four serving plates. Arrange one squab breast on top of each serving of farro. Pour about ¼ cup of the sauce onto each plate and garnish each with 1 tablespoon of quince paste.

BRAISED SHORT RIBS WITH RADICCHIO SLAW AND POTATO SALAD

This is my version of Mediterranean barbecue. It can be eaten hot or cold, so it is one of my favorite picnic dishes. In warm weather, bring along some crusty semolina bread to make cold sandwiches, and in the fall serve the short ribs and potatoes warm for a truly comforting meal. The key to this dish is to get a good, even sear on the short ribs in a hot pan and then to cook them very slowly using low heat in order to break down all of the collagen in the meat and develop the flavor of the sauce. For the best results, the ribs should be made a day before serving (see Chef's Note). MAKES 4 SERVINGS

SHORT RIBS

2 lb boneless beef short ribs

1 tbsp salt

Freshly ground black pepper

¼ cup olive oil

1 Spanish onion, diced

1 carrot, peeled and diced

4 garlic cloves, smashed

1 celery stalk, peeled and diced

2 tsp tomato paste

4 sun-dried tomatoes, packed in oil, diced

1 qt Chicken Broth (page 6), warmed

1 rosemary sprig

1 bay leaf

1 thyme sprig

1 orange, peeled and cut into quarters

1 cup balsamic vinegar

1. Preheat the oven to 300°F.

2. Thoroughly dry the short ribs and season them liberally with the salt and pepper.

3. In a 3-quart oven-safe pot or Dutch oven, heat the olive oil over medium heat. Working in batches to avoid overcrowding the pan, cook the ribs on each side until golden brown, about 8 minutes.

4. Remove the ribs from the pot, add the onion, carrot, and garlic and cook until slightly caramelized, about 5 minutes. Add the celery and continue cooking until the celery has softened, about 3 minutes. Add the tomato paste and the sun-dried tomatoes and continue cooking until the tomato paste becomes aromatic and there is a slight red film on the bottom of the pot, about 2 minutes.

5. Return the ribs to the pot and add the broth, rosemary, bay leaf, thyme, orange quarters, and balsamic vinegar. Increase the heat to establish a simmer and skim off any scum that rises to the surface.

6. Cover the pot, place it in the oven, and cook the ribs until fork-tender, about 2½ hours. Remove the ribs from the oven, transfer them to a dish, and cover with plastic wrap.

7. Return the pot to the stovetop over medium heat and slowly reduce the sauce until it is thick enough to coat the back of a wooden spoon. Return the ribs to the pot and coat with the sauce (see Chef's Note). Remove and discard the bay leaf and herb sprigs.

8. To make the radicchio slaw: In a bowl, combine the onion, honey, vinegar, basil, chives, beet, and olive oil. Add the radicchio and toss to coat well, season with the salt and pepper, and let marinate for at least 30 minutes before serving.

RADICCHIO SLAW

1 red onion, finely chopped, soaked in salted water for 1 hour, drained well, and rinsed

1 tsp lavender honey

½ cup balsamic vinegar, simmered until reduced by one-third

6 basil leaves, chopped

1 tsp finely chopped chives

1 red beet, peeled and grated

2 tbsp olive oil

1 head radicchio, halved and thinly sliced (as cabbage would be for coleslaw)

¼ tsp kosher salt

Freshly ground black pepper, to taste

POTATO SALAD

2 lb Yukon Gold potatoes, peeled and diced

1 tbsp salt, plus more as needed

2 shallots, finely chopped

Finely grated zest and juice of 1 lemon

¼ cup olive oil

1 cup crème fraîche

1 tsp finely chopped tarragon

1 cup peeled, seeded, and sliced cucumber

Freshly ground black pepper, to taste

9. To make the potato salad: Put the potatoes in a large pot and cover with cold water. Add the salt and bring to a boil over high heat. Boil the potatoes until they are fork-tender, about 12 minutes. When the potatoes are tender, drain them in colander, then place the colander back over the hot pot for a few minutes so that the potatoes dry out.

10. While the potatoes are cooking, combine the shallots, lemon zest and juice, olive oil, crème fraîche, tarragon, and cucumber in a bowl. Add the warm potatoes to the mixture and stir to coat well. If necessary, adjust the seasoning with salt and pepper. Serve warm or cold.

11. Divide the slaw and potato salad evenly among four serving plates and place the ribs on top of the slaw.

Chef's Notes *Short ribs are best when made the day before serving. Hold in the refrigerator overnight, and the next day you will be able to skim any excess fat from the top of the cold sauce. Slowly reheat the ribs over medium heat before serving.*

If Yukon Gold potatoes are unavailable, substitute bliss or white creamer potatoes.

VENISON WITH APPLE-VANILLA COMPOTE AND FOIE GRAS BREAD PUDDING

Venison's rich flavor and color has made it one of my favorite meats. It is also low in fat and is now fairly easy to purchase. If venison is unavailable, this recipe can be made using any dark game or poultry; duck is virtually interchangeable with venison. And, if you don't care for game meat, pork or lamb would work here as well. MAKES 6 SERVINGS

VENISON

1 tbsp unsalted butter

2 sage leaves

4½ lb venison saddle, bones removed and reserved, meat trimmed

Olive oil, as needed

1 onion, peeled and sliced ¼ inch thick

1 carrot, peeled and sliced ¼ inch thick

1 celery stalk, sliced ¼ inch thick

1 vanilla bean, split lengthwise

½ cup apple cider

1 apple, peeled and diced

1 bay leaf

1 black peppercorn

1 thyme sprig

1½ cups Pinot Noir

1 qt beef broth

FOIE GRAS BREAD PUDDING

2 tbsp unsalted butter

4 shallots, finely chopped

2 cups whole milk

2 cups foie gras, at room temperature, cleaned and scraped

1 tsp chopped sage

3 large eggs

Salt, to taste

Freshly ground black pepper, to taste

½ loaf white bread, crust removed, cubed or cut into triangles, and dried slightly

1. Preheat the oven to 350°F. Butter six 2- to 3-inch ramekins.

2. Place the sage leaves on top of the venison meat and reserve in the refrigerator until needed.

3. In a roasting pan, toss the venison bones with olive oil. Put the pan in the oven and roast the bones until well browned, about 1 hour, turning the bones over every 20 minutes.

4. Heat a small amount of olive oil in a large pot over medium heat, add the onion, carrot, and celery, and cook until the vegetables are caramelized, about 8 minutes. Add the browned bones to the pot with the caramelized vegetables. Scrape the seeds from inside each half of the vanilla bean into the pot, then add the pod.

5. Pour the apple cider into the roasting pan and deglaze, using a wooden spoon to scrape up all the pan drippings. Add the pan drippings and liquid to the large pot and increase the heat to medium-high to establish a simmer. Add the diced apple, bay leaf, peppercorn, thyme, and wine. Continue simmering until the liquid has reduced by three-quarters, skimming off any scum that rises to the surface. Add the beef broth and continue simmering until the liquid has reduced to 2 cups, skimming as necessary. At this point, the sauce will have simmered for about 1 hour total and should be thick enough to coat the back of a wooden spoon. Strain the sauce through a fine-mesh sieve, cover it with plastic wrap, and reserve.

6. To cook the saddle: Heat a small amount of olive oil in a large pan over medium-high heat. Add the venison and sage leaves and cook until the meat is browned on both sides but still pink in the middle and the internal temperature registers 145°F, about 4 minutes per side. Reserve the venison and keep warm in the oven until needed.

7. To make the foie gras bread pudding: Heat the butter in a high-sided sauté pan over medium heat, add the shallots, and cook until translucent, about 5 minutes. Add the milk and increase the heat to establish a simmer. Simmer for 2 minutes, then remove from the heat and allow to cool slightly.

8. In a blender, process the warm milk mixture, foie gras, sage, and eggs until smooth. Season with salt and pepper.

Continued

APPLE COMPOTE

1 tbsp unsalted butter

1 cup sliced shallots

1½ lb firm, tart apples, peeled and sliced

1 vanilla bean, split lengthwise

¼ cup sugar

¼ cup red wine

9. Place the cubed bread in a mixing bowl, pour the foie gras mixture on top, and allow it to soak into the bread. Transfer the mixture into the prepared ramekins and smooth out the tops with a rubber spatula. Gently place the ramekins in a high-sided roasting pan and pour in enough water to reach halfway up the sides of the ramekins. Bake the bread puddings until set, about 30 minutes. Set aside to cool.

10. To make the apple compote: Melt the butter in a small pot over medium heat. Add the shallots, apples, and vanilla bean and cook until the shallots and apples are translucent, about 5 minutes. Add the sugar and wine, partially cover the pot, and continue cooking until the liquid has reduced to a syrup, about 20 minutes.

11. To serve, let the venison rest on the cutting board for at least 15 minutes before slicing. Slice in ¼-inch-thick slices and serve about 3 slices per plate. Be sure that the sauce is piping hot before it is drizzled over the venison. Serve the foie gras bread pudding with the apple compote on the side.

Chef's Note *An alternative to baking the foie gras bread pudding in individual ramekins is to bake the mixture in a loaf pan. When the bread pudding is completely cool, the loaf can be removed from the pan and sliced into individual portions (see photo).*

LEG OF LAMB WITH GARLIC AND SAVORY

Don't be intimidated by the idea of preparing a leg of lamb; if you aren't feeding a large crowd, simply ask the butcher for a small top round of lamb and follow the same method. By studding the lamb with garlic slices and roasting it slowly, the garlic virtually melts into the meat and the herbs become incredibly aromatic. The technique is fairly simple, but if you decide that you don't want to take the time to stud the lamb with garlic, just process the garlic with the rest of the flavoring ingredients in a food processor to make a paste and coat the outside of the lamb with the paste. MAKES 6 SERVINGS

1 cup fresh savory, rosemary,
or lavender flowers

Zest of 2 lemons

¼ cup olive oil

¼ cup kosher salt

½ tsp cracked black pepper

1 boneless leg of lamb (about 3 lb)

1 head garlic, cloves peeled and thinly sliced

1. Place the savory, rosemary, or lavender, lemon zest, olive oil, salt, and pepper in a food processor and process to a smooth paste.

2. Using the tip of a small paring knife, pierce a ½-inch slit into the lamb and, while the knife is still in the meat, insert a slice of garlic. Continue inserting slits and garlic every ¼ inch or so all the way around the meat.

3. Rub the lamb with the herb mixture and allow to marinate for at least 1 hour or overnight in the refrigerator.

4. Preheat the oven to 400°F.

5. Remove the lamb from the marinade. Put the lamb in a roasting pan fitted with a rack and roast in the oven until a crust has formed on the outside of the meat, about 15 minutes. Reduce the oven temperature to 325°F and continue to roast until the internal temperature registers 140°F, about 2 hours. Remove the lamb from the oven and allow it to rest for at least 30 minutes before carving.

Chef's Note *This preparation is also very good with pork, although pork is not consumed in many areas of the Mediterranean as a result of religious practices.*

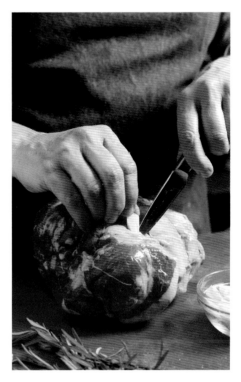

Using the tip of a small paring knife, make 1½-inch slits in the leg of lamb and insert garlic slices into the slits.

RABBIT BRAISED WITH LAVENDER AND HONEY

Although you may not eat rabbit frequently, this dish is sure to make you a convert. The combination of the braised legs with the roasted loin and miniature chops is delicious and allows for total utilization of the rabbit, so there is no waste. If you're not comfortable fabricating the whole rabbit yourself, just ask your butcher to do it for you. The lean meat is complemented by the flavors of the tomato, artichoke, and cipollini onions, making this a light dish that also feels hearty and comforting.

MAKES 4 SERVINGS

1 whole rabbit, legs separated, loin boned, and 1-inch rack from each side

Salt, to taste

Freshly ground black pepper, to taste

1 lavender sprig

¼ cup olive oil

10 cipollini onions, peeled

2 artichokes, leaves removed, choke scooped out, and bottoms sliced ¼ inch thick

1 onion, diced

1 carrot, diced

1 celery stalk, diced

Zest of 1 lemon

2 cups Chicken Broth (page 6), warmed

1 cup dry rosé

3 tbsp honey

8 halves Tomato Confit (page 141)

Savory or other fresh herb, to taste

1. Preheat the oven to 375°F.

2. Season the rabbit pieces with salt and pepper and place in a dish on top of the lavender sprig. Set aside for 20 minutes at room temperature so that the flavor of the lavender permeates the meat.

3. In a large sauté pan, heat the olive oil over medium heat. Place the rabbit loin in the pan and sear until browned on each side, about 4 minutes. Remove the loin from the pan and place it back on top of the lavender in a separate pan.

4. Place the rabbit legs in the hot pan over medium heat and sear until browned on each side, about 4 minutes. Remove the legs from the pan and reserve.

5. Place the cipollini onions in the pan over medium heat and cook until caramelized to a golden brown on each side, about 4 minutes. Remove the cipollini from the pan and reserve.

6. Place the sliced artichokes in the pan over medium heat and cook until caramelized on each side, about 5 minutes. Remove the artichokes from the pan and reserve.

7. Place the diced onion and carrot in the pan and cook until caramelized, about 4 minutes. Add the celery, lemon zest, lavender sprig, and seared rabbit legs and rack chops back to the pan. Add the broth and rosé and increase the heat to establish a simmer. Skim off any scum that rises to the surface. Simmer until the rabbit legs are tender, about 30 minutes. (The meat should easily pull right off the bone.) Transfer the rabbit legs to a separate container and pull the meat off the bones; cover and reserve. Reserve the loin chops separately.

8. Strain the cooking liquid, discard the solids, and return the liquid to the pan. Add the seared cipollini onions back to the strained liquid, bring to a simmer over medium heat, and cook until the liquid has reduced by half. Add the honey and the caramelized artichoke slices. Add the leg meat and rack chops to the pan and continue cooking until the meat is heated through, about 3 minutes.

9. Place the pan with the reserved rabbit loin in the oven and roast for 10 minutes, or until the internal temperature registers 130°F. Remove the loin from the oven and allow to rest for 5 minutes before slicing. Slice the loin on the bias into ¼-inch-thick slices.

10. To serve: Arrange the leg meat in the bottom of a serving platter and place the sliced loin off to one side. Spoon out the artichoke, cipollini, and tomato confit halves and place on the other side of the platter. Top with the little rack chops and sauce the entire platter. Garnish with sprigs of savory. Serve with the rest of the bottle of chilled rosé.

PORCHETTA

Traditional *porchetta* can be made several different ways. I have made it with a small suckling pig with the skin on, but a faster and easier method is to use a pork loin with the belly still attached. This simplified preparation calls for a boneless pork loin cut into quarters, surrounded by Italian sausage with sautéed onions and fennel added, and wrapped in a butterflied pork belly. The whole thing is then tied and slowly roasted. The trick to a moist roast is to be sure to allow it rest for 30 minutes before carving so that the juices have time to redistribute.

MAKES 6 TO 8 SERVINGS

¼ cup olive oil

½ fennel bulb, trimmed and diced, fronds reserved

½ onion, diced

1 lb Italian sausage, casings removed

½ cup chopped fennel fronds

½ cup chopped flat-leaf parsley

Finely grated zest of 2 lemons

½ cup bread crumbs

One 12-inch-square piece pork belly

Salt, to taste

Freshly ground black pepper, to taste

2 lb boneless pork loin, cut in half lengthwise, each half cut into quarters

1. Heat the olive oil in a pan over medium heat, add the fennel and onion, and cook until tender, about 4 minutes. Remove from the heat, transfer to a bowl, and allow to cool. When the fennel and onion are cool, stir in the sausage, fennel fronds, parsley, lemon zest, and bread crumbs and combine well.

2. Season the pork belly liberally with salt and pepper. Place a piece of cheesecloth on a clean work surface and lay the pork belly out flat on top of it. Spoon the sausage mixture on top of the pork belly and spread into a thin, even layer.

3. Arrange the pork loin quarters on top of the sausage layer and, with the help of the cheesecloth, roll the edges of the pork belly up. Continue rolling until the sausage mixture and pork loins are enclosed in the pork belly and the roast is completely wrapped in cheesecloth.

4. Twist the ends of the cheesecloth so that the whole roast is in the shape of a tube, then secure the ends of the cheesecloth with kitchen twine. Tie kitchen twine around the roast every inch or so to help it hold its tubular shape. Place the roast in a roasting pan fitted with a rack and refrigerate overnight.

5. The following day, preheat the oven to 400°F.

6. Place the roasting pan with the porchetta in the oven for 15 minutes to sear the outside. Reduce the oven temperature to 250°F and continue to roast until the internal temperature registers 140°F, about 2 hours. Allow the porchetta to rest for at least 30 minutes before slicing. This resting period will account for any carryover cooking and allow the juices in the meat to evenly distribute.

TOP ROW LEFT TO RIGHT:

Lay the pork belly out on a piece of cheesecloth and spread a generous layer of the ground pork mixture on top. Carefully lay the pork loin quarters on top.

Use the cheesecloth to roll the pork belly around the filling until the pork loin is completely enclosed.

BOTTOM ROW LEFT TO RIGHT:

Wrap the porchetta securely in the cheesecloth and twist the ends to make a tube. Use kitchen twine to tie the cheesecloth in place; this will help keep the porchetta's shape as it cooks.

For the moistest roast, let the porchetta rest for 30 minutes before slicing it in order to allow the natural juices to redistribute.

PORK BRAISED IN MILK

The first time I had this dish, I have to say that I was perplexed. It was the most amazingly tender pork dish that I had ever had. The lactic acid in the milk in combination with the slow-cooking method really makes this melt-in-your-mouth tender. After the pork has cooked, you reduce the milk-broth mixture so that it looks like curds. The result is more like a condiment than a sauce. In Italy you might find a different sauce served with this dish, but the curds taste so good I think it is a shame to waste them. I use a boneless cut of pork for ease of cooking. MAKES 6 SERVINGS

2½ lb boneless pork loin, rolled and tied

Salt, to taste

Freshly ground black pepper, to taste

2 tbsp olive oil

2 tbsp unsalted butter

1 garlic clove, minced

2 shallots, finely chopped

2 rosemary sprigs

3 cups whole milk, warmed

2 cups beef broth, warmed

1 tsp finely grated lemon zest

1. Season the pork loin with salt and pepper.

2. Heat the olive oil and butter in a large, heavy-bottomed pot over medium-high heat, add the pork loin, and cook until browned on all sides, about 2 minutes per side. Reduce the heat to medium. Remove the pork from the pan. Add the garlic, shallots, and rosemary and cook until the shallots are translucent, about 3 minutes. Add the pork back to the pan. Slowly pour the milk and broth over the pork, increase the heat to bring the liquid to a boil, then lower the heat to medium-low. Partially cover the pot with a lid and cook the pork loin until the internal temperature registers 145°F, about 1 hour. Transfer the pork to a platter, cover lightly with aluminum foil, and set aside to rest. Strain the liquid and return it to the pot.

3. Cook the milk-broth mixture over medium-high heat until it begins to reduce. Use a wooden spoon to scrape the bottom of the pan to loosen the milk curds as they form. Continue cooking until the liquid has almost completely reduced and only the milk curds remain; it should look like moist, lumpy curds rather than a smooth sauce. Depending on the amount of fat in the pork loin and the milk, you may need to degrease the surface of the sauce before serving. Stir in the lemon zest.

4. Slice the pork loin into ¼-inch-thick slices. Before plating, spoon the sauce onto the platter and place the pork slices on top of the sauce. The sauce will look curdled and lumpy but it is delicious. Saucing the platter and then placing the pork on top of the curds will prove a bit more user-friendly to your guests because of the appearance.

TOP ROW LEFT TO RIGHT:

Sear the pork in hot oil until it is golden brown on all sides.

Remove the pork from the pan, cook the garlic, shallots, and rosemary, then return the pork to the pan.

BOTTOM ROW LEFT TO RIGHT:

Slowly pour the warm milk and beef broth over the pork.

Slice the pork loin and serve it with the reduced milk sauce. The sauce will look curdled and lumpy.

BISTEEYA

The first time I had this dish was at a Moroccan restaurant in 1979. We were sitting on the floor on pillows and eating with our hands. The restaurant made a version of this classic pie with chicken livers in it as well as the chicken. It was sprinkled with about a quarter inch of confectioners' sugar and a little bit of cinnamon. It was one of the most exotic dishes I had ever eaten. Our recipe does not include the chicken livers but if you would like to try it that way, brown off 1 cup of chicken livers, chop them up, and mix them into the filling. MAKES ONE 8-INCH BISTEEYA (8 TO 10 PORTIONS)

BISTEEYA

¼ cup extra-virgin olive oil, plu more as needed

2 medium onions, diced

1 tsp finely chopped fresh peeled ginger

¼ tsp ground mace

¼ tsp freshly grated nutmeg

⅛ tsp ground cloves

¾ tsp ground cinnamon

1 lb boneless, skinless chicken thighs

Salt, as needed

Freshly ground black pepper, as needed

2¼ cup Chicken Broth (page 6)

2 tbsp unsalted butter

3 tbsp chopped cilantro

3 tbsp chopped flat-leaf parsley

¼ tsp saffron threads, crushed and dissolved in ¼ cup water

2 tbsp light brown sugar

4 large eggs, beaten

½ recipe of rolled Fresh Phyllo Dough (page 212) or 1 package of store-bought phyllo dough

1 cup almonds, toasted and coarsely chopped

GARNISH

2 tbsp confectioners' sugar, plus more as needed

1 tsp ground cinnamon, plus more as needed

1. Preheat the oven to 400°F.

2. Heat the ¼ cup of olive oil in a large pan over medium heat. Add the onions and cook until soft and light golden brown, about 5 minutes. Add the ginger, mace, nutmeg, cloves, and cinnamon and toast until aromatic, about 1 minute. Add the chicken thighs, season with salt and pepper, and continue cooking so that the chicken releases its natural juices. When the juices stop rendering, add the chicken broth and adjust the heat to establish a simmer. Continue simmering until the chicken is tender and cooked through and the broth has concentrated, about 1¼ hours.

3. Remove the chicken thighs from the pan and shred the meat into bite-size pieces. The meat should be tender enough to fall easily off the bone.

4. Add the butter, cilantro, parsley, dissolved saffron, and brown sugar to the pan with the cooking liquid and simmer over medium-high heat until the liquid has reduced by three-quarters, about 30 minutes. Stir in the eggs and cook, stirring constantly to create curds as you would cook scrambled eggs, until the eggs are stiff, about 4 minutes. Remove the egg mixture from the heat. If excess liquid is still present, continue cooking until the liquid has reduced to ¼ cup, then remove from the heat.

5. Place 2 sheets of stretched phyllo dough on a clean work surface with the 2 sheets overlapping by 4 inches. Lightly brush the dough with olive oil. Repeat this step until there are 6 to 8 layers of two overlapping phyllo sheets.

6. Lightly oil an 8-inch-round cake pan. Place the layered phyllo dough into the cake pan and press the dough into the pan until it is fully covered. The dough will overhang the edges of the pan; this excess dough will be used to cover and close the bisteeya.

7. Layer the egg mixture, the shredded chicken, and then the toasted almonds into the phyllo-lined cake pan. Cover the filling by folding the overhanging dough over the top of the bisteeya to seal it. Lightly brush the top with olive oil. Bake the bisteeya in the oven for 15 minutes, reduce the oven temperature to 350°F, and continue baking until the phyllo dough is golden brown and flaky, about 30 minutes. Cool for about 5 minutes before you flip it out onto a serving platter.

8. To serve: Place the serving platter on top of the cake pan and flip the bisteeya over onto the platter. Garnish with a sprinkling of confectioners' sugar and ground cinnamon. If desired, use a lattice or stencil to make a design using the cinnamon.

Chef's Note *If, for aesthetic purposes, you would like to score the phyllo dough into portion sizes before baking, place plastic wrap into the cake pan before layering the dough. Follow the same steps to seal the bisteeya. Chill the bisteeya for 1 to 2 hours before placing it on a sheet pan. Use a serrated knife to cut through the top of the phyllo to portion, then follow the steps for baking. By buttering and chilling, you can pop this out, score the phyllo while it is cold, and then after it has cooked it will be easier to cut and the phyllo will not crumble.*

FLORENTINE-STYLE STEAK

The traditional cut for this steak does not exist in the United States, so I chose to use a T-bone. If you would like to splurge, purchase a nice porterhouse. This is a simple preparation reminiscent of simple Florentine cooking, but it requires a high-quality cut of meat. MAKES 4 SERVINGS

2 T-bone steaks, 1½ inches thick (about 4 lbs)

¼ cup extra-virgin olive oil

¼ cup finely chopped garlic

2 tsp salt

1 tsp freshly ground black pepper

1 tsp finely chopped rosemary leaves

3 tbsp freshly squeezed lemon juice

1. Brush the steaks with 3 tablespoons of the olive oil and season generously with the garlic, salt, pepper, and rosemary.

2. Preheat a grill or grill pan over high heat. Grill the steaks until you can see distinct grill marks, about 2 minutes on each side. Move the steaks to the cooler part of the grill, or reduce the heat under the grill pan, and continue to grill over indirect medium heat until the steaks are medium-rare, another 8 to 9 minutes on each side or 125°F internal temperature.

3. Transfer the meat to a cutting board or a large platter. Drizzle each of the steaks with 1½ teaspoons more of olive oil and finish by sprinkling the steaks with the lemon juice.

4. Let the steaks rest for 10 to 15 minutes before carving into slices. Serve on a heated platter or individual warmed plates.

VEAL CHEEKS OSSO BUCO STYLE

The Italian term *osso buco* can be literally translated to "hole in the bone." Traditional osso buco is made with veal shanks, but in class I actually prefer using veal cheeks so that I don't have to worry about the bone (see Chef's Note). If you do use cheeks, it is not really classical osso buco because of the lack of bone, but the traditional flavors and cooking methods are all there. Osso buco is usually served with a *gremolata*, a condiment made with lemon zest, garlic, and parsley.

MAKES 4 SERVINGS

VEAL

6 tbsp extra-virgin olive oil

1 onion, finely chopped

1 carrot, finely chopped

1½ celery stalks, finely chopped

1 cup chopped plum tomatoes

2 garlic cloves, thinly sliced

8 veal cheeks (or 4 veal shanks)

½ cup white wine

2 cups brown veal stock

1 rosemary sprig

1 thyme sprig

1 bay leaf

Zest of ½ orange

⅛ tsp saffron threads

¾ tsp salt

¼ tsp freshly ground black pepper

GREMOLATA

Finely grated zest of 2 lemons

¼ cup chopped flat-leaf parsley

1 garlic clove, finely chopped

1 anchovy fillet, rinsed, dried, and finely chopped

1. To prepare the veal: In a large, oven-safe, heavy-bottomed pot or enameled casserole, heat 2 tablespoons of the olive oil over medium heat. Add the onion, carrot, celery, tomatoes, and garlic. Cover the pot and cook until the vegetables are tender and have reached a jamlike consistency, about 9 minutes.

2. In a sauté pan over medium-high heat, heat the remaining 4 tablespoons olive oil. Place the veal cheeks in the pan and cook until they are a deep golden brown, about 10 minutes. Work in batches to avoid overcrowding the pan. When the veal cheeks are browned, transfer them to the pot with the vegetables.

3. Pour the white wine into the sauté pan used to cook the cheeks and deglaze it. Cook over medium heat until the wine has reduced by three-quarters, then pour the reduced white wine into the pot.

4. Add the brown veal stock, rosemary, thyme, bay leaf, orange zest, and saffron. Cover the pot and braise the veal cheeks until fork-tender, about 1 hour and 15 minutes. If, at any point, the braising liquid becomes too thick, add some more of the veal stock. If the braising liquid is too runny, remove the lid to allow some of the liquid to evaporate as it braises in the oven. When the veal cheeks are fork-tender, carefully remove them from the pot and reserve them, covered with some of the cooking liquid, until ready to serve.

5. Strain the braising liquid and adjust the seasoning with salt and pepper. Pour it back into the pot and simmer until lightly reduced until you have achieved a light napping consistency *(nappé)*.

6. To make the gremolata: Stir together the lemon zest, parsley, garlic, and anchovy until well combined.

7. Serve the veal cheeks in the strained braising liquid and top with the gremolata.

Chef's Note *Veal cheeks are available online. You might also inquire at your local butcher shop as they may be able to order them for you.*

FISH AND SHELLFISH

Mediterranean countries have always been dependent on the sea, particularly in coastal areas. During the Age of Discovery, every culture seemed to have a dish that involved salt cod, for example. The indigenous species in the Mediterranean and its surrounding sister seas were, no doubt, different than those we are used to eating. When writing this chapter, I tried to create a feeling of Mediterranean dishes using fish we might find more familiar and available here in the United States.

I have also included a few items to inspire you to explore some new possibilities. Be sure to find a reputable seafood market in your area and try to buy fresh whenever possible. When fish has been frozen, it loses a lot of moisture after it defrosts, leaving it dry and less flavorful. On the shores of the Mediterranean Sea, locals have the luxury of fresh fish daily. Whether you live by the sea or not, find the best source possible for the best result.

These days, there are some very reputable fish farms that are producing sustainable seafood. You might inquire at your fishmonger about sustainably farmed species or check out Web sites like the Monterey Bay Aquarium Seafood Watch to get updates on which fish species are the most sustainable. Talk to your local fishmonger about sustainable substitutions that they have in stock that can be used in the recipes in this chapter.

There are several important things to remember when selecting fish. If the fish is whole, look at the eyes; they should be clear and bright. The next thing is the gills; they should be a vivid reddish color, not brown or oxidized. These two indicators can be seen even if you can't touch the fish. For the next two indicators you will have to get pretty close up and personal with the fish. Here is a little secret you should know: Fish should not smell fishy! If it smells like anything, that should be the ocean and nothing else. If it smells, don't buy it. And finally, if you are lucky enough to be able to touch the fish, it should be somewhat firm. If your finger leaves an indent in the flesh, that is an indication that it is not so fresh. When preparing any of these dishes, freshness is really important and can make or break the dish. Don't compromise.

When purchasing fish from your local fish counter, it is helpful to know some terms that describe how the fish is sold. Whole fish is just that, the fish as it was caught, completely intact. Drawn fish have had the guts removed, but the head, fins, and scales are still intact. Dressed fish have the guts, gills, scales, and fins removed; the head may or may not be removed. Portion cuts from the fillets of large fish, such as tuna and swordfish, are also commonly called steaks. A fillet is a boneless piece of fish, removed from either side of the backbone, and is one of the most common ways to purchase fish. The skin may or may not be removed before cooking.

SEA SCALLOPS SEARED WITH TURNIPS AND PISTACHIOS

Be sure to use sea scallops and not bay scallops for this recipe; bay scallops are too small. The sweetness of the scallop pairs really well with the sweetness of the turnips and shallots that is brought out by the roasting. Enjoy this dish with a glass of Crémant d'Alsace. MAKES 4 SERVINGS

TURNIP AND SHALLOTS

12 baby turnips

4 shallots

1 leek, washed and cut into 1-inch sections

Olive oil, as needed

Salt, as needed

Freshly ground black pepper, as needed

1 cup Vegetable Broth (page 4)

1 tsp finely chopped thyme

2 tbsp crème fraîche

4 oz pistachio nuts

SCALLOPS

1 lb sea scallops, muscle tabs removed

Salt, as needed

Freshly ground black pepper, as needed

2 tbsp plus 1 tsp olive oil, plus more as needed

1 thyme sprig

1 cup panko bread crumbs

1. To prepare the turnips and shallots: Preheat the oven to 350°F.

2. Peel the turnips and shallots. Toss the turnips, shallots, and leek with olive oil and place in a roasting pan or on a sheet pan. Season with salt and pepper and roast in the oven until tender and caramelized. Add the vegetable broth to the roasting vegetables, as needed, to keep them from drying out or burning. When the turnips are tender, season with half of the thyme and reserve.

3. Toast the nuts for 5 minutes in the oven, cool, then chop them in a food processor.

4. To prepare the scallops: Using paper towels, dry off the scallops and season both sides with salt and pepper.

5. Heat 2 tablespoons of the olive oil in a sauté pan. Add the scallops to the pan, being careful not to overcrowd them. Cook the scallops on one side until golden brown, about 4 minutes, and then turn them over. Add the thyme sprig to the pan and finish the cooking in the oven for an additional 4 minutes.

6. Finish the vegetables by mixing them with crème fraîche, half of the toasted pistachios, and the remaining thyme.

7. To serve: Spoon the turnips and vegetables onto a platter and arrange the scallops around the turnips.

8. Toss the panko bread crumbs with the remaining toasted pistachios and the 1 teaspoon olive oil and season with salt and pepper. Toast in a 300°F oven for 3 minutes and then sprinkle the panko mixture on top of the turnips and scallops just before serving.

SKATE WINGS WITH BRUSSELS SPROUTS AND VERJUS

Skate is an unusual fish that is worth seeking out. It has two wings that look similar to that of a stingray. These wings are the edible part of the fish that are slightly meaty in texture because they are well exercised. Try to find skate wings that have already been cleaned with their skin removed or have the fishmonger clean them for you. MAKES 6 SERVINGS

1 pint Brussels sprouts

4 skate wings, skinned

Salt, to taste

Freshly ground black pepper, to taste

1 cup all-purpose flour

½ cup olive oil

2 shallots, sliced

2 cups seedless red grapes, halved

1 cup verjus (see page 50)

3 tbsp unsalted butter

1 tbsp finely chopped chives, plus more to taste

1. Preheat the oven to 200°F.

2. Pull off the tough outer leaves from the Brussels sprouts, cut them in half and remove the core, and thinly slice the sprouts.

3. Prepare an ice bath. Bring a medium pot of salted water to a boil over high heat. Add the Brussels sprouts and allow the water to return to a boil. Once the Brussels sprouts are tender, about 4 minutes, remove from the boiling water and plunge them into the ice bath to stop the cooking process. Drain and reserve.

4. Prepare the fish by seasoning both sides of each skate wing with salt and pepper. Lightly coat each wing in flour and shake off the excess flour as needed.

5. Preheat a large sauté pan or skillet over medium-high heat. Add 2 tablespoons of the olive oil to the pan and allow the oil to come up to the temperature of the pan. Once slight ripples appear in the oil, place the skate in the pan and sauté on the presentation side first for about 4 minutes; the fish should be golden brown and slightly crisp. Turn and sauté on the opposite side for 4 minutes more. Repeat step 5 as needed to cook all skate wings.

6. Transfer each skate wing, as it is cooked, to a warm platter and reserve in the oven until ready to serve.

7. Add the shallots to the same pan that the fish was cooked in and sauté over medium heat. Once the shallots begin to caramelize, add the blanched Brussels sprouts and increase the heat. Cook the Brussels sprouts until they are lightly caramelized. Season the shallots and Brussels sprouts with salt and pepper and add the grapes. As soon as the grapes are hot, spoon the vegetable-fruit mixture onto a plate and keep warm in the oven.

8. Increase the heat below the pan, add the verjus, bring to a boil, and deglaze the pan, scraping the bottom of the pan with a wooden spoon to gather all the caramelized bits; the pan must be hot in order to deglaze appropriately. Once the liquid has been added, reduce it to ⅓ cup. Once reduced, whisk in the butter and finish the sauce with the chives.

9. Arrange the vegetables and skate wings on a serving platter and finish with the pan sauce. Garnish the dish with more chives, if desired.

PAN-ROASTED HALIBUT WITH CORN AND FAVA BEANS

Halibut is one of my favorite fishes. It is meaty yet mild and usually readily available. It is quite versatile and can be sautéed or roasted. This simple recipe highlights the flavor and freshness of the fish as well as its accompaniments. MAKES 4 SERVINGS

HALIBUT

4 halibut fillets (about 6 oz each)

Salt, as needed

Freshly ground black pepper, as needed

¼ cup olive oil

1 tarragon sprig

Zest and juice of 1 lemon

CORN AND FAVA BEANS

3 tbsp olive oil

3 shallots, finely chopped

2 tbsp finely chopped pancetta

3 ears corn, kernels cut off the cob

1 lb fava beans, shelled, blanched, and peeled (see page 35)

Salt, to taste

Freshly ground black pepper, to taste

1 cup Vegetable Broth (page 4)

1 tbsp finely chopped chives

1. Preheat the oven to 350°F.

2. To prepare the fish: Rinse the halibut fillets under cold running water and pat them dry with paper towels. Season both sides of each fillet with salt and pepper.

3. Preheat a large, oven-safe sauté pan over high heat. Add the olive oil and heat until it ripples slightly. Add the fish fillets to the pan, cut side down, and sauté until lightly browned, about 5 minutes.

4. Turn each fillet over and add the tarragon, lemon zest, and lemon juice to the pan. Transfer the pan to the oven and cook until the fish flakes when prodded with a fork, about 5 minutes.

5. Transfer the fish from the sauté pan to a serving platter and place in a 200°F oven.

6. To prepare the corn and fava beans: Return the pan to the stovetop over medium-high heat and add the olive oil. Add the shallots and pancetta and sauté until the shallots are aromatic and the pancetta and shallots are slightly golden, about 3 minutes.

7. Add the corn and sauté for about 3 minutes until warmed through. Add the fava beans and season with salt and pepper. Arrange the corn and fava bean mixture on the platter with the fish.

8. Over medium-high heat, add the broth and to the pan and deglaze, using a wooden spoon to scrape the caramelized bits off the bottom of the pan. Allow the broth to simmer until reduced by half. Pour the sauce over the fish and vegetables and serve. Garnish with the chives.

SOFT-SHELL CRABS WITH GRILLED SCALLIONS AND LEMON POLENTA

Soft-shell crabs are in season in the spring, so keep your eye out because the soft-shell season doesn't last that long. Be sure to have the apron, lungs, and eyes removed by your fishmonger and use the crabs as soon as possible. MAKES 6 SERVINGS

PRESERVED LEMON ZEST
3 Meyer lemons
2 tbsp salt

SCALLIONS
2 bunches scallions
¼ cup olive oil
1 tsp salt
Freshly ground black pepper, to taste

POLENTA
4½ cups water
2 tbsp salt
2 shallots, finely chopped
2 cups polenta
Zest of 1 Meyer lemon
2 tbsp unsalted butter
2 tbsp finely chopped chives

CRABS
2 tbsp olive oil
6 soft-shell crabs, cleaned
Salt, to taste
Freshly ground black pepper, to taste

GARNISH
1 Meyer lemon, sectioned and seeded
Olive oil, as needed

1. To prepare the lemons: Peel the zest from the lemons, leaving the white pith behind, and cut into thin strips. Squeeze the juice from the lemon over the strips of zest and combine with the salt. Allow the mixture to sit for at least 1 hour. Rinse the lemon zest before using.

2. To prepare the scallions: Remove the dried outer layers and roots and wash the scallions. In a baking dish, toss the scallions in the olive oil and season with the salt and pepper. Cover with plastic wrap and let the scallions sit at room temperature for 30 minutes; the scallions will start to sweat.

3. To make the polenta: Preheat the oven to 325°F.

4. In a large, oven-safe pot, bring the water to a boil with the salt and shallots. Slowly stream the polenta into the boiling water while whisking constantly to incorporate and prevent lumps from forming. Bring the polenta back to a simmer and cover the pot. Place the covered pot in the oven for about 30 minutes. While the polenta cooks, continue to prepare the crabs and scallions.

5. Finish the scallions: Preheat a grill pan and slowly grill the scallions until they are soft; they should have nice grill marks for presentation.

6. To prepare the soft-shell crabs: Preheat a large sauté pan over medium-high heat. Add the olive oil and allow to heat. Season the crabs on both sides with salt and pepper. Once the oil begins to ripple, add the crabs, shell side down, and sauté for about 4 minutes.

7. Remove the polenta from the oven and whisk in the lemon zest, butter, and chives.

8. Mound the polenta on a serving platter and arrange the grilled scallions on top of the polenta. Once the crabs are cooked, place them on top of the scallions. Finish the plate with the rinsed preserved lemon zest and the lemon sections. Drizzle with olive oil, as needed, just before serving.

OLIVE OIL–POACHED TUNA PROVENÇAL

This is one of my favorite ways to prepare tuna for a Salade Niçoise (page 130) but you can also pair it with other accompaniments for a really nice meal. I suggest serving the tuna confit along with some haricots verts in garlic on crispy polenta. This olive-oil poach works best with denser, high-activity fish, such as swordfish or other deep-water fish. It really infuses a lot of flavor into the fish while gently cooking it. For the best tuna salad you have ever had, poach fresh tuna and use it instead of canned. MAKES 4 TO 6 SERVINGS

1 qt olive oil
2 thyme sprigs
2 rosemary sprigs
4 bay leaves, preferably fresh
1 head garlic, peeled
1½ lb tuna fillet

1. In a small saucepan, combine the olive oil with the thyme, rosemary, bay leaves, and garlic and heat to 200°F for 10 minutes. Cool the oil mixture and refrigerate overnight.

2. The following day, remove and discard the thyme, rosemary, and bay leaves and pour the olive oil into a heavy-bottomed pot. Place the tuna in the oil so that it is totally submerged. Heat the oil to 160°F and hold the temperature between 160°F and 180°F for 5 minutes. The tuna is now ready to serve and should still be pink inside. Serve the tuna warm or cold.

Chef's Note *If you want to reuse the oil, bring it to a simmer then cool and refrigerate it. It can be used again for poaching, or even in a vinaigrette for a Niçoise salad.*

BOUILLABAISSE

Bouillabaisse is a classic French fish stew that's found in different forms and with different names along the Mediterranean coast. It truly showcases the bounty of the sea. Feel free to use whatever fish is the freshest at the market that day. Almost any type will work well with the flavor profile of this dish. MAKES 4 SERVINGS

ROUILLE

3 garlic cloves, peeled

¼ tsp kosher salt

¼ tsp cayenne

½ tsp powdered saffron, dissolved in 1 tbsp boiling water

¼ tsp fresh bread crumbs

1 large egg yolk, at room temperature

1 tsp freshly squeezed lemon juice

1 cup olive oil

FISH STEW

2 tbsp olive oil

½ cup sliced onions

½ cup sliced well-washed leeks

¼ cup sliced, trimmed fennel bulb

1 garlic clove, chopped

1 cup plum tomatoes, peeled and seeded, or 8 oz whole canned plum tomatoes, chopped

1½ tsp tomato paste

½ tsp crumbled saffron threads

½ cup potatoes, peeled and cut into ½-inch dico

3 cups fish stock

Kosher salt, as needed

Freshly ground black pepper, as needed

Cayenne, as needed

12 oz assorted seafood (John Dory, red mullet, red snapper, porgy, monkfish, lobster), cut into 3-inch chunks

2 tbsp chopped flat-leaf parsley

2 tbsp chopped chervil

1 baguette, thinly sliced and toasted

Rouille, as needed (see above)

1. To make the rouille: Using a food processor or a mortar and pestle, process (or pound) the garlic, salt, and cayenne to make a paste. Mix in the dissolved saffron and bread crumbs.

2. Add the egg yolk and lemon juice and combine thoroughly.

3. Add the olive oil in a slow steady stream and process (or whisk) until the sauce emulsifies and thickens. Reserve in the refrigerator until needed.

4. To make the fish stew: In a large, heavy-bottomed stockpot, heat the olive oil over medium-high heat, add the onions, leeks, fennel, and garlic and sweat until translucent, about 5 minutes.

5. Add the tomatoes, tomato paste, saffron, potatoes, and fish stock and simmer until the potatoes are cooked, 10 to 15 minutes. Season with salt, pepper, and cayenne.

6. Add the seafood in order of firmness and cooking time, with the denser, longer-cooking items placed on the bottom and the delicate fillets on top. Cook until the seafood is done. Once the seafood is cooked, add the parsley and chervil.

7. To serve, carefully remove the fish and shellfish and arrange it on a large serving platter or in a warm bowl. Ladle the broth and potatoes over the fish and serve with the bread and rouille.

Chef's Note *Rouille is a garlic and saffron mayonnaise that is traditionally served with bouillabaisse. The difference in flavor when you make your own mayonnaise will surprise you. It is completely different from what you buy at the store because the flavors of the ingredients in the emulsion really shine, especially the eggs. If you don't have time to make the rouille, simply finely chop the garlic cloves, dissolve the saffron, and stir it into 1 cup of store-bought mayonnaise.*

GALICIAN OCTOPUS FAIR-STYLE

Pulpo á feira is a Spanish dish that was originally served at traditional rural fairs. Although it is Spanish, every time I make this dish I remember my first trip to Greece. There always seemed to be a shift of older women down by the seaside beating larger octopuses on a stone wall to tenderize them. I recommend that you find some smaller octopuses for this dish, but large will work as well. Just simmer slowly until tender, unless of course you are feeling aggressive! After you cook the octopus, peel it before you cut it. Just take a kitchen towel and rub off the dark outer skin. This step is not absolutely necessary, but it will make the texture more palatable. MAKES 5 SERVINGS

OCTOPUS

2 qt water

3 tbsp salt

3 bay leaves

1½ tsp black peppercorns

3 garlic cloves, crushed

1 lb octopus, cleaned

ESCABECHE MARINADE

1 cup white wine vinegar

1 medium Spanish onion, sliced

½ red bell pepper, seeded and cut into 2-inch strips

4 garlic cloves, very thinly sliced

¾ tsp black peppercorns

3 bay leaves

1 cup extra-virgin olive oil

1. To prepare the octopus: Bring the water and salt to a boil and add the bay leaves, peppercorns, and garlic. Dip the octopus into the boiling water 3 times until the tentacles fully curl. Once the tentacles have curled, drop the octopus into the boiling aromatic liquid and reduce the heat.

2. Allow the octopus to simmer until tender, about 1 hour. Remove the octopus from the water and cut it into 1-inch pieces.

3. To prepare the marinade: Bring the vinegar to a boil and add the onion, bell pepper, garlic, peppercorns, and bay leaves. Simmer the mixture for 2 minutes. Add the olive oil and simmer until the onion is translucent, about 5 to 7 minutes.

4. Remove the marinade from heat and allow it to cool slightly. Add the octopus to the marinade and continue to cool together. It is best to marinate the octopus overnight, but in a pinch, 2 hours will do.

5. Serve the octopus chilled or at room temperature.

SQUID WITH CARAMELIZED ONIONS

This recipe for *calamares encebollados* comes from the memory of José Andrés, who worked as a young chef on the Spanish coast. During the summers, one of his favorite meals was this beachside griddled squid dish that was prepared after a long night of revelry. The old fishermen used a classic technique that allowed the squid to be trapped without releasing their ink. The young chefs would then light up the *plancha,* or griddle, and sear the squid while they were still alive without cleaning them. Today this is still one of Chef Andrés's all-time favorite breakfasts. Squid that are really fresh will have a nice brilliant finish and a slightly gray color and, if so, they don't necessarily need to be cleaned. The outer skin turns pink when the squid is no longer fresh. MAKES 6 SERVINGS

1 cup Spanish extra-virgin olive oil

4 garlic cloves, unpeeled

4 Vidalia or Spanish onions, thinly sliced

4 bay leaves, preferably fresh

2½ lb squid, cleaned and cut into triangles

Salt, to taste

¼ cup dry white wine

1 bunch flat-leaf parsley, chopped

1. Heat the olive oil in a large sauté pan over medium heat.

2. Split open the garlic cloves and add to the pan.

3. Add the onions and bay leaves and cook slowly until the onions are golden brown, about 35 to 40 minutes.

4. Using a slotted spoon, transfer the onions to a plate, leaving the oil in the pan. Set the onions aside. Increase the heat to high under the pan.

5. Dry the squid and season with salt. Add to the hot pan and sauté in small batches for 20 to 30 seconds. Once all the squid has been cooked, return all the squid to the pan, add the caramelized onions, and stir to combine.

6. Pour the wine over the squid and cook for about 20 seconds. Remove and discard the bay leaves.

7. Sprinkle with the parsley and serve immediately.

SALT-CRUSTED SEA BASS

This is one of the most aromatic ways to cook sea bass. The crust forms a nice cooking vessel for the fish and citrus, and when you crack the crust the smell is incredible. Bring the fish to the table in the crust and then crack it open in front of your guests so that they can savor the aroma—but make sure to let them know that the crust is not edible! MAKES 4 SERVINGS

SALT CRUST
4 large egg whites

3 cups salt

2 cups all-purpose flour

2 tbsp chopped thyme

SEA BASS
1 orange, thinly sliced

1 lemon, thinly sliced and seeded

1 lime, thinly sliced and seeded

1 fennel bulb, trimmed and thinly sliced

1 red onion, thinly sliced

¼ cup olive oil

Salt, as needed

Freshly ground black pepper, as needed

4 sea bass fillets (about 6 oz each)

4 thyme sprigs

1. To prepare the salt crust: Mix together the egg whites, salt, flour, and thyme in an electric mixer fitted with the paddle attachment until a dough forms.

2. Roll out the dough into approximately 4- to 6-inch circles or into 2 large ovals.

3. To prepare the sea bass: Preheat the oven to 350°F.

4. Layer the citrus slices on the bottom of the dough.

5. In a bowl, toss the fennel and onion with the olive oil and season with salt and pepper.

6. Lay the fish fillets, skin side out, on top of the citrus slices and then the fennel and onion mixture on top of the fish. Scatter the thyme sprigs on top. Season with salt and pepper.

7. Place the top piece of dough over the fish. Crimp the top piece of dough together with the bottom piece to seal so that all the steam and juices are contained while baking.

8. Place the salt-crusted fish on a sheet pan and bake in the oven for about 30 minutes.

9. Transfer the baked salt crust sea bass to a serving platter and serve immediately. Crack open the crust while still hot.

TOP ROW LEFT TO RIGHT:

On a floured work surface, roll the dough out so that there is a 2-inch border on all sides when the fish is placed on top.

After layering the fish with the fennel and citrus fruit, place a second piece of rolled dough on top of the fish and the flavoring ingredients.

BOTTOM ROW LEFT TO RIGHT:

Seal the edges of the dough by crimping it with your fingers as you would a piecrust.

Crack the crust open at the table and remove the fish before serving. Remember that although the crust is beautiful, it is not edible.

COUSCOUS-CRUSTED SALMON WITH FREGOLA, ZUCCHINI, AND PINE NUTS

Fregola is a toasted pasta similar to couscous that hails from Sardinia. The crunch of the couscous combined with the buttery texture of the salmon gives this dish a really nice contrast, and serving the salmon with fregola is a fun way to go. Slathering the salmon fillet with pesto allows the pasta to stick to the salmon when it is dredged in the couscous. The salmon will then develop a nice crust when it is sautéed in olive oil. If you have leftovers, turn them into a salad by flaking the salmon into the fregola and adding lemon juice and olive oil. It makes a great lunch. MAKES 4 SERVINGS

SALMON

4 salmon fillets (about 6 oz each)

½ cup Pesto Genovese (page 245)

Salt, to taste

Freshly ground black pepper, to taste

1 cup couscous

¼ cup olive oil

FREGOLA

1 qt water

1 tbsp salt

1½ cups fregola

2 tbsp olive oil

1 garlic clove, finely chopped

2 zucchini, diced

½ cup Chicken Broth (page 6)

2 tbsp chopped flat-leaf parsley

1. To prepare the salmon: Brush each salmon fillet with the pesto until fully coated on the top and bottom. Season with salt and pepper.

2. Place each piece of salmon on top of the couscous and press it into the salmon as though you were breading the fish.

3. Heat the olive oil in an oven-safe sauté pan over medium heat until fairly hot and sauté the salmon, cut side down first, for 4 to 5 minutes. Turn the salmon over and finish on the stovetop or in a 350°F oven, about 5 minutes. Keep warm until ready to serve.

4. To prepare the fregola: Bring the water and salt to a boil. Pour the fregola into the water as though you were cooking pasta. Check for doneness after 3 to 4 minutes; it should be tender. Drain and reserve.

5. In a sauté pan, heat the olive oil and add the garlic. Sauté the garlic until aromatic. Add the zucchini and sauté until golden, about 2 minutes more.

6. Add the chicken broth to the zucchini and reduce by half. Once the broth has reduced, add the cooked fregola to the sauté pan and mix well. Add the chopped parsley.

7. To serve: Arrange the zucchini and fregola mixture on a serving platter. Remove the salmon from the warm oven and arrange on top of the fregola.

FLOUNDER WITH SALSA VERDE

Growing up, my father, Anthony, was an avid fisherman. Dad taught me how to fish at a very early age. We used to go off shore in New Jersey and sometimes to the back bays. I still remember catching my first seven-pound flounder at the age of six. It was quite a feat, and neither my father nor my grandfather could believe his eyes. That fish fed the entire family that night, and there is nothing like the flavor of fresh flounder. If you can't catch your own, be sure to go to a reputable fishmonger. Any kind of sole or flounder will do for this recipe. The salsa verde is easy; just whip it up in your food processor. Serve the fish on a bed of salad greens and croutons as a light meal. MAKES 4 SERVINGS

FLOUNDER

1½ lb skinless flounder fillets

Salt, to taste

Freshly ground black pepper, to taste

1 cup all-purpose flour

¼ cup olive oil

SALSA VERDE

4 tomatillos, stemmed and cut into large dice

1 bunch flat-leaf parsley, roughly chopped

½ cup capers

4 cornichons

2 tbsp finely chopped chives

2 shallots, finely chopped

¼ cup olive oil

4 cups salad greens

Juice of 1 lemon

2 tbsp olive oil

Salt, to taste

Freshly ground black pepper, to taste

2 cups croutons *or* toasted baguette slices

1. To prepare the fish: Season the flounder fillets with salt and pepper. Fold them in half with what was the skin side in. This will make them easier to handle. Dust the fillets with flour and unfold them.

2. Heat the olive oil in a sauté pan over medium heat until fairly hot but not smoking. When the oil begins to ripple, place the flounder fillets in the pan, presentation (skin) side down, being careful not to overcrowd the pan. Sauté each fillet on the first side until golden brown, about 4 minutes. Turn them over and cook until golden brown on the opposite side.

3. To make the salsa verde: Place the tomatillos, parsley, capers, cornichons, chives, shallots, and olive oil in the bowl of a food processor fitted with the metal blade and pulse until evenly chopped.

4. To serve: Toss the salad greens with the lemon juice, olive oil, salt, pepper, and croutons or baguette slices. Place the greens on a plate and top with the warm flounder. Pour any remaining juices from the sauté pan onto the fish just before serving. Top the fish with the salsa verde.

CLAMS WITH FRESH FAVA BEANS

This is one of the most delicious and easy summer dishes I can remember ever making. Use the freshest clams possible, and fresh favas in season. If you can't get fresh favas, use frozen peas; the dish will still be delicious. Serve this with some fresh pasta, or alone in a bowl along with some crusty bread. MAKES 4 SERVINGS

1 lb fresh fava beans

2 tbsp olive oil, plus as needed

2 shallots, thinly sliced

1 garlic clove, finely chopped

4 oz finely chopped pancetta *or* prosciutto

1 cup white wine

1 lemon, juiced

1 lb clams (Manila or another small variety), carefully washed

2 cups clam juice

½ cup chopped flat-leaf parsley

½ cup panko bread crumbs

Finely grated zest of 1 lemon

1. Prepare the fava beans as instructed on page 35.

2. Heat 2 tablespoons of the olive oil in a pot over medium heat. Add the shallots and garlic and sauté until tender, about 5 minutes. Add the pancetta and sauté until almost crispy, about 5 minutes. Add the white wine and lemon juice and reduce by three-quarters, about 5 minutes.

3. Add the clams and clam juice, cover the pot, and steam the clams until they open, 5 to 8 minutes. Discard any clams that do not open.

4. Remove the lid from the pot and, while the liquid is simmering, add the reserved fava beans. Transfer the clams to a serving bowl.

5. Reduce the liquid in the pot by half and add half of the parsley to the broth.

6. Mix the remaining half of the parsley with the panko bread crumbs and lemon zest. Moisten the mixture with a little olive oil.

7. Pour the fava beans and broth over the clams and then sprinkle with the panko-parsley mixture.

BREADS, PIES
AND TARTS

Many cuisines have what we refer to as a "trinity." In Cajun cuisine the trinity is onions, celery, and green peppers; Asian cuisine has ginger, garlic, and scallions. In the Mediterranean, the trinity is wheat, wine, and olives. Wheat has been one of the most important grains in the Mediterranean basin dating back to the time of the ancient Egyptians.

As we mentioned in chapter 4, the grain Kamut has been found in Egyptian tombs, and farro has been called the grain of the Roman soldiers. Beyond simply eating these grains in their natural form, the Egyptians ground them and made them into pastas, porridges, and bread. There are certain cultures that actually use bread to pick up their food rather than utensils. If you go to Morocco, you will find yourself eating with your hands and using bread as the vehicle to lift the food to your mouth. This chapter features flatbreads as well as yeast-raised breads.

And though we have been bombarded with low-carbohydrate diets in the past ten to twenty years, I still maintain that everything is good in moderation. There is nothing better than a loaf of crusty bread. Although I couldn't possibly include all of the breads I would like to in this chapter, I have provided a sampling of some of my favorites.

PISSALADIÈRE

Pissaladière is simply a French version of pizza, traditionally topped with onions that have been melted down in olive oil, and with anchovies and Niçoise olives. It is best made with sweet onions, and a good-quality olive oil is a must. If possible, use an oil with more floral notes than the grassy-flavored kind you often find in grocery stores. It will make a big difference. To make pitting the olives easier, smash them with the side of your chef's knife and the pits will pull right out; no need to buy a fancy olive pitter. I also recommend using white anchovies because they are a bit milder. If they are unavailable, use canned anchovies or just smear the pissaladière crust with a little anchovy paste. MAKES 1 PISSALADIÈRE

DOUGH

¾ tsp instant dry yeast

2 cups (9½ oz) bread flour

1 tbsp sugar

1 tsp salt

¾ cup plus 2 tbsp (7 oz) water, warmed to about 105°F

BOUQUET GARNI

1 thyme sprig

3 parsley stems

1 bay leaf

2 leek leaves, cut into 3-inch pieces

TOPPING

1 tbsp olive oil

1 lb onions, thinly sliced

2 garlic cloves, crushed

20 anchovy fillets, packed in oil, preferably white

20 black or Niçoise olives, pitted

1. To make the dough: Combine the yeast, flour, sugar, and salt in the bowl of an electric mixer fitted with either the dough hook or the paddle attachment. Add the water and mix on medium speed until the mixture forms a smooth dough, about 10 minutes. Cover the bowl with a damp cloth and put it in a warm place for 1 to 1½ hours until the dough has doubled in size.

2. To make the bouquet garni: Gather the thyme, parsley, and bay leaf together and wrap in the leek leaves. Tie securely together with a piece of kitchen twine.

3. Preheat the oven to 450°F. Lightly oil a half sheet pan or rimmed cookie sheet.

4. To make the topping: Heat the olive oil in a large saucepan over low heat. Add the onions, garlic, and bouquet garni and cook until the onions are very soft but not colored, about 10 minutes, stirring frequently so that the onions and garlic do not burn. Remove from the heat and reserve.

5. Once the dough has risen, using a rolling pin, roll it into a rectangle the size of the sheet pan, allowing for a ½-inch overhang around the edges of the pan. Carefully place the rolled dough onto the prepared pan and turn up the overhang to make an even edge all the way around. Set the dough aside to rest for 15 minutes and to allow it to finish rising. Bake the crust for 10 minutes.

6. Remove the bouquet garni from the onions and spread the onions out in a thick layer over the dough. Arrange the anchovy fillets in an X, or crosshatch, patterns on top of the onions, leaving ½ inch of space in the center of each X. Place an olive upright in the center of each anchovy X. Serve immediately.

WHOLE WHEAT PITA

Pita is a leavened flat bread that puffs up during the baking process like a balloon. I love watching it puff in the oven and as soon as it's done, I grab it out, dip it in some olive oil, and have at it. You can also make large batches of pita and freeze them after they have been baked. MAKES 15 PITAS

1 packet active dry yeast

½ tbsp sugar

1¼ cups (10 oz) water, warmed to about 100°F

1½ tsp sugar

1⅔ cups (8 oz) bread flour, plus more for dusting

1¾ cups (8 oz) whole wheat flour

1 tbsp salt

¼ cup olive oil, plus more as needed

1. In a large measuring cup or a small bowl, combine the yeast, sugar, and warm water and mix well.

2. In the bowl of an electric mixer fitted with the dough hook, blend all the ingredients and mix until an elastic dough forms, about 3 minutes.

3. Place the dough into a large oiled bowl or an oiled storage container and mist the dough with additional oil. This adds flavor and will facilitate removing the dough from the bowl or container. Cover the bowl with plastic wrap and place in a warm area. Allow the dough to bulk ferment until it doubles in size, about 2 hours.

4. Line a sheet pan with parchment paper and lightly oil it. Punch down the dough and remove it from the bowl or container. Cut the dough into 3-ounce balls and place them on the prepared sheet pan. Dust the dough balls with flour and wrap the sheet pan with plastic wrap. Allow the dough to proof in a warm area until the balls have doubled in size.

5. On a floured work surface, roll out each ball of dough into a round 7 inches in diameter. Dust each round heavily with flour and store between sheets of parchment paper.

6. Preheat the oven to 450°F. If you have a pizza stone, preheat the oven with the stone in it. If you don't have a stone, place a plain sheet pan or cookie sheet in the oven while it is preheating.

7. When the oven is fully preheated, place a round of dough onto the stone or sheet pan and shut the oven door. As you look through the oven door, you will see bubbles start to pop up on the surface of the dough; this is steam building up in the dough. Eventually the dough will puff up into a pillow. After it is fully inflated, bake for 1 minute more, then remove from the oven. Be careful as the steam will be very hot. The steam inside the bread will finish cooking it. Bake the pita, one or two at a time, until they are all baked. Cool slightly and eat right away, refrigerate, or freeze in plastic zipper-lock bags.

SARDINIAN SHEET MUSIC

This flat bread, called *carta da musica,* from Sardinia is an unleavened flat bread that is so thin you can see through it. Hence its name, because it resembled the parchment that music was once written on. Be sure to bake these one at a time, as they are so thin, they may go up in smoke before you know it. MAKES 20 THIN BREAD SHEETS

¾ cup (4 oz) bread flour *or* all-purpose flour

¾ cup (6 oz) water

2 tbsp extra-virgin olive oil

1½ tsp salt

FINISHING

½ cup olive oil

2 tbsp coarse salt

1. Preheat the oven to 450°F.

2. Combine the flour, water, extra-virgin olive oil, and salt in the bowl of an electric mixer fitted with the dough hook. Mix for about 5 minutes to develop the gluten and tighten the dough; the dough should be firm to the touch and smooth. The water needed may vary depending on the flour. Adjust the dough with additional flour or water, as needed, to achieve the desired consistency. The dough should look like a very soft pasta dough but it should not be sticky, and should be firm but soft.

3. Form the dough into a ball and wrap it in plastic wrap. Allow the dough to rest, about 30 minutes.

4. Divide the dough into 3-ounce pieces. Flour each piece well and then run it through a pasta machine. Using the tines of a fork, prick the entire surface of the flat bread; this will allow steam to escape.

5. Bake the bread on a sheet pan until golden brown, 3 to 4 minutes.

6. As soon as the bread is removed from the oven, brush it with the olive oil and sprinkle it with the coarse salt. The olive oil can be infused with garlic, rosemary, and thyme or other aromatics, if desired.

PIZZA MARGHERITA

It is by no coincidence that *pizza margherita* is reminiscent of the Italian flag; it was created for Queen Margherita and the ingredients represent the colors of the Italian flag: The red is the tomato sauce and sliced tomatoes, the green is the fresh basil leaves, and the white is the fresh mozzarella. It is a simple preparation that should not be overloaded; the tomato sauce should be applied in a nice thin layer, not poured on as we have a tendency to do in the United States.

You might consider making multiple batches of pizza dough at one time and freezing them. Then you can thaw them, as needed, and they are ready to roll and bake. If you are going to make pizza, it also may be worthwhile to purchase a pizza stone, since standard ovens don't get as hot as pizza ovens; a wood-burning pizza oven can reach upwards of 800°F. Since you probably don't have one of those, nor do you want to burn your house down, a preheated 500°F oven with a pizza stone will do nicely. MAKES THREE 12-INCH PIZZAS

DOUGH

3 cups (1 lb 8 oz) water, warmed to about 100°F

2 tsp instant dry yeast

2 tbsp extra-virgin olive oil

2 tsp salt

5¼ cups (1 lb 8 oz) all-purpose flour

Cornmeal for dusting

QUICK MARINARA SAUCE

¼ cup olive oil

2 cups finely chopped onion

4 garlic cloves

2 lb 8 oz canned plum tomatoes, preferably San Marzano (4 cups)

Salt, as needed

Cracked black pepper, as needed

1. To prepare the dough: Place the water, yeast, olive oil, and salt in the bowl of an electric mixer fitted with the dough hook. Add the flour and mix on medium speed until an elastic, homogenous dough forms.

2. Transfer the dough to a large bowl or container and allow it to rest at room temperature until it has doubled in size, about 45 minutes. Fold the dough over on itself to release any gas that has built up.

3. Meanwhile, make the sauce: Heat the oil in a medium sauce pot over medium heat and sauté the onions and garlic until aromatic, 6 to 8 minutes.

4. Add the tomatoes to the pot, crushing them with your fingers while adding them. Cook the sauce until thickened, about 45 minutes, seasoning with salt and pepper as the sauce cooks.

5. Purée the sauce using a food mill and adjust the seasoning.

6. Once the dough has doubled in size, cut the dough into three equal pieces. Cup them in your hands and roll them on a work surface in a circular motion to form nice even, round balls. Cover the balls with a clean dish towel and set aside to rest for 10 minutes to relax the gluten.

continued

1 lb fresh mozzarella cheese, cut into ⅛-inch slices (see page 227)

½ cup basil, cut into thin chiffonade

6 plum tomatoes, thinly sliced

¼ cup extra-virgin olive oil, placed in a squirt bottle

1 tbsp dried Mediterranean oregano

Salt, to taste

Freshly ground black pepper, to taste

7. After the dough balls have rested, flour the work surface and flatten a ball out with your hands. Using a rolling pin, roll out the dough piece into a 12-inch round about ¼ inch thick. Be sure to keep the bottom floured as you roll so that it does not stick to the surface.

8. Preheat the oven with a pizza stone to 450°F. Sprinkle your pizza peel with some cornmeal and then slide the dough onto it. The cornmeal will help the dough slide off the peel and will also add crunch. If you don't have a pizza peel, just line a sheet pan with parchment paper and sprinkle with cornmeal. Roll out the dough and place it on the sheet pan.

9. Prebake the pizza crust for 2 minutes to set the dough, then remove from the oven.

10. Ladle about 4 ounces of sauce over the set dough. Spread the sauce out with the bottom of the ladle until it reaches the edge of the dough.

11. Distribute one-third of the mozzarella slices around the dough, leaving about ½ inch between the slices. Sprinkle some of the basil on top of the pizza. Distribute one-third of the tomato slices on the pizza. Drizzle the pizza with some olive oil and sprinkle with some oregano and additional salt and pepper.

12. Put or slide the pizza back into the oven and bake for another 10 to 15 minutes. Remove from the oven and let cool for 2 minutes before slicing. Repeat making the pizzas with the remaining ingredients, making sure to serve the pizzas warm.

Chef's Note *For a really tasty marinara, save your Parmigiano-Reggiano cheese rinds along with your basil stems and simmer them with the sauce. It will add a bit of depth to this simple, quick sauce.*

COCA

Coca is the Spanish version of pizza. The toppings may vary, but it can be as simple as thinly sliced potato, paprika, and olive oil. For our version, we chose to use caramelized onions and red peppers: It is just delicious. If you have a pizza stone, it will help achieve a crispy exterior. If not, be sure to oil your pan before baking so the crust will crisp up. MAKES THREE 12-INCH COCAS

DOUGH

3 cups (1 lb 8 oz) water, warmed to about 100°F

2 tsp instant dry yeast

2 tbsp olive oil

2 tsp salt

8½ cups (2 lb 8 oz) all-purpose flour

Cornmeal for dusting

TOPPING

Extra-virgin olive oil, to taste

1 lb onions, thinly sliced

2 lb red bell peppers, roasted, seeded, and thinly sliced

½ cup sugar

6 tbsp sherry vinegar

1 tbsp pimentón (Spanish paprika)

Salt, to taste

Freshly ground black pepper, to taste

1. To make the dough: In the bowl of an electric mixer fitted with the dough hook, combine the water, yeast, olive oil, and salt. Add the flour and mix on medium speed until a homogenous dough forms, about 15 minutes.

2. Transfer the dough to a large bowl or container and rest at room temperature until the dough has doubled in size, about 20 minutes. Fold the dough over on itself to release any gas that has built up. Cover the dough with a clean dish towel and set aside to rest at room temperature until the dough has doubled in size, about 20 minutes.

3. Meanwhile, make the topping: In a pan over medium heat, heat the olive oil. Add the onions, cover the pan, and cook until the onions reach a jamlike consistency, about 30 minutes.

4. Add the roasted peppers and continue cooking, stirring to combine the two ingredients. Add the sugar, vinegar, and just enough water to dissolve the sugar. Add the pimentón and continue cooking, covered, until the liquid has reduced to a syrupy consistency, about 20 minutes. Season with salt and black pepper and reserve.

5. Once the dough has doubled in size, cut the dough into three equal pieces. Cup them in your hands and roll them on a work surface in a circular motion to form even, round balls. Cover the balls with a dish towel and set them aside to rest for 10 minutes to relax the gluten.

6. After the dough balls have rested, flour the work surface and flatten a ball out with your hands. Using a rolling pin, roll out the dough into a 12-inch round about ¼ inch thick. Be sure to keep the bottom floured as you roll so that it does not stick to the surface.

7. Preheat the oven with a pizza stone to 450°F. Sprinkle your pizza peel with some cornmeal and then slide the dough onto it. The cornmeal will help the dough slide off the peel and will also add crunch. If you don't have a pizza peel, just line a baking sheet with parchment paper and sprinkle with cornmeal. Roll out the dough and place it on the sheet pan.

8. Prebake for 2 minutes to set dough, then remove from the oven. Add the topping and bake for 15 minutes. Allow to cool for a few minutes before slicing and serving.

PAN BAGNAT

Pan bagnat literally means "bathed bread." This sandwich is basically a Niçoise salad in a round bun—it is "bathed" in the tangy dressing. You can purchase pan bagnat rolls in some French bakeries. If you can't find them, just remember that the bread should be nice and crusty on the outside and soft on the inside, like a round baguette. MAKES 10 SANDWICHES

DRESSING

⅓ cup red wine vinegar

1 bunch basil, chopped

¾ bunch flat-leaf parsley, chopped

4 anchovy fillets

1 jalapeño pepper, roasted, peeled, seeded, and chopped

1 cup extra-virgin olive oil

10 hard rolls (see Chef's Note)

1 lb drained oil-packed tuna, flaked

Tomato concassé (see page 122) *or* 5 plum tomatoes

1¾ cups marinated roasted bell peppers

⅓ cup black olives, pitted and roughly chopped

1 cucumber, peeled, seeded, and chopped

½ cup finely chopped red onion

2 large, hard-boiled eggs, chopped

2 tbsp capers

4 garlic cloves, finely chopped

Salt, to taste

Freshly ground black pepper, to taste

1. Place the vinegar, basil, parsley, anchovies, and jalapeño in a blender and process until smooth. With the blender running, slowly pour in the olive oil in a steady stream to emulsify the mixture.

2. Cut the rolls in half lengthwise and scoop out the interior, leaving a shell about ½ inch thick. Crumble the bread removed from the interior.

3. Combine the crumbled bread with the tuna, tomatoes, roasted peppers, olives, cucumber, red onion, hard-boiled eggs, capers, and garlic. Add just enough dressing to moisten and bind the filling together. Season with salt and black pepper.

4. To assemble each sandwich: Brush the scraped sides of the hard roll with some of the remaining dressing. Fill the roll with 5 ounces of the filling and firmly press the sandwich closed. Wrap each sandwich tightly with parchment paper or waxed paper. Allow the sandwiches to rest at room temperature for at least 1 hour before serving.

Chef's Note *The success of this tasty sandwich depends on excellent, fresh, crusty bread; without that key element, the recipe will produce only an ordinary sandwich.*

SEMOLINA BREAD

Semolina flour is made from the larger particles left behind after fine pasta flour has passed through the mill. Semolina has a grittier texture than the "00" flour we use for fresh pasta, that is good for making dried pastas, dumplings, and especially bread. It is makes a beautiful yellow-loaf with great texture.

MAKES TWO 1½-POUND LOAVES

POOLISH
1½ cups (10 oz) semolina flour

1¼ cups (10 oz) water, warmed to 105°F

Pinch of instant dry yeast

FINAL DOUGH
1½ cups (10 oz) semolina flour

2 cups (10 oz) bread flour

¼ tsp instant dry yeast

1½ cups (12 oz) water, warmed to 105°F

1¼ tsp salt

1. To make the poolish: In a large bowl, combine the flour, water, and the yeast and mix together by hand until well incorporated. Cover the poolish with a clean dish towel and allow to proof at room temperature until it has risen and begun to recede and looks bubbly and frothy on top, 10 to 15 hours.

2. To make the final dough: In the bowl of an electric mixer fitted with the dough hook, combine the flours and yeast. Add the poolish, water, and salt and mix on low speed for 5 minutes and then on medium speed for 2 minutes until the dough is smooth, strong, and very elastic.

3. Transfer the dough to a large bowl or container and allow to rest at room temperature until it has nearly doubled in size, about 30 minutes. Gently fold the dough over on itself, then allow the dough to rest for another 30 minutes at room temperature.

4. Divide the dough into two equal pieces and form a log with each piece. Roll the log out into a long loaf that is tapered on the ends like a torpedo. Place on a sheet pan and let rest. Cover and let sit in a warm area for 20 minutes before baking.

5. Score the top of the loaves with a razor blade, if desired, just before baking.

6. Twenty minutes before the end of the final fermentation, preheat the oven with a baking stone to 475°F. Ten minutes before baking the loaves, place a tray filled with 3 cups of warm water below the baking area in the oven to help produce steam.

7. Uncover the dough and place each piece, seam side down, on a peel lined with parchment paper. Spray each loaf with water and allow it to rest for 5 minutes. Score each loaf and spray each one again.

8. Transfer the loaves and parchment paper to the baking stone and immediately reduce the oven temperature to 450°F. Bake for 12 minutes. Remove the steam tray and parchment paper and rotate each loaf. Continue baking for another 10 to 12 minutes until the crust has a deep color and doesn't give when pressed.

9. Remove the loaves from the oven and transfer to a wire rack to cool.

FRESH PHYLLO DOUGH

Phyllo is the Greek word for "leaf." The art of stretching phyllo dough as leaf-thin as the kind available at the market is something that takes a lot of practice. If you have some spare time on a rainy day, it is a lot of fun and well worth the effort to make phyllo from scratch, but most often the home cook will want to use the store-bought boxed sheets. The best way to handle phyllo while working with it is to lay out a sheet of plastic wrap on the countertop, stack the phyllo sheets on top of it, cover them with another layer of plastic wrap and squeeze all the air out. The most important thing to remember is that moisture is the enemy of phyllo. I do not recommend using a damp towel as many recipes do, because it will just make the dough too moist. For the same reason, I use clarified, not just melted, butter when working with phyllo. Removing the milk solids, or white stuff, from the melted butter will help keep the dough from getting soggy. The flour that you use will also affect the consistency of the dough. I like a combination of high-gluten or bread flour for structure and the fine "00" flour for texture. MAKES 1 POUND 4 OUNCES DOUGH

1 tsp salt

1½ cups (12 oz) water, warmed to about 105°F

2¼ cups (11 oz) "00" flour

2¼ cups (11 oz) high-gluten flour

Cornstarch for dusting

1. Dissolve the salt in the warm water and add the flours. Mix and knead until a smooth dough forms, about 15 minutes.

2. Allow the dough to rest at room temperature for at least 1 hour and up to overnight.

3. Cup the dough in your hands and roll it on the table in a circular motion to form an even round ball. Cover with a clean dish towel and let rest for 10 minutes to relax the gluten.

4. Lightly flour the dough and flatten it out with a rolling pin. Place a white cotton tablecloth over a 4-foot kitchen table and lightly flour the cloth.

5. Start to roll out the dough with the rolling pin, rolling it out as thinly as you can, about ⅛ inch thick, being careful to roll it out evenly. Let the dough rest for 10 minutes.

6. Once the dough has rested, you can start to stretch it. Work your way around the dough, pulling the edges out a little at a time from underneath; you will be circling the table and stretching the dough toward the edge of the table. Be careful not to poke your fingers through the dough while you are stretching it; I usually work with the backs of my hands. If you are having trouble visualizing this, go to YouTube and search "How It's Made: Phyllo Dough." You will see the mechanical version of making the dough as well as the hand-stretching method. Finally, if you are about to give up, get out the pasta machine and roll it in strips.

7. If the dough starts to resist, cover it with another tablecloth and let it rest for 10 minutes, then start again.

8. Toward the end of the stretching process, the edges should be hanging off the table and the dough should be so thin that you can see through it. When you have gotten to this stage, you can cut off the thick edges and you are left with the thin dough. By this time the dough should also have dried a bit so that it will not stick together.

9. Now you have to cut the dough. Traditionally a *senida* is used to wrap the dough. It is a wood plank that is about 8 inches wide by however long your table is. You can fashion one out of cardboard by wrapping pieces of cardboard in aluminum foil.

10. Dust the surface of the dough lightly with some cornstarch; do not use too much or it will burn holes in the dough. Lay the *senida* on one edge of the dough and flip the board over until all of the pastry is wrapped around the board. Now you should have one large rectangle of dough.

11. Cut the edges loose from the sides of the board and you will have multiple sheets of dough. Now cut the dough into 1-foot lengths and stack on top of each other. You now have your own homemade box of phyllo. Fold the dough in half and then roll it up. Wrap the roll in plastic wrap. You can use the dough right away or freeze it until you need it. Defrost in the refrigerator before using.

PARMESAN BISCOTTI

When we think of "biscotti" in the United States, we usually think about little biscuits or cookies, sweet and studded with fruit or nuts. But the name actually refers to the method in which they are baked—twice—so that they can be stored for long periods of time at room temperature. There are many versions of biscotti, both sweet and savory. These tasty little biscotti are great with cheese and sliced prosciutto, or just by themselves. MAKES ABOUT 30 BISCOTTI

3 cups (13 oz) all-purpose flour

2 cups grated Parmigiano-Reggiano

1 cup cold unsalted butter, cubed

2 tsp coarsely ground black pepper

2 large eggs

1. Preheat the oven to 350°F. Line sheet pans with parchment paper.

2. In the bowl of an electric mixer fitted with the paddle attachment, mix the flour and cheese.

3. Cut in the cold butter until the mixture looks crumbly and the butter is evenly distributed. Add the pepper. Add the eggs and mix on medium speed until it just comes together.

4. Form the dough into logs 12 inches long by 2 inches in diameter, wrap in plastic wrap, and refrigerate for 20 minutes, or until firm.

5. Slice the logs crosswise into ¼-inch-thick slices and place the slices on the prepared sheet pans. Bake until the edges are golden brown, about 10 minutes.

BRIOCHE

Buttery, rich, and delicious, brioche is one of those breads that may not be good for you but sure does taste good. As long as you are going to the trouble, make an extra loaf and freeze it. You can use it for hors d'oeuvre, French toast, or even sandwiches. MAKES 1 LOAF OR BRIOCHE À TÊTE

BRIOCHE DOUGH

3⅓ cups (1 lb) bread flour

1 tbsp instant dry yeast

2 cups unsalted butter, softened

3 large eggs

6 tbsp (3 oz) whole milk

3½ tbsp sugar

1 tbsp salt

EGG WASH

2 large eggs, combined with 1 tbsp milk

1. To make the brioche dough: In the bowl of an electric mixer fitted with the dough hook, combine the flour and yeast. Add ½ cup of the butter, the eggs, milk, sugar, and salt and mix on low speed for 4 minutes. Increase the speed to medium and, with the mixer running, gradually add a scant 1¼ cups of the butter, scraping down the sides of the bowl as necessary. After the butter is fully incorporated, mix on medium speed for 15 minutes, or until the dough pulls away from the bowl.

2. Line a sheet pan with parchment paper, grease it with butter, and place the dough on top. Cover the dough tightly with plastic wrap and refrigerate overnight.

3. You have several options for shaping brioche dough. You can use a standard loaf pan if you want to use it for slicing, or you can use a fluted brioche mold for a traditional *brioche à tête*.

4. For the loaf pan, hand roll the dough out to the length of your pan. Grease the pan lightly with butter and place the dough in the pan. Cover with plastic wrap and let proof in a warm place for 20 minutes.

5. To shape the dough for a brioche mold, pinch off a piece of dough the size of a ping-pong ball and reserve it. Form the rest of the dough into a ball between your cupped hands by rolling it in a circular motion on a lightly floured work surface.

6. Grease the brioche mold lightly with butter and place the ball into the mold. Shape the little reserved ball of dough into a nice little round by placing it under the cupped palm of your hand and rolling it in a tight circular motion on the work surface. Apply the ball to the top of the brioche so that it looks like a little hat. Cover and let proof for 20 minutes in a warm place before baking.

7. For a pan loaf, preheat the oven to 400°F and then reduce the heat to 350°F. Brush the loaf with egg wash, then bake for 20 minutes. Rotate and bake for an additional 8 to 10 minutes, until golden brown. Remove from the pan immediately and transfer to a wire rack to cool.

8. For a brioche à tête, preheat the oven to 375°F. Brush the loaf with egg wash and bake for 12 minutes. Rotate and bake for an additional 3 to 5 minutes until golden brown. Remove from the pan immediately and transfer to a wire rack to cool.

FOCACCIA SANDWICHES

Once you have mastered making focaccia, you can use it to make one of my favorite sandwiches. I used to sell this sandwich in my shop and it was a favorite. Forget the subs, make this instead! MAKES 8 LARGE SANDWICHES OR UP TO 30 COCKTAIL-SIZE SANDWICHES

FOCACCIA

Cornmeal, as needed

2¼ cups (18 oz) water

1 tbsp (½ oz) fresh compressed yeast

¼ cup extra-virgin olive oil

6½ cups (1 lb 12 oz) bread flour

2 tsp salt

1 tbsp (1 oz) sea salt *(optional)*

Fresh rosemary leaves for top, as needed *(optional)*

ONION RELISH

1½ cups red onions, thinly sliced

2 tbsp extra-virgin olive oil

1 tbsp red wine vinegar

1 tsp chopped oregano

Salt, to taste

Freshly ground black pepper, to taste

SANDWICH AND FILLING

1 cup Pesto Genovese (page 245)

½ cup mayonnaise

8 oz mortadella, thinly sliced

8 oz aged provolone, thinly sliced

8 oz sopressata, thinly sliced

1 cup sun-dried tomatoes, cut into julienne

1 lb arugula, well washed

¼ cup olive oil

1. To make the focaccia: Line a half sheet pan with parchment paper and sprinkle with cornmeal.

2. In the bowl of an electric mixer fitted with the dough hook, combine the water, yeast, and olive oil until the yeast has dissolved. Add the flour and salt and mix on medium speed until it forms a smooth, elastic dough, about 10 minutes. Cover the bowl with a clean dish towel and allow it to rest for 1 hour and 15 minutes to ferment.

3. Punch down the fermented dough with your hand to remove any air pockets. Divide the dough into 10-ounce portions per focaccia. Using your hands, round each portion of dough into a ball. Set each ball on a prepared sheet pan and allow to rest at room temperature for 1 hour.

4. Press the balls of dough flat and stretch slightly toward the edges of the pans to create a flat rectangle the size of the sheet pan. Brush the dough with olive oil and, if desired, add any optional garnishes such as sea salt and rosemary. Allow the focaccias to rest for an additional 30 minutes on the prepared sheet pans. Meanwhile, preheat the oven to 425°F.

5. Bake the focaccias until the crust is golden brown and does not give way when pressed, about 30 minutes. Allow to cool completely.

6. To make the onion relish: In a nonreactive bowl, combine all the ingredients and allow them to marinate for 1 hour.

7. To assemble the sandwiches: Combine the pesto and mayonnaise. Split a focaccia in half horizontally. Spread each half of the focaccia with the pesto mayonnaise and onion relish and layer with the remaining ingredients. Top with the other focaccia half and cover with plastic wrap or parchment. Cover with another sheet pan of the same size and place a weight on top of the second pan. Place in the refrigerator for about 30 minutes. Skewer sandwiches with picks, cut each into 8 pieces (or more for cocktail-size), and serve.

Chef's Note *Focaccia bread may be served on its own, lightly brushed with garlic and olive oil, dressed with a virtually endless number of garnishes, or used as the base of a sandwich.*

BRUSCHETTA

Bruschetta were originally created as way to utilize bread that was going stale. Just slice some pieces of bread and rub them with a cut garlic clove, then brush them lightly with olive oil and grill. The toppings can be anything you have on hand: some thinly sliced prosciutto, fresh mozzarella, a tomato and onion salad, sautéed greens, chicken liver pâté spread, or an assortment of all the above. Bruschetta are quick and easy snacks to serve for a casual cocktail hour. MAKES 8 SERVINGS

TOMATO-BASIL TOPPING

4 plum tomatoes, cut into small dice

2 shallots, finely chopped

6 basil leaves, chopped

2 tbsp extra-virgin olive oil

2 tbsp red wine vinegar

BRUSCHETTA

1 baguette

1 garlic clove, cut in half

¼ cup olive oil

1. To make the topping: Combine all the ingredients and let marinate for 1 hour at room temperature.

2. To make the bruschetta: Slice the bread slightly on the bias into ½-inch-thick slices and let sit for a hour to firm up; this will give the texture of stale bread.

3. Rub each piece of bread with the cut side of the garlic clove. Lightly brush each piece with the olive oil on both sides and grill for 1 to 2 minutes per side. Top with 1 table-spoon topping and serve.

Chef's Note *For additional toppings, consider tapenade or Pesto Genovese (page 245), Sun-dried Tomato Pesto (page 246), Tomato Confit (page 141), Chicken Liver Pâté (page 240), or Pork Rillettes (page 238). You can also go with a thin slice of prosciutto, a half fig, and a teaspoon of mascarpone, drizzled with balsamic vinegar. Use your imagination to create many more possibilities.*

ONION TART WITH CANTAL AND CARAMELIZED APPLES

Cantal is considered a favorite, or even the national cheese, of France because it is one of the oldest cheeses still being produced. It is named after the Cantal mountains in the Auvergne region of France and is available in a variety of ages, each of which has its own flavor. If you cannot find Cantal, substitute sharp Cheddar.

MAKES ONE 8-INCH TART

TART SHELL
1½ cups all-purpose flour
¾ cup unsalted butter
¼ cup lard *or* duck fat
½ cup ice water
Pinch of salt

FILLING
¼ cup olive oil
1 onion, thinly sliced
8 sage leaves, 2 chopped and 6 whole
Salt, to taste
Freshly ground black pepper, to taste
2 tbsp unsalted butter
2 tbsp sugar
1 apple (Gala, Fuji, or any tart-crisp variety), cored, peeled, if desired, and cut into small dice
1 tbsp sherry vinegar
½ cup grated Cantal *or* white Cheddar
1 cup heavy cream
6 large egg yolks
1 tbsp Dijon mustard

1. To make the tart shell: In the bowl of a food processor fitted with the metal blade, pulse the flour with the butter and lard or duck fat until it is the consistency of cornmeal.

2. Add the water and salt and process for 30 seconds, or until it forms a ball. Flatten the ball of dough, wrap it in plastic wrap, and allow to rest for at least 30 minutes in the refrigerator.

3. On a board or work surface lightly dusted with flour, using a rolling pin, roll out the dough into a 10-inch circle with a thickness of ⅛ inch. Line an 8-inch tart pan with the dough and chill the tart shell for at least 30 minutes in the refrigerator.

4. Preheat the oven to 325°F.

5. Prick the bottom of the tart shell with the tines of a fork and line it with parchment paper or wax paper. Weight down the paper with some dried beans, lentils, or rice.

6. Blind bake the tart shell for 20 minutes. Remove the paper and the beans and continue to bake for another 10 minutes so that the bottom dries out a bit. Remove from the oven and reserve until needed.

7. To make the filling: Heat the olive oil in a sauté pan over medium heat and add the onions. Cook the onions very slowly, stirring frequently, until they are golden brown, about 10 minutes. When the onions are starting to color, add the chopped sage and season to taste with salt and pepper. When the onions are totally caramelized, about 15 minutes, remove from the heat, transfer to a bowl and set aside.

8. In the same pan, melt the butter with the sugar, add the apples, and sauté over high heat until they are lightly browned, about 10 minutes. Deglaze the pan with sherry vinegar and cool.

9. Layer the caramelized onions on the bottom of the reserved, prebaked tart shell and then sprinkle with the cheese. Evenly distribute the apples on top of the cheese.

10. To make the custard: Heat the cream until it is slightly warm and then whisk it into the egg yolks. Season the custard with salt and pepper and the Dijon mustard and then pour it over the filling in the shell. Place the whole sage leaves on top.

11. Bake the tart until the custard is set, about 20 minutes. Remove from the oven and let cool before cutting and serving.

TOMATO TART WITH OIL-CURED OLIVES

This tart makes a wonderful lunch with a simple salad on the side. The typically Provençal ingredients are simple yet have an amazing amount of flavor. If you want to, you can also turn this into little tartlets for a cocktail party. Just be sure to chop all the ingredients small enough to fit into 1-inch tartlet pans. The baking time will be less but the result just as delicious! MAKES ONE 8-INCH TART (5 TO 6 PORTIONS) OR TWENTY-FOUR 1-INCH TARTLETS

TART SHELL

1½ cups all-purpose flour

1 tbsp chopped basil

¼ tsp cracked black pepper

¾ cup unsalted butter

¼ cup lard

½ cup ice water

Pinch of salt

FILLING

1 cup heavy cream

6 large egg yolks, at room temperature

8 Tomato Confit halves (page 141)

24 oil-cured olives, pitted

1 tbsp chopped basil

1 tsp chopped oregano

1. To make the tart shell: In the bowl of a food processor fitted with the metal blade, pulse the flour with the basil and pepper and then pulse in the butter and lard until it is the consistency of cornmeal.

2. Add the water and salt and process for 30 seconds, or until it forms a ball. Flatten the ball of dough and wrap in plastic wrap. Allow the dough rest for at least 30 minutes in the refrigerator.

3. Preheat the oven to 325°F.

4. On a board or work surface lightly dusted with flour, using a rolling pin, roll out the dough into a 10-inch circle with a thickness of ⅛ inch. Line an 8-inch tart pan with the dough and chill the tart shell for at least 30 minutes in the refrigerator.

5. Prick the bottom of the tart shell with the tines of a fork and line with parchment paper or wax paper. Weight down the paper with some dried beans, lentils, or rice.

6. Blind bake the tart shell for 20 minutes. Remove the paper and the beans and continue to bake for another 10 minutes so that the bottom dries out a bit. Remove from the oven and reserve until needed.

7. To make the filling: In a small saucepan, heat the cream until it is slightly warm and gradually whisk in the egg yolks to temper.

8. Arrange the tomato halves in the prebaked tart shell along with the olives. Sprinkle the basil and oregano over the tomatoes and olives.

9. Place the tart on a sheet pan and pour the custard into the shell. Bake for 20 to 30 minutes until the custard is set. Let cool before cutting and serving.

LEEK, POTATO, AND KALE PIE

Okay, here is your chance to try your hand at homemade phyllo. See page 212 for instructions, or just use store-bought phyllo. You may actually like it better as it may be thinner and crispier. MAKES 4 SERVINGS

PHYLLO DOUGH

2¼ cups (11 oz) "00" flour

2¼ cups (11 oz) high-gluten flour

1 tsp salt

1½ cups (12 oz) water, warmed to 105°F

FILLING

5 tablespoons extra-virgin olive oil, plus as needed

1 lb leeks, well washed, and thinly sliced

1 bunch Tuscan kale

½ lb Yukon Gold or creamer potatoes, peeled and thinly sliced

Salt, to taste

Freshly ground black pepper, to taste

1 tbsp chopped dill

1½ tsp chopped thyme

1. To make the dough: In the bowl of an electric mixer fitted with the dough hook, mix all of the ingredients together on medium speed and knead until smooth, about 15 minutes.

2. Allow the dough to rest at least 1 hour. However, it is best to make it the day before and allow it rest overnight in the refrigerator See the directions for Fresh Phyllo Dough on page 212 for shaping instructions.

3. Preheat the oven to 425°F. Lightly oil a 10-inch cake pan with extra-virgin olive oil.

4. To make the filling: In a large, wide, heavy-bottomed pot or rondeau, sweat the leeks slowly in about 1 tablespoon of the oil, covered, until they are fully cooked, about 10 minutes; covering them with a lid helps to keep them moist and to cook evenly.

5. Strip the kale leaves from the stems and wash the leaves. Boil in salted water until tender and cooked, about 15 minutes. Drain and add to the leeks.

6. When the leeks and kale are three-quarters of the way cooked, add the potato slices and gently fold them in. Stir in the salt, pepper, and herbs and drizzle ¼ cup olive oil onto the potatoes. Replace the lid and cook for 15 minutes, until the potatoes are cooked. Remove the pan from the heat and allow the filling to cool.

7. Lightly brush a 1-foot-square piece of phyllo with olive oil. Layer another piece on top and continue until you have four layers. Brush the top layer with oil and invert over the cake pan. Press the corners in, letting the extra dough hang over the sides.

8. Fill with the cooled filling and then fold the sides on to the top of the filling.

9. Repeat the layering process with 4 more pieces of phyllo and olive oil. Cut a 10-inch circle out of the dough. Place it on top of the folded over phyllo.

10. Bake the pie for 10 minutes. Reduce the oven temperature to 350°F and continue to bake for 30 minutes more.

11. Remove the pie from the oven and cool for 10 minutes. Invert the pie onto the bottom of a cookie sheet and return to oven for a final browning. Bake for another 10 minutes or so until the top is golden brown.

12. Remove from oven and let set for 10 minutes before slicing. The pie is good warm or at room temperature.

CHEESES & YOGURT
DIPS & SPREADS

Cheese has been a very important part of Mediterranean civilization since the ancient Sumerians. If you think about it, cheese is the ultimate food. It is full of protein and nutrients and, in some cases, it has an extensive shelf life depending on the salt content and hardness of the cheese.

Cheese was probably discovered by accident as our ancient ancestors carried milk in the stomach of a smaller animal; it was a perfect little pouch that did not leak. But what they probably did not know was that the stomach contained natural rennet, a coagulant used in cheese making. And so the milk coagulated and they found themselves with a creamy new food source, and thus the ultimate travel food was born. This chapter will introduce you to basic fresh cheeses and yogurt that you can make at home; some are incredibly easy and fun to make. The recipes will also teach you how to make some cheeses that might be fairly pricey at your local cheese counter or not available at all. If you want to get into cheese making in more depth there are many books and Web sites available to the home cheese maker.

DIPS AND SPREADS

There are so many possibilities for dips and spreads in Mediterranean cuisine. The meze table alone gives us more than a dozen vegetable, yogurt, and fruit- and nut-based dips and spreads. The beautiful thing about dips and spreads is that they are really versatile—they can usually also be used as a sauce or garnish for main courses. Tapenade, for instance, is a nice spread for crostini but it can be a great accompaniment to roasted lamb as well. Tzatziki is a really good dip, but thin it down with some buttermilk and it makes a tasty salad dressing. When you are preparing these dips and spreads, think outside the box and consider what else you can do with them.

HARISSA FETA SPREAD

This spread combines the fairly spicy harissa with some nice salty feta cheese. Just put the ingredients in the food processor and pulse away. The moral of the story is, treasure your condiments; you never know how you might use them.

MAKES 1 QUART

1 lb Feta Cheese (page 225 or purchased)

1 cup Greek-style Yogurt (page 224 or purchased)

1 cup cream cheese

¼ cup Harissa (page 14)

1. Place all the ingredients in the food processor and pulse until evenly mixed.

2. Let sit for 1 hour in the refrigerator before serving.

GREEK-STYLE YOGURT

Fresh yogurt is really easy and fun to make. The secret to making Greek-style yogurt is to strain it after it sets, which makes it thick and rich, even if it's made with low-fat milk. Cleanliness is an absolute must in yogurt making, so be sure that your pot and the container you are going to store the yogurt in have been sterilized. Some recipes call for yogurt starter, but honestly, you just need a little yogurt to make yogurt. It is cheaper, and once you get your first batch made, you can use some of that for the starter for your second batch, and so on. MAKES 1 QUART

1 qt milk (preferably a hormone-free local milk)

3 tbsp plain yogurt, with live cultures

1. In a sterilized pot, heat the milk to 180°F, stirring so that it does not burn on the bottom. Let the milk cool to 110°F and whisk in the yogurt. Cover with a clean cloth or plastic wrap and let it sit out in a warm place (110°F) for 10 to 12 hours. You can either put it on top of your refrigerator, or place in a gas oven with a pilot light. Another option would be to place it on a heating pad on top of your counter.

2. Line a colander with damp cheesecloth and spoon the thickened yogurt into the cheesecloth and tie the top. Place the colander in a bowl and let the yogurt drain overnight in the refrigerator. The next day most of the whey (liquids) will have drained off leaving you with a really thick rich yogurt, even if it's low-fat milk that you used to start.

Chef's Note *Be careful to monitor the temperatures so that your yogurt thickens properly. If it does not firm up after 12 hours, you may have gotten the milk too hot and killed the starter. Be sure to clean and rinse your pot or container thoroughly to remove soap residue, which might also inhibit or kill the starter.*

FETA CHEESE

Feta cheese is a fairly salty sheep or goat cheese that originated in Greece. In my wonderful travels to the Greek islands, my daily lunch was a Greek salad that consisted of a very different feta than we have here in the States. It was creamy and crumbly, not too salty, and did not appear to have been brined, as is most feta sold in the United States. Since goat's milk is easier to find here, I suggest you use that, but if you have a source for sheep's milk, the result is very nice and subtle. Don't bother brining the cheese—it will be so delicious that it will be eaten before you know it. MAKES 1 POUND

1 gal pasteurized goat's or sheep's milk

½ tsp liquid rennet or ½ rennet tablet dissolved in ¼ cup cool water (preferably not chlorinated)

1 packet mesophilic starter

¼ cup kosher salt

1. In a sterilized pot, heat the milk to 86°F and add the diluted rennet and starter. Stir for a few minutes until thoroughly mixed, then let it stand at 86°F for an hour.

2. Cut the curd into ½-inch cubes and let them stand for 15 minutes.

3. Using a rubber spatula, stir the curds gently for 20 minutes and then pour them into a cheesecloth-lined colander. Tie the cloth in a knot and hang over a bowl at room temperature for 4 hours to drain.

4. Remove the curds from the bag and cut into 1-inch cubes. Sprinkle with salt and put in a covered, sterilized container to age in the refrigerator for anywhere from 3 to 5 days. The longer the aging, the drier the cheese. Weight the top of the cheese down for a firm block that you can slice.

Chef's Note *You can find mesophilic starter online.*

FRESH MOZZARELLA CHEESE

Fresh mozzarella is readily available in most markets, but it is also fun to make. Honestly, it is just cow's milk cheese curd melted in salted water and formed into any number of shapes. The thing to remember is that the more you pull it, the firmer it becomes. Cow's milk curd can be found at specialty foods or gourmet shops and delis as well as online. MAKES 2 POUNDS

5½ oz salt (about ¾ cup)

1 gal water

2 lb cheese curd, cut into ½-inch cubes

1. In a sterilized pot, add the salt to the water and bring to 160°F. Remove the pot from the heat.

2. Place the cheese curd in a colander and lower the colander into the hot water. The curds must be completely submerged.

3. Work the curd in a circular motion with wooden spoons, stretching it until it becomes a smooth but stringy mass. Maintain the water temperature at a constant 155°F during this process, rewarming the pot as needed.

4. Remove the cheese from the water and continue stretching until the curd is smooth.

5. Shape the cheese into 4-ounce balls or a log and allow the cheese to cool slowly in the liquid in which it was melted. Store the cheese wrapped in plastic wrap or in brine. Cover and refrigerate for up to 5 days.

BURRATA CHEESE

Cheese makers came up with a delicious and inventive use for the little shards of mozzarella left over in the salt water after forming it: burrata. A true burrata is composed of these little shards and some fresh cream surrounded by melted mozzarella. When you cut it open, the cream and the little shards spill out. An easy way to re-create this is by using a good-quality ricotta; try the Lemon Ricotta on page 231. If you like, spoon a teaspoon of fresh cream on top before sealing the cheese. MAKES 1 POUND 4 OUNCES (ABOUT 6 SERVINGS)

1 gal water

7 oz salt (about 1 cup)

1 lb fresh cheese curd, cut into 4-oz pieces

½ cup fresh ricotta cheese

2 tbsp heavy cream (optional)

1. In a sterilized pot, heat the water and salt to 160°F. Prepare 4 pieces of plastic wrap, approximately 8 by 8-inch squares, one for each piece.

2. Dip the curd in the salt water maintaining a temperature between 160°F and not over 180°F until it is soft and pliable approximately 4 minutes. Flatten the curd on a piece of plastic wrap, working quickly so that it does not cool off.

3. Place the plastic wrap in your hand or, if it is easier, in a 4-ounce ramekin and spoon the ricotta into the center. Top off with fresh cream, if using, and quickly fold the corners of the mozzarella over the top and twist up into a ball; the rolling is similar to that of making a sausage link.

4. Let the burrata cool before cutting.

Chef's Note *If you think that it cooled off too much before it sealed, dip the plastic-wrapped ball back in the hot water for a few minutes until it feels soft again. Take it out and twist the seal a little more.*

TOP ROW, FROM LEFT TO RIGHT:

Melt the cheese curd in warm salted water until it's soft and forms a mass.

Stretch the melted cheese curd until it is shiny. To prepare it for filling, gently stretch the melted curd.

BOTTOM ROW, FROM LEFT TO RIGHT:

To shape the burrata, wrap your hand in plastic wrap. Press the flattened cheese curd into the plastic wrap between your thumb and fingers to form a well. Fill the well with ricotta. Wrap the cheese curd around to cover the filling. Wrap the curd completely with the plastic wrap and tie the ends with kitchen twine or just twist well to secure it in place.

After softening the cheese in the warm water and then firming it in cold water, the burrata filling should be completely enclosed in the fresh mozzarella and hold its shape when cut.

229

STRING CHEESE

String cheese is mozzarella that has been pulled like taffy, creating a cheese that can be pulled off in strings. It is firmer than mozzarella because it has been pulled so much. It makes a delicious snack and it is a lot of fun to make as well.

MAKES 1 POUND ROPE OR SIXTEEN 1-OUNCE LOGS

1 gal water

7 oz salt (about 1 cup)

1 lb fresh cheese curd, cut into 1-inch pieces

1. In a sterilized pot, heat the water and salt to 160°F.

2. Dip the curd in the salt water maintaining a temperature between 160°F and not over 180°F until it is soft and pliable, 4 to 8 minutes.

3. Drain the curd and, while it is still warm, start pulling it like taffy into 2-foot-long strands, then fold it in half and pull again. Continue to pull the curds approximately a dozen times or so until it starts to firm up. If it will no longer pull, you can dip it back into the hot water for a few minutes, holding it by the ends.

4. To form the string cheese, you can either roll it into a series of logs 6 inches long and about 1 inch in diameter, or take the entire thing and twist it into a rope knot like Armenian string cheese.

RICOTTA PESTO CHEESE

This is a simple little cheese that combines lemon ricotta and Genovese pesto. It is easy to make and will be ready to eat in a day. All you have to do is layer the two in a piece of cheesecloth and then drain for 1 to 2 days. MAKES 1 QUART

3 cups Lemon Ricotta (page 231)

1 cup Pesto Genovese (page 245)

1 cup pine nuts, toasted and ground in a food processor

1. Dampen a 1-foot-square piece of cheesecloth and wring it out. Line a 3-cup soufflé dish with the cheesecloth.

2. Layer 1 cup of the ricotta on the bottom of the dish. Follow with ½ cup pesto, then layer another 1 cup ricotta, followed by another ½ cup pesto. Finish with the final 1 cup ricotta.

3. Gather the overhanging cloth up and tie the cheese into a tight bundle. Hang the cheese in the refrigerator over a bowl to drain for 24 to 48 hours.

4. Unwrap the cheese ball and roll in the pine nuts. Serve with some toasted focaccia, pita bread, or grissini bread sticks.

ARTICHOKE RICOTTA

This makes a great dip or a topping for crostini. Be sure to thoroughly cook the artichokes until they are softened, or they might oxidize. They are also much more pleasing to the palate when they are nice and tender. MAKES 1 QUART

3 artichokes

Finely grated zest and juice of 1 lemon

2 tbsp olive oil

2 shallots, finely chopped

1 cup leeks, well washed, halved lengthwise and cut into ¼-inch-thick slices

1 tsp chopped thyme

2 cups ricotta cheese

1 tbsp chopped flat-leaf parsley

Salt, to taste

Freshly ground black pepper, to taste

1. Cover the artichokes with water and the lemon juice. Bring the water to a simmer and cook the artichokes for approximately 40 minutes, or until a knife inserted in the center of the artichoke bottom easily pierces the bottom. Let the artichokes cool and pull off all the leaves. Then scoop out and discard the chokes.

2. Dice or grate the rest of each artichoke and reserve. Heat the olive oil in a sauté pan and sauté the shallots, leeks, and thyme until tender. Remove from the heat and cool, then add the lemon zest.

3. Combine the ricotta with the shallot-leek mixture and the grated or diced artichokes. Season with the chopped parsley, salt, and pepper. Cover tightly and let sit for at least 2 hours before serving.

Chef's Note *You may also use store-bought artichokes that are jarred, canned, or frozen.*

LEMON RICOTTA

Ricotta is so easy to make that I am not sure why we buy it. The key to good ricotta is good milk and careful temperature control. I recommend that you use a local milk with no added hormones or antibiotics. If you can get milk that has not been homogenized, that is even better. The less the milk is handled at the dairy, the better the end result. MAKES 1 POUND

½ gal whole milk

Juice of 2 to 3 lemons

Finely grated zest of 2 lemons

Salt, to taste

1. In a sterilized pot, heat the milk to between 185°F and 200°F. Add the juice of 2 of the lemons and stir. Cover the pot and let sit for approximately 15 minutes; the milk should start to separate into curds and whey. If this does not happen, add a little more lemon juice to the milk until it starts to set.

2. Line a colander with cheesecloth and pour the curds into the lined colander. Tie the cheesecloth into a bundle with kitchen twine and hang it over a bowl to drain for 1 to 2 hours in the refrigerator until it stops dripping.

3. Remove the cheese from the cloth and fold in the lemon zest and salt to taste. Store in a sterilized container in the refrigerator, covered, for up to 2 weeks.

MEDITERRANEAN VEGETABLE AND GOAT CHEESE CAKE

This was one of the most popular items on my catering menus when I owned Gigliotti Culinary Concepts Ltd. Probably 75 percent of all the parties I catered in that ten-year period had this on their menu. I am not sure how many I have made, but it is probably upward of a thousand by now. It does require a little time, but the end result is really worth it. It tastes better and holds together better after a few days in the refrigerator under a weight, so plan ahead and that will free up time to prepare other dishes for your party. MAKES 6 TO 9 SERVINGS

1 lb eggplant, sliced ⅛ inch thick

1 tbsp salt, plus as needed

½ cup olive oil

2 shallots, finely chopped

1 lb zucchini, seeded and cut into julienne

1 lb yellow squash, seeded and cut into julienne

Freshly ground black pepper, to taste

3 garlic cloves, finely chopped

2 red bell peppers, seeded and cut into julienne

2 yellow bell pepper, seeded and cut into julienne

1 lb spinach leaves

1 lb shiitake mushrooms, sliced

Two 7-ounce goat cheese logs

1 rosemary sprig, chopped

1 bunch basil, chopped

Finely grated zest of 1 lemon

1 cup sun-dried tomatoes, cut into julienne

1. Salt the eggplant slices and cover them. Set aside to sweat and release their excess moisture, about 30 minutes. Rinse the eggplant slices and pat them dry.

2. Preheat a grill pan and grill the eggplant on both sides until totally soft inside. Set aside.

3. In a sauté pan, heat 2 tablespoons of the olive oil, add the shallots, and sauté until translucent. Add the zucchini and yellow squash separately and cook quickly until tender but without coloring. Season with salt and black pepper; reserve until needed and then drain well.

4. In a sauté pan, heat 2 tablespoons of the olive oil, add 1 garlic clove, and sauté until aromatic. Add the red bell peppers and cook until tender. Season with salt and black pepper. Remove from the pan, reserve until needed, and then drain well. Repeat the entire step to cook the yellow bell peppers and keep them separate.

5. In the same pan, sauté the remaining garlic clove, add the spinach, and cook quickly until it wilts. Reserve until needed and then drain well.

6. Heat 2 more tablespoons of the olive oil in the pan. Add the shiitake mushrooms and sauté over relatively high heat until all of their liquid evaporates. Season with salt and black pepper; reserve until needed, and then drain well.

7. In the bowl of an electric mixer fitted with the whisk attachment, whip the goat cheese until slightly soft. Add the rosemary, basil, and lemon zest.

8. Spray an 8-inch cake pan with vegetable oil spray and line it with plastic wrap, making sure that there is plenty of wrap hanging over the sides of the pan.

9. Begin layering the cake. The bottom of the pan will be the top of the cake so be sure to arrange the first layer of vegetables in an attractive manner. You might use only an eighth of the vegetables for this layer. Evenly layer the reserved eggplant, zucchini, yellow squash, red bell peppers, yellow bell peppers, spinach, mushrooms, the sun-dried tomatoes, and the goat cheese until everything is used, using the vegetables to make 3 layers and the goat cheese to make 2 layers.

10. Fold the plastic wrap over the top of the cake and place it on a sheet pan. Put another cake pan on top of the cake and weight it down with something heavy like a can. Refrigerate for 2 days.

11. To serve, unwrap the bottom of the cake and invert a plate on top of it. Flip it over and gently pull on the wrap until the vegetable cake releases from the pan. Serve the cake with fresh pita bread or toasted pita chips.

MINT, CUCUMBER, AND YOGURT DIP

This is one of the most refreshing dips, and I have loved it for years. I remember traveling in the Greek Islands and being so hot that I all I could do was just sit in the shade. My traveling companion and I would go to a taverna and order a glass of wine and some of this salad along with a basket of pitas. It was just the ticket for exhausted, dehydrated travelers. We were instantly revived—and no, it wasn't the wine. MAKES 1 QUART

1 bunch mint leaves

1 tbsp olive oil

1 shallot, finely chopped

Finely grated zest of 1 lemon

Finely grated zest of 1 orange

2 cups plain Greek-style yogurt (page 224 or purchased)

1 hothouse cucumber, grated, sprinkled with salt, and water squeezed out

Salt, to taste

Freshly ground black pepper, to taste

1. Plunge the mint leaves into boiling water, immediately remove, and plunge into ice water to set the color. Reserve.

2. In a small pan, heat the olive oil, add the shallot, and sauté until aromatic. Remove from the heat and cool. Fold in the citrus zests.

3. Chop the blanched mint finely and fold it into the yogurt. When the shallot has cooled, fold the shallot-zest mixture into the mint yogurt. Squeeze the cucumber again and fold it into the yogurt mixture. Season with salt and pepper. Cover and let sit for at least 1 hour in the refrigerator before serving.

WHITE BEAN AND DUCK SPREAD

As I noted in the recipe for Duck and White Bean Soup (page 23), duck and beans are a classic combination in southwest France, as exemplified in their traditional cassoulet. You really have to cook the duck thoroughly as well as the beans. The meat must be melt-in-your-mouth tender and the beans should be soft enough to crush on the roof of your mouth with your tongue. Make the entire recipe and freeze some so you have it on hand. MAKES 2 QUARTS

1 lb dried white beans

DUCK STOCK
1 whole duck (about 4 pounds)
3 qt water
2 onions
1 carrot
1 celery stalk
1 bay leaf
1 thyme sprig
1 head garlic, cloves peeled

WHITE BEAN AND DUCK SPREAD
2 tbsp plus ½ cup olive oil, plus more for drizzling
1 onion, finely chopped
Salt, to taste
Freshly ground black pepper, to taste
2 tbsp finely chopped chives

1. To prepare the beans: Put the white beans in a large bowl, cover with cold water by at least 2 inches, and soak overnight.

2. To make the duck stock: Place the duck in a pot with the water to cover and simmer for 2 hours. After 1 hour, add the vegetables, herbs, and garlic. Continue to cook until the duck meat pulls easily off the bone.

3. Remove the duck from the stock and reserve. Strain and reserve the stock; discard the onions, carrot, celery, and herbs. Reserve the garlic cloves. Pick the duck meat off the bones and shred it by hand. Discard the skin.

4. To make the spread: In a sauce pot, heat 2 tablespoons of the olive oil, add the onion, and sauté until tender. Drain the soaked white beans, add to the pot, and cover with the reserved duck stock. Bring to a simmer and skim off any foam that rises to the surface. Continue to simmer until the beans are falling apart.

5. Drain the beans and reserve the cooking liquid. Place the beans in a food processor and run until the purée is smooth, adding the reserved bean cooking liquid as needed.

6. Reduce the remaining bean cooking liquid to a syrup and return it to the bean purée. Fold in the shredded duck meat and season with salt and pepper.

7. Drizzle in the remaining ½ cup olive oil and fold in the chives. Cover and refrigerate for 2 hours before serving. Serve cold or warm, drizzled with olive oil.

FAVA BEAN PURÉE

When I worked at Jean-Louis at Watergate, Jean-Louis made the most fantastic fava bean purée I have ever had. He seemed to be a magician with food. This is a perfect example of how he took a few simple ingredients and turned them into something special. The purée is bright green, flavorful, and tastes like a little bit of heaven. This is my best recollection of how he made it. Even if it's not exactly the same it's still pretty great. MAKES 3 CUPS

2 lb fresh fava beans

1 cup olive oil

Juice of 1 lemon

Salt, to taste

Freshly ground black pepper, to taste

1. Prepare the fava beans as instructed on page 35.

2. After you have squeezed all the favas out of their skins, place them in a blender. Add the olive oil and blend on high until very smooth. Season with lemon juice, salt, and pepper.

3. Serve with fresh pita as a dip, or serve as a side vegetable with dinner.

TOP ROW, FROM LEFT TO RIGHT:

Use a paring knife to carefully slice down the seam of the pod, then use your fingers to remove the fava beans.

After the beans have been blanched, squeeze each bean between your thumb and forefinger to pop it out of its outer skin. If the beans are not popping out easily, make a small cut in the seam of the skin with a paring knife before squeezing them.

BOTTOM ROW, FROM LEFT TO RIGHT:

In a blender, purée the ingredients until smooth and homogenous.

Serve the purée with a few fresh fava beans, a drizzle of olive oil, and some crusty bread.

PORK RILLETTES

Rillettes were made in the farmhouse kitchen after the slaughter to utilize some of the fatty, tougher cuts of the animal. It is simply a French potted meat that, when made properly, can last for months without spoiling. Due to lack of refrigeration, the farmers had to find ways of preserving their food for longer periods of time. This is a traditional method. MAKES ABOUT 1 POUND

SACHET D'ÉPICES

1 thyme sprig

3 or 4 parsley stems

1 bay leaf

2 or 3 leek leaves and/or 1 celery stalk, cut in half crosswise

1 carrot, cut in half lengthwise (optional)

RILLETTES

1 lb pork butt, very fatty, cubed

2 cups onion, diced

1 cup carrot, diced

1 cup celery, diced

3 cups Chicken Broth (page 6) or white beef stock, plus more as needed

1 tsp salt, plus more to taste

½ tsp freshly ground black pepper, plus more to taste

1. To make the sachet d'épices: Place all the ingredients in a piece of cheesecloth and gather the edges to form a bag around the ingredients. Tie the pouch with kitchen twine and reserve until needed.

2. You can choose to cook the pork in a heavy-bottomed pot on the stovetop or braise it in an oven-safe, heavy-bottomed pot or enameled casserole in the oven. If braising, preheat the oven to 350°F.

3. If cooking on the stovetop, place the pork, onion, carrot, celery, and sachet in a heavy-bottomed pot. Add enough broth to almost cover.

4. Simmer, covered, very slowly on the stovetop, or braise, covered, in the oven until the meat is cooked and very tender, at least 2 hours.

5. Remove the pork from the pot and set aside. Reserve the stock and rendered fat. Discard the vegetables and sachet. Let the meat cool slightly.

6. Transfer the meat to a chilled bowl of an electric mixer fitted with the paddle attachment. Add the salt and pepper. Mix on low speed until the meat breaks into pieces. Test for appropriate seasoning and consistency; the consistency should be spreadable, not runny or dry. Adjust the consistency by adding some of the reserved fat and stock. Make any adjustments before filling the mold.

7. Pack the rillettes in small earthenware molds. Ladle some of the reserved fat over the top and allow to cool before serving. Once cool, the fat can be scored for a decorative effect. The rillettes will keep in the refrigerator for 2 to 3 weeks.

Variations

DUCK RILLETTES: *Substitute duck meat for the pork and add a small sprig of rosemary to the sachet.*

SALMON RILLETTES: *Substitute cubed salmon for the pork and fish stock for the chicken broth.*

TOP ROW, FROM LEFT TO RIGHT:

Cut the pork into cubes.

Cook the pork until it is extremely tender and breaks easily into pieces.

BOTTOM ROW, FROM LEFT TO RIGHT:

In a chilled mixer bowl, whip the chilled pork on low speed until it is a spreadable consistency. If necessary, add some of the reserved fat to adjust the consistency.

Pack the pork into jars or molds and pour in enough reserved fat to cover the pork completely.

CHICKEN LIVER PÂTÉ WITH APPLES AND COGNAC

I love this pâté. My friend and former chef, George Pechin, taught me how to make this back in the 1970s. It is still as good today as it ever was. I like to make the entire recipe and freeze some. The apples, cognac, and chicken livers are a really nice combination of savory and subtle sweetness and this will appeal even to those who think that they don't like liver. If you like, you can make it with duck livers instead. MAKES 2 QUARTS

1 lb chicken livers, cleaned and dried

Salt, as needed

Freshly ground black pepper, as needed

2 tbsp olive oil

1 cup unsalted butter, cubed

3 shallots, sliced

1 garlic clove, sliced

1 thyme sprig

1 bay leaf

1 apple, Gala or Fuji, peeled, cored, and sliced

¼ cup cognac

1. Season the livers with salt and pepper.

2. In a sauté pan, heat the olive oil, add the livers, and sear on a high heat. Remove the livers from the pan and set aside on a plate. Reduce the heat, add 2 tablespoons of the butter, and melt in the pan. Add the shallots, garlic, thyme, and bay leaf and cook slowly until the shallots are tender.

3. When the shallots are tender, add the apple and increase the heat. Cook until the apple is tender, then return the livers to the pan and increase the heat.

4. Pour the cognac into the pan and light it with a match. Cook until the flame goes out, about 1 minute. Remove and discard the thyme sprig and bay leaf. Transfer the liver and apple mixture to a blender, add the remaining butter, and blend until velvety smooth. Season with salt and pepper.

5. Pour the pâté into ramekins or a larger soufflé dish to chill. Once chilled, place plastic wrap directly onto the surface so it won't oxidize. You can spread it on toasts or serve it along with fresh apple slices.

Chef's Note *You will want to slightly oversalt the pâté because once it is chilled, the salt flavor is muted quite a bit.*

TOP ROW, FROM LEFT TO RIGHT:

Sear the dried chicken livers, being careful not to overcrowd the pan.

In a blender, purée the ingredients until completely homogenous and velvety smooth.

BOTOM ROW, FROM LEFT TO RIGHT:

Pour the pâté mixture into a container and refrigerate until set. Once the pâté is firm, you can use a knife or toothpick to gently score a decorative pattern on top.

You may serve pâté family style in its container, as you would a dip, or scoop it into individual portions (as shown here). Garnish with the apple compote.

HUMMUS BI TAHINI

Hummus is a Middle Eastern staple that is so easy to make and is delicious when put on just about anything. You can flavor the hummus with any number of ingredients, such as spicy chiles, roasted garlic, or puréed roasted red peppers.

MAKES 1 QUART

8 oz dried chickpeas (about 1¼ cups)

Salt, as needed

Juice of 2 lemons

2 garlic cloves, crushed to a paste with salt (see Chef's Note, page 97)

6 tbsp tahini

¼ cup extra-virgin olive oil

GARNISH

Chopped flat-leaf parsley, as needed

2 tbsp olive oil (optional)

1. Put the chickpeas in a large bowl and add enough cold water to cover them by 2 inches. Immediately discard any chickpeas that float to the surface. Soak the chickpeas overnight.

2. The following day, place the soaked chickpeas in a pot, cover with fresh water, and put a lid on the pan. Simmer the chickpeas until tender, about 1 hour. Be sure to maintain the proper amount of cooking liquid. If the liquid evaporates, add more while cooking. After they are very tender, drain and reserve the cooking liquid.

3. Place the chickpeas in a food processor and purée with some of the reserved cooking liquid to a smooth paste.

4. Add the salt, lemon juice, garlic, tahini, and olive oil. Taste and adjust the seasonings and consistency.

5. Garnish with chopped parsley and the olive oil, if desired.

OPPOSITE PAGE: *Clockwise from top: Tzatziki (page 245), Sun-Dried Tomato Pesto (page 246), Baba Ghanoush, Hummus bi Tahini, Pine Nut and Feta Cheese Dip (page 244).*

BABA GHANOUSH

The puréed eggplant gives a silky smooth texture to this baba ghanoush. Enjoy it as a dip for vegetables or serve with pita bread. Its versatility makes it a natural candidate to put out on a meze table alongside other dips and spreads. MAKES 1 QUART

2 large eggplants

½ cup tahini, plus more as needed to taste

4 garlic cloves, crushed with salt (see Chef's Note, page 97)

Juice of 2 lemons

Freshly ground black pepper, to taste

Salt, to taste

1. Wash the eggplant and roast on a rack in the oven or directly on the grill until completely soft in the middle. Remove the eggplant from the heat and allow it to cool until it can be handled.

2. Peel the eggplant and place into a fine-mesh sieve. Allow any excess juices to drain for about 15 minutes. Mash the eggplant to a purée consistency.

3. In a food processor fitted with the metal blade, mix the tahini, garlic, lemon juice, pepper, salt, and a little cold water until the purée is homogenous. Pulse in the eggplant and purée until smooth. Taste and adjust the seasoning and consistency.

PINE NUT AND FETA CHEESE DIP

The unusual combination of ingredients in this dip will surprise and delight you. Smooth and rich, the dip pairs well with lighter vegetables and can add complexity when used as the spread on the base of a canapé. It is sure to become a favorite and one you will want to have on hand. MAKES 3 CUPS

12 oz feta, drained

1½ cups pine nuts

¾ cup whole milk

3 tbsp extra-virgin olive oil

¼ tsp cayenne

Salt, to taste

Paprika, to taste

1. Place one-third of the cheese, pine nuts, milk, and olive oil in a blender. Blend until smooth. Repeat this process in three stages. Stir together the three batches of dip with the cayenne.

2. Refrigerate for at least 1 hour before serving.

3. Remove from the refrigerator before serving. Taste and add salt, if needed. Garnish with paprika and serve.

TZATZIKI SAUCE

Tzatziki is a wonderfully simple dish that can be made in no time at all. It can be used as a condiment or a dip and is wonderful in a falafel sandwich. MAKES 1½ CUPS

½ cup plain yogurt

½ cup sour cream

½ cup grated cucumber

1 tsp finely chopped garlic

1 tbsp extra-virgin olive oil

1 tbsp chopped dill

1 tbsp chopped mint (optional), plus as needed for garnish

1 tsp freshly squeezed lemon juice

½ tsp finely grated lemon zest

Salt, to taste

Freshly ground black pepper, to taste

1. Combine the yogurt, sour cream, cucumber, and garlic in a food processor and blend until smooth. Transfer to a bowl and fold in the olive oil, dill, mint, if using, lemon juice, and lemon zest.

2. Stir until combined and season to taste with salt and pepper. Keep refrigerated until ready to serve. Garnish with chopped mint, if desired.

PESTO GENOVESE

The city of Genoa is said to be the origin of the classic pesto as we know it today. Genoa was a major port and its inhabitants were probably the first Italians to see the imported basil plant. Although its origins are thought to be either Indian or North African, basil is one of those ingredients we now think of as classically Italian—when in fact it is a food immigrant. The first written recipe for pesto Genovese was seen in the Italian cookbook *La Cuciniera Genovese* written in 1863. MAKES 2 CUPS

6 garlic cloves

Salt, as needed

⅓ cup pine nuts

4 cups basil leaves, tightly packed

½ cup extra-virgin olive oil, plus more as needed

1 cup grated Parmigiano-Reggiano

1. Mash the garlic and salt together to a smooth paste.

2. Place the garlic paste and pine nuts in a food processor and blend until smooth. Add the basil and olive oil and blend slowly until a smooth, fluid consistency is achieved.

3. Add the cheese and more olive oil, if needed, and blend until smooth. Taste and adjust with salt.

SUN-DRIED TOMATO PESTO

Sun-dried tomato pesto is a favorite because of its slightly sweet and savory deliciousness. Although you might think of pesto as the traditional Pesto Genovese (page 245), made with basil, the Italian word *pesto* simply means "paste," so you can make it out of anything including garlic scapes, mint, cilantro, spinach, or anything else you can think of. It is nice to have an assortment of pestos in your refrigerator or freezer, so make many types to use instead of processed condiments. MAKES 2 CUPS

6 garlic cloves

Salt, as needed

⅓ cup pine nuts

2 cups sun-dried tomatoes, packed in oil

½ cup extra-virgin olive oil, plus more as needed

1 cup basil leaves, plus as needed for garnish

1 cup grated Parmigiano-Reggiano

1. Mash the garlic and salt together to a smooth paste.

2. Place the garlic paste and pine nuts in a food processor and blend until smooth. Add the sun-dried tomatoes and olive oil and blend slowly until a smooth, fluid consistency is achieved. Add the basil leaves and continue to blend until the basil is incorporated

3. Add the cheese and more olive oil, if needed, and blend until smooth. Taste and adjust with salt, as needed. Garnish with basil leaves.

DESSERTS
AND BEVERAGES

DESSERTS

Every culture has its own varieties of desserts. Mediterranean desserts are natural as the sun, warm as a sunflower, and aromatic as lavender. Mediterranean desserts tend to be simpler and not at all like the rich, sugary American desserts that we are accustomed to. I prefer the less sweet version of any dessert that I eat. If you like the sweeter varieties, add more sugar to the recipes to your taste.

In the Mediterranean, there are not many cakes per se and not nearly as much decorative license. Mediterranean desserts take raw ingredients and accentuate their flavors without embellishing with unnecessary garnish. The premise might be that you have a fig that has been perfectly ripened by the sun. Now the task is to take that perfect creation and highlight its flavor, shape, color, and aroma. The key is not to lose the fig in the dessert.

For most of the desserts, you might also consider using agave nectar. It has a natural flavor without being overpowering. That and the fact that it does not spike your blood sugar make it one of my favorite sweeteners.

RAISIN AND ROSE WATER TART

This tart is a bit unusual and has the flavor of hosaf, a Middle Eastern condiment made with raisins and rose water. It is a nice alternative to the usual suspects for dessert. If you don't like raisins, use dried cranberries or even dried cherries.

MAKES 6 SERVINGS

TART SHELL

1½ cups all-purpose flour

¼ cup sugar

½ cup unsalted butter, cubed and chilled

½ cup ice water

1 large egg yolk

FILLING

¼ cup freshly squeezed lemon juice

¼ cup rose water

1 lb golden raisins or other dried fruit

1 cup heavy cream

1 vanilla bean, split lengthwise and scraped

¼ cup sugar

3 large eggs

1. To make the tart shell: In the bowl of a food processor fitted with the metal blade, pulse the flour, sugar, and butter until the butter is evenly distributed in the flour; it should have the appearance of coarse cornmeal. Add the water and egg yolk and process for 1 minute or less, just until it forms a ball. Flatten the ball and wrap it in plastic wrap.

2. Lightly flour a board or workspace. Lightly flour the top of the chilled dough and, using a rolling pin, roll it out into a 12-inch round with a thickness of about ¼ inch. Fold the dough into quarters and place into a 10-inch tart pan. Be sure to press the inside edges in so that the edges of the tart will be straight once baked. To do this, use a dough scrap to push the dough along the edges, which will prevent breaking through the dough.

3. Trim the edges so that they hang ¼ inch over the tart pan and chill for at least 30 minutes in the refrigerator before baking.

4. Preheat the oven to 325°F.

5. Prick holes in the bottom of the chilled tart shell every 2 inches with the tines of a fork and then line the shell with parchment paper. Weight down the paper with some dried beans, lentils, or rice.

6. Blind bake the tart shell until the sides start to set, about 20 minutes. Remove the parchment paper and beans and bake for another 10 minutes so that the bottom dries out a bit.

7. To make the filling: In a small saucepan over medium high heat, bring the lemon juice and rose water to a simmer and then add the raisins. Turn off the heat, cover, and allow the raisins to plump and cool.

8. In a separate small saucepan, bring the cream just to a simmer along with the scraped vanilla bean, including the pod, and sugar and cook, stirring to dissolve the sugar; let cool slightly. Remove the vanilla bean pod.

9. Whisk the cream gradually into the eggs to temper and then add the raisins. Fill the prebaked tart shell and continue to bake for another 30 minutes until set. Cool and serve.

POLENTA CAKE WITH GRAPPA, BERRIES, AND MINTED MASCARPONE

This cake is dense and not too sweet, almost like a sweet cornbread. I like to use coarse polenta so that it also has an interesting texture, but if you have to use regular cornmeal, that works as well. MAKES 6 SERVINGS

POLENTA CAKE

¼ cup unsalted butter, at room temperature

1 vanilla bean, split lengthwise and scraped, pod reserved for compote

2½ cups confectioners' sugar

2 large eggs

1 large egg yolk

¾ cup coarse polenta or cornmeal

¾ cup all-purpose flour

1 tsp baking powder

½ cup whole milk

GRAPPA BERRY COMPOTE

½ cup grappa

½ cup sugar

Reserved vanilla bean pod

1 pint fresh blueberries

1 pint fresh blackberries

1 pint fresh raspberries

MINTED MASCARPONE

1 cup mascarpone

¼ cup confectioners' sugar

2 tbsp chopped mint

1. To make the polenta cake: Preheat the oven to 350°F. Grease an 8-inch cake pan with butter or vegetable spray and line the bottom with parchment paper. Dust with flour and tap out the excess flour.

2. In an electric mixer fitted with the paddle attachment, cream the butter and vanilla bean seeds until soft and fluffy. While still beating, add the sugar gradually until it is all incorporated. Add the whole eggs and egg yolk, one at a time, beating to incorporate before adding the next.

3. In a bowl, combine the polenta or cornmeal, flour, and baking powder. Using a rubber spatula, fold them by hand into the butter-sugar mixture, alternating with the milk until combined. Be sure not to overmix or the cake will be tough.

4. Pour the batter into the prepared pan and shake to level the top. Bake the cake until a toothpick inserted in the center comes out clean, about 45 minutes

5. Remove from the oven and transfer to a wire rack to cool. When cool, turn the cake out onto a plate or a piece of parchment paper. Cut into wedges to serve.

6. To make the grappa berry compote: Combine the grappa and sugar in a sauté pan and bring to a boil. Tilt the pan away from you, so that the grappa catches fire and flames up (flambés) and cook until the flame goes out. Add the reserved vanilla bean pod. Add the blueberries then the blackberries. Increase the heat and cook until the syrup has reduced slightly and the berries have started to soften.

7. Add the raspberries last and toss with the other berries and syrup. The compote is ready and should be served warm with the cake.

8. To prepare the minted mascarpone: Combine the cheese, sugar, and mint and mix until smooth. Serve with the cake and berries.

PANNA COTTA

You can flavor panna cotta with many things, including vanilla, lemongrass, chocolate, mint, or anything else you fancy. For different flavors simply add the flavoring ingredient to the milk and let infuse for about 30 minutes while it is heating and then strain it out, if necessary. Panna cotta is the perfect dessert if you are watching your fat intake because you can make it with low-fat milk if you want to. The gelatin in it still makes it seem like a rich pudding. MAKES 5 SERVINGS

1 qt milk
½ cup sugar
2 tsp pure vanilla extract
2 envelopes gelatin
6 tbsp water
1 pint fresh raspberries or blackberries

1. In a saucepan, heat the milk and the sugar until the sugar has dissolved. Add the vanilla to the milk and strain through a fine-mesh sieve.

2. Sprinkle the gelatin onto the water and let bloom for 10 minutes. Prepare an ice bath. Melt the bloomed gelatin for 20 seconds in the microwave until it is liquid. Whisk the melted gelatin into the milk mixture. Place the mixture over the ice bath and stir until it begins to thicken. Pour into five 5-ounce ramekins and cool in the refrigerator until set, about 1 hour.

3. Serve with fresh berries.

SORBET

All the sorbets that we shot for the photos in this book were made with purées from Perfect Purée out of Napa Valley. You can source them through the Internet for really easy prep, or you can make your own fruit purées. If you do decide to make your own, the process is fairly straightforward. Go out in your garden or to your farmers' market and select your fruit. Make a simple syrup with half sugar and half water. Simmer until the sugar melts. Purée the fruit that you want to make the sorbet with in the blender with some simple syrup. You will know it is ready when it tastes good. If you are using something tart like lemon juice, you may use as much as 50 percent syrup, but if you are blending raspberries, just add enough syrup so that the berries taste pleasantly sweet. If your fruit is prone to oxidizing, you might consider adding some ascorbic acid to set the color. One of the things that you will also need to keep in mind is that when foods are frozen, the flavor dulls. Taking that into account, you may want to make the purée a little extra sweet. Process your sorbets in an ice cream machine according to the manufacturer's instructions until thick and then finish in your freezer.

So make your own purée, or take the easy route by buying it—but do make sorbet. Following is a basic recipe for fresh raspberry sorbet. MAKES 1 QUART

2 cups fresh raspberries
1 cup sugar
1 cup water
Juice of 1 lemon

1. Blend the raspberries thoroughly in a blender and strain through a fine-mesh sieve.

2. Bring the sugar and water to a simmer and cook until the sugar dissolves. Allow the syrup to cool.

3. Stir the lemon juice into the raspberry purée and add enough simple syrup to sweeten the purée.

4. Process in an ice cream maker according to the manufacturer's instructions.

MEYER LEMON GRANITA

Granitas are simply icy mixtures of fruit and sugar that are scraped as the surface freezes. After the initial freeze of 45 minutes or so, you go back into the freezer every 30 minutes and scrape until it is all scraped off the pan. If you like, you can use purchased fruit purées to make your granitas, but you may have to adjust the purée by adding water so that you achieve a little more crystallization. MAKES 1 QUART

½ cup sugar

½ cup water

2 cups freshly squeezed Meyer lemon juice (see Chef's Note)

1. In a saucepan, bring the sugar and water to a simmer and cook, stirring, until the sugar has dissolved, then cool. Add the lemon juice and pour the mixture into a flat nonreactive, metal pan or other container. Place in the freezer for approximately 40 minutes.

2. Using a spoon, scrape up the frozen edges as they set up, then return to the freezer for 30 minutes. Repeat every 30 minutes until all the mixture has been scraped and the granita has frozen completely.

Chef's Note *If you don't have Meyer lemons, which are sweeter than the supermarket variety, use regular lemons. You may have to increase the amount of sugar by ¼ cup.*

GELATO

We always had a selection of gelato on our menu at Grappa, and the flavors depended on what was seasonal or available. The recipe that follows is my gelato base. It is easy to make and, if you want to add different flavors, you can. We frequently added fresh ripe bananas to our milk while it was steeping and then puréed them into the custard. You might also consider adding gianduja, a hazelnut-flavored chocolate, or even fresh peach, cherry, or guava purée. The more moisture the added fruit has, the more sugar you may need to add. MAKES 1½ QUARTS

2 cups whole milk

2 cups heavy cream

1 cup sugar

1 vanilla bean, split lengthwise

6 large egg yolks

1. In a saucepot, heat the milk, cream, and sugar with the vanilla bean.

2. In a heatproof bowl, whisk the egg yolks lightly. Slowly whisk the warm cream mixture into the egg yolks. Place the bowl over a saucepan of not-quite-simmering water and whisk for 10 minutes.

3. Strain through a fine-mesh sieve and chill overnight to ripen. Check the flavor and process in an ice cream maker according to the manufacturer's instructions.

Clockwise from left: white peach gelato, cherry gelato, pink guava gelato.

BAKLAVA

I have always loved the crispiness of baklava but not its extreme sweetness. Here, I have adapted the recipe to include dried cherries, apricots, pears, hazelnuts, and pistachios. I also prefer to use agave nectar instead of honey, and less of it than is traditional. So my version is not traditional, but then neither am I. It is, however, delicious.

When working with phyllo, there are a few things that you need to remember. Always use clarified butter because the milk solids in melted butter will soften the dough and make it soggy. The next thing to think about is how you are going to keep the dough from drying out while working with it. I spread out some plastic wrap on the countertop and then place the phyllo on top of the sheet. Then I cover it with another sheet of plastic wrap. It is like making a bed for your phyllo. Then, while you are working with it, you can just pull the covers up when you aren't working with it. The edges dry out first, so when working with the sheets, be sure to butter from the outside edges in. MAKES 117 1-INCH PIECES

¼ cup pistachios, toasted and chopped

¼ cup hazelnuts, toasted and chopped

¼ cup dried cherries, cut into rough dice

¼ cup dried pears, cut into rough dice

¼ cup dried apricots, cut into rough diced

12 sheets phyllo dough

1 cup clarified unsalted butter (see Chef's Note)

2 cups agave nectar

¼ cup rose water

1. Preheat the oven to 325°F.

2. In a bowl, mix together the pistachios, hazelnuts, cherries, pears, and apricots.

3. Lay a sheet of phyllo on your countertop and brush it with clarified butter. Place another layer of phyllo on top and brush it with clarified butter. Place the phyllo in the bottom of a 9 x 13 baking pan. Sprinkle with a light layer of the nut and fruit mixture and then drizzle with about ¼ cup of the agave nectar.

4. Repeat step 3 until all the ingredients are used and the phyllo is the finishing layer. Press down on the baklava, using a sheet of plastic wrap so that it won't stick to your hands, then refrigerate for 30 minutes.

5. Using a sharp knife, lightly score the phyllo into square- or diamond-shaped pieces about 1 inch wide so that when it is baked it will be easier to cut. Combine the remaining agave nectar and the rose water and drizzle the baklava with ½ cup of the mixture. Bake in the oven until golden and crisp, about 20 to 30 minutes. Cool, cut, and serve.

Chef's Note *Although it is extra work to make clarified butter, it is important to use it in this recipe so that the dough doesn't get soggy from the milk solids. Melt 1¼ cups unsalted butter over medium heat and allow the butter to come to a gentle simmer. Soon the milk solids will start to float to the top of the butter. Skim off as much of the milk solids as possible so that you are just left with the butterfat. Allow the butter to cool to room temperature before using.*

TOP ROW LEFT TO RIGHT:

Brush the clarified butter between the sheets of phyllo dough. Remember to keep any reserved phyllo dough between two sheets of plastic wrap to keep it from drying out while you work.

Cut the phyllo sheets to fit the size of your baking dish. Place the phyllo, butter side down, brush with butter, add a layer of the fruit-nut filling, then drizzle generously with agave nectar.

BOTTOM ROW LEFT TO RIGHT:

Before baking, score the baklava into square- or diamond-shaped pieces. Drizzle the agave–rose water mixture evenly over the top and bake for 30 minutes.

When finished, the warm, gooey filling will be a textural contrast to the crispy phyllo layers. Serve warm or at room temperature.

KATAIFI CHEESE NESTS

Kataifi is a strange-looking, nestlike dough that looks like shredded wheat. When baked, these nests are crispy and delicious. There are many variations of this dessert, but the one I like best is filled with nuts and cream cheese. If not available in your supermarket or gourmet store, you can source it online. Kataifi is kind of messy to work with, so you might consider placing some parchment paper on your work surface before beginning. That way, when you are done, you can gather up the edges of the paper and not end up with dough shards all over your kitchen.

MAKES 12 SERVINGS

SYRUP

¾ cup sugar

¾ cup honey

½ cups water

Two 4-inch strips orange zest

⅔ cup freshly squeezed orange juice

2 tbsp freshly squeezed lemon juice

FILLING

1 cups ricotta cheese

¾ cup cream cheese

3 tbsp honey

1½ tsp finely grated orange zest

¼ tsp ground cinnamon

One 1-pound package kataifi, thawed if frozen

½ cup (1 stick) unsalted butter, melted

½ cup pine nuts, toasted

Whipped cream (optional)

1. To make the syrup: In a saucepan, bring the sugar, honey, water, zest, and juices to a boil over moderate heat. Boil until the sugar has dissolved, then reduce the heat and simmer for 8 minutes. Cool the syrup.

2. To make the filling: Stir together the cheeses, honey, zest, and cinnamon.

3. Preheat the oven to 350°F. Butter the wells of a standard 12-cup muffin pan.

4. In a large bowl, pull apart the strands of kataifi to loosen them and toss with the melted butter. Divide equally among the muffin wells and pack evenly.

5. Poke a 1-inch-deep depression in the top of each mound to form a nest. Spoon the filling into holes, then sprinkle the pine nuts over the filling. Bake the nests on the upper rack of the oven until the nests are pale golden, about 35 minutes.

6. Drizzle all the syrup over the nests; the syrup will gradually be absorbed. Cool the birds' nests in the pan on a wire rack. Serve warm or at room temperature dusted with some powdered sugar and maybe even some whipped cream.

MASCARPONE-STUFFED FIGS WITH SABA

This is one of the easiest and most decadent desserts you will ever eat. The key is to find the freshest figs, good-quality mascarpone, and saba. Saba, which is made from sweet grape must (and is what balsamic vinegar is made from), was the ancient Italian sweetener of choice; sugar was not readily available in those days. These days, you might have to look a bit to find saba. Try sourcing it online, or ask for it in a gourmet shop. Sweetened mascarpone, fresh figs, and a drizzle of saba: a dessert that is as delicious as it is simple. MAKES 6 SERVINGS

½ cup mascarpone cheese

2 tbsp confectioners' sugar, plus more as needed

12 fresh figs, well washed

½ cup saba

1. Sweeten the mascarpone with the confectioners' sugar and transfer it to a disposable pastry bag fitted with a small round tip.

2. Split the figs lengthwise to the stem, but not completely in half, and fill with about 2 teaspoons of the sweetened mascarpone. Arrange on a plate and drizzle with the Saba. Sprinkle with more confectioners' sugar and serve.

TARTE TATIN

Although tarte Tatin seems quite elegant and, in some restaurants, liberties have been taken to fancy it up, it is really just a simple apple tart. I am not sure how many versions of this tart I have eaten over the years, but I maintain that simpler is better. Remove all the bells and whistles and keep it simple—a good pastry dough; flavorful, firm, tart apples; and maybe a little Chantilly cream (sweetened whipped cream) on the side. Enough said. MAKES 6 SERVINGS

DOUGH

1½ cups all-purpose flour

¼ cup sugar

Finely grated zest of 1 lemon, lemon reserved for the apples

1 vanilla bean, split lengthwise and scraped, pod reserved for the apples

1½ cups unsalted butter, cubed and chilled

1 large egg yolk

½ cup ice water

CARAMELIZED APPLES

6 crisp-tart apples, such as Honeycrisps or Granny Smiths

1 cup sugar

Juice of 1 lemon, from the reserved lemon

Reserved vanilla bean pod

2 tbsp unsalted butter, at room temperature

Lightly sweetened soft whipped cream, as needed (optional)

1. To make the dough: In the bowl of a food processor fitted with the metal blade, pulse the flour, sugar, lemon zest, and vanilla bean seeds with the butter until it looks like cornmeal.

2. Add the egg yolk and water and pulse again just until it just forms a ball. Flatten the ball, wrap in plastic wrap, and refrigerate for at least 30 to 40 minutes.

3. On a lightly floured board or work surface, roll out the chilled dough into a 10-inch round about ¼ inch thick and refrigerate, covered.

4. To make the caramelized apples: Peel and core the apples and cut them in half. Preheat the oven to 350°F.

5. Sprinkle the sugar into a 8-inch nonstick sauté pan and then pour in the lemon juice. Turn the heat to medium, add the vanilla pod, and cook until the sugar starts to brown. When the sugar is a dark caramel and almost burned, remove and discard the vanilla bean pod and place the apples, round side down, in the pan, along with the butter, and press them into them into the caramelized syrup. Cook the apples for about 10 minutes before placing the dough on top.

6. Reduce the heat while you apply the dough. Place the dough round on top of the sauté pan and, using a rubber spatula, press the sides down into the pan, tucking it in so that it forms a small rim. This way, when the tart is flipped out of the pan, the little rim will catch any extra caramel.

7. Prick the top of the dough several times with a paring knife to allow steam to escape. Place the entire pan in the oven for about 30 minutes. When the crust is baked and golden brown, remove the tart from the oven and cool for 5 to 10 minutes.

8. Place a plate upside down on top of the pan and invert the sauté pan onto the plate. Serve the tart warm or at room temperature with some whipped cream, if desired.

Chef's Notes *If the apples are peeled ahead of time, hold them in water sprinkled with lemon juice, but be sure to dry them off well before placing in the caramelized sugar.*

Be very careful when flipping over the tart, as the sugar is dangerously hot.

TOP ROW LEFT TO RIGHT:

Place the apple halves into the pan, round side down, and lightly press them into the caramelized syrup.

After cooking the apples for about 10 minutes on the stovetop, cover the pan with the rolled dough, tucking it in with a rubber spatula around the inside edge of the pan.

BOTTOM ROW LEFT TO RIGHT:

Bake until the dough is golden brown.

After removing the tart from the oven, allow it to cool for about 5 to 10 minutes, then invert it onto a serving platter, so that the apples are on the top.

PLUM TARTS

These are little tarts filled with plums and baked free-form. You simply cut out rounds of the dough, apply the topping, and twist the rim over so that it looks like a mini pizza. Chill the tarts and then bake on a sheet pan. Simple and delicious.

MAKES 6 SERVINGS

1 recipe Tarte Tatin dough (page 262)

FILLING
6 plums, halved and pitted
2 tbsp unsalted butter
6 tbsp granulated sugar
Juice of 1 orange
2 tbsp Armagnac or cognac
6 tbsp prune or plum jam
¼ cup confectioners' sugar
6 tbsp mascarpone

1. Preheat the oven to 350°F. Line a sheet pan with parchment paper.

2. Divide the dough into 6 small, equal balls and flatten them. Cover them with plastic wrap and refrigerate.

3. When chilled, roll each ball out into a 5-inch round and place on the prepared sheet pan. Refrigerate the dough while you are making the filling.

4. In a sauté pan, heat the plums, butter, granulated sugar, and orange juice over medium heat. Cook the sliced plums slowly until somewhat tender, about 8 minutes. Add the Armagnac or cognac and flambé; when the flame goes out, increase the heat and reduce the liquid in the pan to a syrup. Cool before assembling the tarts.

5. To assemble the tarts: Spread each dough round with a tablespoon of the jam. Divide the plum filling evenly among the rounds of dough on top of the jam. Twist the edges of the dough up onto the plums until you work your way around. Sprinkle each tart with the confectioners' sugar and bake until golden brown, about 35 minutes.

6. Serve each tart on an individual dessert plate, topped with a tablespoon of mascarpone cheese.

Chef's Note *Should you decide to make a larger version, increase the baking time by about 10 minutes. After you remove a large tart from the oven, let it cool slightly before slicing it into wedges. Serve the wedges topped with the mascarpone cheese.*

CANNOLI CHEESECAKE

This ricotta cheesecake tastes like a really good cannoli. I served it frequently to my catering clients and it was always a hit. It has a creamy texture without being too rich. I use sun-dried cherries and shaved chocolate in the mix, which makes it really tasty. For the crust, I crush cannoli shells in the food processor to make a graham cracker–type crust for the bottom of the cheesecake. Bake the cheesecake in a 10-inch cake pan and be sure to cool and refrigerate overnight before attempting to remove it from the pan. MAKES 12 SERVINGS

CHEESECAKE

1 lb 8 oz ricotta cheese

1 lb cream cheese

12 oz sugar (about 1⅔ cups)

5 large eggs

2 large egg yolks

1 vanilla bean, split lengthwise and scraped

1 cup dried cherries, roughly chopped

1 cup chocolate chips or chopped semisweet chocolate

CRUST

2 cups crushed cannoli shells

1 cup sugar

Pinch of ground cinnamon

½ cup melted unsalted butter

1. To make the cheesecake: Preheat the oven to 300°F. Spray a 10-inch cake pan with nonstick cooking spray and line with a circle of parchment paper.

2. In an electric mixer fitted with the paddle attachment, cream the ricotta and cream cheese on medium speed until very smooth and soft, about 10 minutes. Slowly add the sugar and mix until it is completely incorporated. Add the whole eggs, one at a time, incorporating each before adding the next and then add the egg yolks and the vanilla bean seeds and incorporate. Reserve at room temperature.

3. Using a rubber spatula, fold in the cherries and chocolate and mix just until incorporated.

4. To make the crust: In the bowl of a food processor fitted with the steel blade, combine all the ingredients for the crust. Pulse until they are evenly distributed.

5. Sprinkle the crust mixture into the bottom of the prepared pan, press into an even layer, and refrigerate for 10 minutes.

6. Pour the room-temperature batter into the chilled crust and place the cake pan in a roasting pan and pour in enough water to come halfway up the side of the cake pan.

7. Bake for about 2 hours; remove from the oven when the cake appears to be set and no longer jiggles when the pan is lightly shaken. Let the cake cool in the water bath to room temperature. When it is at room temperature, cover the top of the pan with plastic wrap and refrigerate the cake overnight.

8. The following day, cut out another circle of parchment paper and put it on a 10-inch flat, serving plate. Put the cheesecake on a burner and heat just the bottom of the pan to slightly melt the butter in the crust; this will allow the cake to release from the pan. Using a paring knife, cut around the sides of the pan to be certain the cake will release from the sides. Place the parchment paper over the top of the cheesecake and then put the flat plate upside down over the cake pan. Invert the cake and shake lightly until you feel the cake drop to the plate. Place the plate on the countertop and remove the pan from the cake. Place another cake plate over the bottom of the cake and flip it right side up. Return the cake to the refrigerator for 10 minutes to let the butter in the crust set again. Cut the cake into portions and serve.

GRAPPA WITH BERRIES

This recipe can be made with any fruit that is in season. The recipe makes six portions, but you can make as much or as little as you like. Keep replenishing the fruit as you use it so that you'll have a supply on hand whenever you need it.

MAKES 6 SERVINGS

1 cup fresh blueberries
1 cup fresh strawberries
1 cup fresh blackberries
1 cup red and green grapes
¼ cup sugar
1 quart grappa

1. Wash the fruit and place each type in a separate clean jar.

2. Sprinkle 1 tablespoon of the sugar over the fruit in each of the jars. Pour 1 cup of grappa into each jar and allow to sit for 2 days before using. Store in the refrigerator. The berries can be served over gelato, sorbet, or a simple cake. You can also just eat them out of a glass with a spoon.

BEVERAGES

Nonalcoholic beverages are very important in many areas of the Mediterranean basin. Islam, practiced by much of the population of the Middle East, prohibits consumption of alcoholic beverages. The arid climate in many Mediterranean countries also makes hydration a necessity. Beverages, besides being a means to rehydrate, are also a way to socialize. In the United States you might drop in on a friend and have either iced tea or lemonade offered to you as a beverage. In the countries of the Mediterranean, you may be offered something a little more interesting. The following are recipes can expand your nonalcoholic repertoire, quench your thirst, and leave your palate refreshed.

SAFFRON TEA

This is traditionally a Pakistani tea, but since saffron is readily available in the Mediterranean basin, I think this qualifies as a good Mediterranean beverage. I enjoy this hot or cold; just be sure to steep the tea for several minutes before drinking so that the saffron really infuses. MAKES 4 SERVINGS

4 cups water
Pinch of saffron threads
Sugar, to taste

In a small saucepan, bring the water to a boil over medium heat. Add the saffron and sugar to taste. Let infuse for several minutes if you are drinking it hot, or for 1 hour if pouring it over ice.

TAMARIND TEA

Tamarind pods are messy to work with, but the fruit surrounding the seed is a tasty treat. In certain cultures, people often just nibble the flesh off the seeds. The seeds are large and the flesh is dark, so it may stain your teeth. Tamarind paste takes the work out of preparing the fruit, but remember to strain it to get rid of the seeds. This tea is tart, delicious, and refreshing. MAKES 6 SERVINGS

5 cups water
1 cup tamarind paste
1 cup sugar

In a small saucepan, bring the water to a simmer over medium heat. Add the tamarind and sugar and stir for about 5 minutes, then let soak for 2 hours. Strain through a fine-mesh sieve and serve cold.

SUMAC BERRY TEA

The sumac berry used in this recipe is not our native sumac; these little red berries are imported. There are two ways to buy sumac: in whole dried berry form and ground. The ground sumac berries are easier to find, but I prefer the whole berries because I find that lightly crushing the berries before steeping results in a much more tart and refreshing beverage. Some types of native sumac are poisonous, so don't go picking by the roadside. MAKES 6 SERVINGS

½ cup dried grand sumac *or* 1 cup dried sumac berries

5 cups warm water

1 cup sugar

6 lemon slices *(optional)*

In a nonreactive bowl, soak the sumac berries in the water and sugar for 2 hours. Refrigerate overnight, then strain garnish with lemon, if desired, and drink. If using ground sumac, some may remain in the glass after straining.

CARDAMOM TEA

Cardamom is one of my favorite spices. When it has been ground, it has the most amazing aroma and just awakens the senses. You can make this tea with cardamom pods or ground cardamom. It is great iced, but in the winter, if you prefer, you can drink it hot. MAKES 8 SERVINGS

6 cups water

¼ cup cardamom pods crushed *or* 2 tbsp ground cardamom

¼ cup green tea leaves

1 cup sugar

1 cup whole milk

In a small saucepan, bring the water to a boil over high heat. Add the cardamom, tea leaves, and sugar and let steep until cool. Add the milk and refrigerate overnight.

Clockwise from left: Hibiscus Flower Water (page 274), Fresh Mint Tea (page 273), Sumac Berry Tea

Clockwise from left: Basil Water (page 274),
Lemon Balm Tea, Hibiscus Flower Water (page 274)

LEMON BALM TEA

Every summer, my lemon balm comes back up in my garden with a vengeance. It is often difficult to figure out what to do with it because it grows so profusely. I have been making iced tea out of it for the past several years. If you can't find lemon balm, try lemongrass, which is readily available in most markets. Be sure to crush the lemongrass to bring out its fragrant oils. MAKES 6 SERVINGS

3 bunches lemon balm leaves, well washed

6 cups water

Sugar, to taste

6 lemon slices

Put the washed lemon balm in a heatproof container. In a small saucepan, bring the water to a boil over high heat and pour over the fresh lemon balm leaves. Cool and let steep in the refrigerator overnight. Sweeten as desired and serve garnished with a lemon slice.

Chef's Note *If substituting lemongrass, use 3 stalks lemongrass, cut into ½-inch lengths and crushed with the side of a knife.*

FRESH MINT TEA

Mint, like lemon balm, comes back year after year and has a tendency to take over your garden. Mint tea is a standard in both my summer and winter beverage repertoire. Mint has an amazing cooling effect on the body. If you want a refreshing face mask, mix the leftover tea leaves with ½ cup yogurt, refrigerate until cool, and smooth on your face. It's a nice hydrating and cooling remedy for a little too much sun. MAKES 6 SERVINGS

3 bunches mint, well washed

1 cup sugar

6 cups water

1 tbsp mint chiffonade

Put the mint and sugar in a heatproof container. In a small saucepan, bring the water to a boil over high heat and pour over the fresh mint and sugar. Let cool and steep overnight. Strain before drinking and garnish with the mint chiffonade. Drink hot or cold.

CUCUMBER WATER

This light, refreshing cooler is sure to find its place alongside the iced tea in the refrigerator over the summer. Be sure to seed the cucumbers or they will impart a bitter flavor when the cucumber is blended. MAKES 6 SERVINGS

1 cucumber, peeled and seeded

Juice of 1 lime

5 cups water

Sugar, to taste

1 lime, sliced for garnish

1. In the jar of a blender, blend the cucumber and lime juice and then strain through a fine-mesh sieve for 1 hour. If you have a juice extractor you won't have to strain it; the machine will do that for you.

2. Add the juice to the water along with a little sugar to taste.

3. Serve garnished with a lime slice.

HIBISCUS FLOWER WATER

This is one of the most flavorful, refreshing drinks I have ever had. You can find dried hibiscus flowers, also known as *flor de jamaica,* in your local health food store or online. This is a great alternative to iced tea. MAKES 8 SERVINGS

1 cup dried hibiscus flowers

1 cup sugar

2 quarts boiling water

8 small mint leaves *(optional)*

Pour boiling water over hibiscus flowers and sugar. Stir and let steep for at least an hour, then strain and cool. Garnish with a mint leaf, if desired. The hibiscus water can be served hot or iced.

Chef's Note *Basil can be substituted for the hibiscus flowers to make the basil water pictured on page 272.*

TURKISH COFFEE

This coffee is a little tricky to make but worth the effort. It is traditionally served warm in coffeehouses and is a very social ritual. The coffeehouses are a place to socialize, and since alcohol consumption is not acceptable in Muslim regions of the Middle East, beverages like this coffee are standard fare. This drink is delicious hot, but can be served iced as well. Just be careful not to pour the grounds into your glass MAKES 4 SERVINGS

1 qt water

¼ cup sugar

¼ cup Turkish coffee, very finely ground

1. Put the water, sugar, and coffee in a small pot, ideally a Turkish coffeepot. The coffee should float on top of the water, forming a seal between the water and the air.

2. Start heating the water over moderate heat but do not let the water boil. The coffee will start to foam, and soon the foam will cover the top of the pot. Quickly remove the pot from the heat and the foam will go down.

3. Return the pot to the heat, stir down the foam, then remove the pot from the heat. Return to the heat and this time when it foams, don't stir down the foam. Scoop the foam out into small espresso style cups and let the coffee sit so that the grounds settle a bit.

4. Pour the coffee into the cups but be careful not to pour the last of it as it contains all the grounds.

Chef's Note *Don't panic if some of the grounds go into the cup, they will settle at the bottom.*

ROSEMARY LEMON ICED TEA

One of my favorite flavor combinations is lemon and rosemary. I use both in combination frequently with lamb, pork, chicken, and even fish. Since I love the flavors so much, I thought I would try making a tea with them, and it was instant love. This tea is refreshing and thirst quenching and the ingredients are easy to find. MAKES 5 SERVINGS

1 bunch rosemary, well washed

Zest of 2 lemons

Juice of 2 lemons

1 cup sugar

5 cups water

Put the rosemary, lemon zest, lemon juice, and sugar in a heatproof container. In a small saucepan, bring the water to a boil and pour it over. Stir and let infuse for 2 hours. Strain and serve over ice.

GLOSSARY

"00" FLOUR A finely ground flour often used for making pasta.

A

AIOLI A garlic mayonnaise

AL DENTE Literally translates to "to the tooth"; refers to an item, such as pasta or vegetables, cooked until it is tender but still firm, not soft.

ANTIPASTO Literally translates to "before the pasta." Typically, a platter of cold hors d'oeuvre that includes meats, olives, cheese, and vegetables.

ARBORIO RICE A high-starch, short-grain rice traditionally used in the preparation of risotto.

B

BABA GHANOUSH A purée of roasted or grilled eggplant and tahini. The same dish with less tahini in Palestine is known as *mutabbal*.

BASMATI A long-grain, needle-shaped rice from the Northern Himalayan foothills of India and Pakistan with a delicate, distinctive flavor.

BISCOTTI Italian for "biscuit"; a twice-baked cookie that can be either sweet or savory.

BISQUE A soup based on crustaceans or a vegetable purée. It is classically thickened with rice and finished with cream.

BISTEEYA A savory meat pie of pigeon, encased in a paper-thin layered crust.

BLIND BAKE To partially or completely bake an unfilled pastry crust.

BOCCONCINI Small, bite-size balls of fresh cheese; similar to mozzarella.

BOLOGNESE Indicating that something comes from Bologna; usually refers to a meat sauce better known as *ragù alla Bolognese*.

BOTTARGA Cured fish roe, usually shaved or grated over pasta or salads.

BOUILLABAISSE A hearty fish and shellfish stew flavored with saffron. A traditional specialty of Marseilles, France.

BOUQUET GARNI A small bundle of herbs tied with string, used to flavor stocks, braises, and other preparations. It usually contains bay leaf, parsley, thyme, and possibly other aromatics wrapped in leek leaves.

BRANDADE A purée of salt cod, olive oil, potato, and garlic.

BREAD FLOUR A hard wheat flour made from the finely milled endosperm with a protein content ranging from 11 to 13 percent.

BROCCOLI RABE A deep green long stemmed member of the cabbage family with small florets and a strong bitter flavor.

BRUISE To partially crush a food item in order to release its flavor.

BRUNOISE Small dice; 1/8-inch/3 mm square is the standard. For a brunoise cut, items are first cut in julienne, then cut crosswise. For a fine brunoise, 1/16-inch/1.5-mm square, cut items first in fine julienne.

BUCATINI A long tubular pasta.

BULGUR Processed grain from durum wheat, parcooked and dried for preservation purposes.

BURRATA A type of mozzarella with a cream-filled center.

C

CALASPARRA RICE Short- and fat-grain rice with a high-starch content often used for the preparation of paella.

CANNELLINI BEANS A white kidney-shaped bean often used in minestrone, salads, stews, and side dishes.

CANTAL Firm and mild cow's milk cheese.

CAPELLINI Long thin strands of pasta. Also known as angel hair.

CARAMELIZATION The process of browning sugar in the presence of heat. The caramelization of sugar occurs from 320° to 360°F/160° to 182°C.

CARNAROLI RICE A short-grain rice with a high starch content often used for risotto.

CARPACCIO A dish traditionally made with thinly pounded slices of raw beef; may also be made with seafood such as scallops.

CARRY-OVER COOKING Heat retained in cooked foods that allows them to continue cooking even after removal from the cooking medium. Especially important to roasted foods.

CASSOULET A stew of beans baked with pork or other meats, duck or goose confit, and seasonings.

CATAPLANA A clamshell-shaped piece of cooking equipment used to make a seafood dish of the same name.

CAVATELLI A type of small pasta with a slightly rolled shape.

CHANTERELLES Trumpet-shaped mushrooms with a golden-apricot color and a nutty flavor.

CHELOW A Persian method of steaming basmati rice in a mixture of oil or butter, yogurt, and seasonings, until it is fluffy, tender and has developed a dark golden crust known as a *tah dig*.

CHIFFONADE Leafy vegetables or herbs that are stacked and then cut crosswise into fine ribbons; often used as a garnish.

CIPOLLINI ONIONS Small onions with a flattened shape and slightly sweet flavor.

COCA A Spanish type of pizza.

COMPOTE A dish of fruit, fresh or dried, cooked in syrup flavored with spices or liqueur.

CONCASSÉ To pound or chop coarsely. Concassé usually refers to tomatoes that have been peeled, seeded, and chopped.

CONFIT Meat, usually goose, duck, or pork, cooked and preserved in its own fat.

COULIS A thick purée, usually of vegetables but possibly of fruit. Traditionally refers to meat, fish, or shellfish purée; meat jus; or certain thick soups.

COUSCOUS A durum wheat product made from the endosperm of the wheat known as the semolina. It is cooked by steaming in a couscousière.

COUSCOUSIÈRE A set of nesting pots, similar to a steamer, used to cook couscous.

CRÈME FRAÎCHE Heavy cream cultured to give it a thick consistency and a slightly tangy flavor. Used in hot preparations since it is less likely to curdle when heated than sour cream or yogurt.

CROSS CONTAMINATION The transference of disease-causing elements from one source to another through physical contact.

D

DANGER ZONE The temperature range from 40° to 140°F/4° to 60°C; the most favorable condition for rapid growth of many pathogens.

DEGLAZE To use a liquid, such as wine, water, or stock, to dissolve food particles and/or caramelized drippings left in a pan after roasting or sautéing. The resulting mix then becomes the base for the accompanying sauce.

DURUM A species of hard wheat primarily milled into semolina for use in dried pasta.

E

EGG WASH A mixture of beaten eggs (whole eggs, yolks, or whites) and a liquid, usually milk or water, used to coat baked goods to give them a sheen.

EMULSION A mixture of two or more liquids, one of which is a fat or oil and the other of which is water based, so that tiny globules of one are suspended in the other. This may involve the use of stabilizers, such as egg or mustard. Emulsions may be temporary, permanent, or semipermanent.

ESCABECHE A cooking technique in which the main item, typically fish, is cooked and then marinated in an acidic liquid for several hours before serving.

F

FARRO An ancient form of wheat; often used in salads, soups, or ground for baked goods.

FATTOUSH A broad term for bread salad using leftover pita bread.

FERMENTATION The breakdown of carbohydrates into carbon dioxide gas and alcohol, usually through the action of yeast on sugar.

FETA A tangy, salty, and crumbly fresh cheese that can be made from cow, sheep, or goat milk.

FOCACCIA A yeast bread flavored with olive oil and typically topped with various items such as herbs, garlic, sun-dried tomatoes, etc.

FOIE GRAS The fattened liver of a duck or goose.

FOND The French term for stock. Also describes the pan drippings remaining after sautéing or roasting food. It is often deglazed and used as a base for sauces.

FORBIDDEN RICE A black-colored grain once only eaten by royal dynasties in China.

FRITTO Italian term for a fried dish.

G

GELATO An Italian-style ice cream that is denser than American-style ice cream.

GNOCCHI Small dumplings typically consisting of flour and potatoes or ricotta.

GRANITA A frozen dessert based on sugar, water, and a flavored liquid with the texture of crushed ice.

GRAPPA A grape-based Italian brandy.

GREMOLATA A condiment consisting of minced herbs, lemon zest, and garlic.

H

HARICOTS VERTS A special variety of green beans.

HARISSA A hot chili paste used to season many Maghreb foods.

HIGH-GLUTEN FLOUR A flour that is milled from the entire endosperm with a protein content between 13 to 14 percent; often used for bagels and hard rolls.

HUMMUS BI TAHINI A purée of chickpeas and sesame seed paste. The name *hummus* actually means "chickpeas" in Arabic.

I

INFUSION Steeping an aromatic or other item in liquid to extract its flavor. Also, the liquid resulting from this process.

ISRAELI COUSCOUS A larger, round form of couscous often used in pilafs, salads, and soups.

J

JULIENNE Vegetables, potatoes, or other items cut into thin strips; 1/8 inch by 1/8 inch by 1 to 2 inches/3 mm by 3 mm by 3 to 5 cm is standard. Fine julienne is 1/16 inch by 1/16 inch by 1 to 2 inches/1.5 mm by 1.5 mm by 3 to 5 cm.

K

KAFFIR LIME LEAF The leaves of a particular citrus plant that can be used either fresh or dry to impart a citrus flavor to foods.

KALAMATA OLIVE A black olive named after the city in Greece.

KIBBEH Patties made of ground lamb, green wheat, mint, and various spices; it can also be made in a cake form or breaded and fried.

L

LARDON A strip of fat used for larding; may be seasoned. Also refers to a browned piece of slab bacon cut in the shape of a baton.

LEMONGRASS A tough, yellow green blade used for flavoring soups, stocks, stir-fries, or steamed preparations.

LEMON VERBENA An herb with a delicate lemon flavor.

M

MANDOLINE A slicing device of stainless steel with carbon-steel blades. The blades may be adjusted to cut items into various shapes and thicknesses.

MEZE A Middle Eastern term for small dishes or bites.

MIREPOIX A combination of chopped aromatic vegetables—usually two parts onion, one part carrot, and one part celery—used to flavor stocks, soups, braises, and stews.

MIRIN Rice wine often used for cooking.

MORTADELLA An Italian cold cut made from pork, which resembles bologna; often contains pistachios.

N

NIÇOISE OLIVE A small black olive from France.

O

ONION PIQUÉ An aromatic combination of onion, clove, and bay leaf used to flavor stocks, soups, and stews. To make an onion piqué, cut a slit in the onion and insert the bay leaf, then stud the onion with three cloves.

ORECCHIETTE Small, ear-shaped pasta.

OSSO BUCO A traditional dish of braised veal shanks; the delicacy of the dish being the bone marrow.

P

PAELLA A typical dish from Valencia made with rice, saffron, and either vegetables, fish, meats, or all combined.

PAILLARD A scallop of meat pounded until thin; usually grilled.

PAN BAGNAT Literally translates as "bathed bread," it is a sandwich stuffed with tuna, olives, vegetables, and eggs.

PANISSE A cooked mixture of chickpea flour and liquid that is sliced and sautéed; typically used as an hors d'oeuvre or side dish.

PANZAROTTI Stuffed fried gnocchi.

PARCH Heating a grain in hot fat or oil in order to begin gelatinizing the starches.

PÂTÉ A rich forcemeat of meat, game, poultry, seafood, and/or vegetables, baked in pastry or in a mold or dish.

PHYLLO A paper-thin pastry used to make the savory pies and sweet pastries of Greece; literally translates as "leaf."

PIMENTÓN DULCE Sweet Spanish paprika.

PIQUILLO A small slightly hot pepper from Navarre, fire roasted, hand peeled, and jarred in its own juices.

PISSALADIÈRE A pizzalike dish from France topped with caramelized onions, anchovies, and olives.

PITA BREAD A round bread that puffs in the oven when baked.

POMEGRANATE A deep red round-shaped fruit indigenous to the Middle East. It ranges in flavor from sweet to sour-sweet, and is popular in savory as well as sweet cooking.

POMEGRANATE MOLASSES A dark liquid sweetener made from the juice of the seeds of the pomegranate fruit.

POOLISH A semiliquid starter dough with equal parts (by weight) of flour and water blended with yeast and allowed to ferment for 3 to 15 hours.

PORCHETTA Traditionally a boned pig, stuffed with wild fennel, etc. cooked on a spit and sliced for panini sandwiches. The version in this book has been simplified and is a boneless pork loin cut into quarters, surrounded by Italian sausage, sautéed onions, and fennel, and wrapped in a butterflied pork belly.

PRESERVED LEMON Lemons salted and stored in their own juices; often used chopped in tagines. An important salty and sour condiment of the Maghreb.

Q

QUINCE A yellow-skinned, apple-shaped fruit that must be cooked before consumed in order to eliminate its astringent flavor; often used in jams, jellies, pastes, and preserves. Quince paste is an indispensable Mediterranean ingredient used in many preparations.

R

RADICCHIO A bitter salad green with a round or oblong head and reddish purple leaves.

RAMP Wild garlic. A long cylindrical member of the onion family with a white stem, green tops, and strong garlicky flavor.

RAS EL HANOUT Literally translates as "top of the shop." A North African spice mixture whose ingredients vary depending on the region or the person making it.

RICER A pierced hopper with a lever that pushes cooked foods (often potatoes) through the openings in the hopper in order to create a smooth purée.

RICOTTA A fresh cheese made by acidifying and heating the whey left over from cheese making; often used for cannoli, cheesecake, or ravioli filling.

RILLETTES Potted meat, or meat that is slowly cooked in seasoned fat, then shredded or pounded with some of the fat into a paste. The mixture is packed in ramekins and covered with a thin layer of fat.

RONDEAU A shallow, wide, straight-sided pot with two loop handles.

ROULADE A slice of meat or fish or cheese rolled around a stuffing. Also, filled and rolled sponge cake.

ROUX Equal parts of flour and fat (usually butter) used to thicken liquids. Roux is cooked to varying degrees (white, blond, or brown), depending on its intended use. The darker the roux, the less thickening power it has, but the fuller the taste.

S

SACHET D'ÉPICES Literally translates as "bag of spices." Aromatic ingredients, encased in cheesecloth, that are used to flavor stocks and other liquids. A standard sachet contains parsley stems, cracked peppercorns, dried thyme, and a bay leaf.

SAFFRON Threadlike stigmas of the crocus flower that impart a yellow color and distinct flavor to food; traditionally used in paella, Risotto Milanese, soups, pilafs, etc.

SEMOLINA The coarsely milled hard wheat endosperm used for gnocchi, some pasta, and couscous.

SOFRITO Sweated tomato, onion, garlic; this base and olive oil is used to season other preparations.

SOPRESSATA A cured and dried salami common in Italian cuisine.

SUMAC A Middle Eastern spice with a tart, lemony flavor; from the dried, ground berries of the sumac plant.

T

TAGINE The name of a conical glazed earthenware vessel that is used to braise the famous stews of the Maghreb.

TAGLIATELLE A type of pasta with the shape of long, flat ribbons.

TAH DIG The brown crispy layer of rice found at the bottom of the pan after making chelow.

TAHINI A sesame seed paste.

TAMARIND A pod-bearing fruit tree whose seeds offer a sour flavor popular throughout the Middle East and Asia.

TAPAS From the word *tapar*, which means "to cover," now refers to finger foods served on top of a slice of bread.

TORTELLI A type of stuffed pasta.

TURMERIC An orange-colored spice often used in curry mixes. Fresh turmeric resembles ginger and is in the rhizome family.

TZATZIKI A Greek condiment made from strained yogurt and cucumbers.

V

VERJUS Literally translates as "green juice"; it is the juice of unripe grapes.

W

WHEY The liquid left after curds have formed in milk.

Z

ZA'ATAR A dry spice condiment of thyme, sesame seeds, sumac, and salt.

ZEST The thin, brightly colored outer part of citrus rind. It contains fragrant oils, making it ideal for use as a flavoring.

INDEX

Page numbers in *italics* indicate illustrations